LONDON AND ITS RAILWAYS

R. DAVIES AND M. D. GRANT

With 158 black & white photographs
13 colour plates
29 maps and diagrams

DAVID & CHARLES

Newton Abbot London North Pomfret (Vt)

Facing Title Page:

The Grand Style *As befitted London's first trunk railway the London
& Birmingham spared no expense in providing its Euston terminus with
the trappings of splendour in its Doric arch entrance and the magnificent
Great Hall waiting room, both of which were sacrificed to progress with
the rebuilding of the station in the 1960s.* G. M. Kichenside

Rus in urbe *In July 1952 Johnson 0-4-4T No 58054 with the 14.33
from Romford to Upminster calls at Emerson Park Halt. Opened by the
London Tilbury & Southend Railway in 1909 to serve middle-class
housing development in the area, the outward growth of urban London
has still not fully dispelled its rural atmosphere.* Brian Morrison

*'For myself, when on a train into London,
I feel almost invariably a sense of some pathos and of some poetry'*
THE SOUL OF LONDON Ford Madox Hueffer

Davies, R.
  London and its railways.
  1. Railways—London (England)
  I. Title   II. Grant, M. D.
  388.4' 2' 0942   HE3019.L8

  ISBN 0-7153-8107-5

Typeset by Typesetters (Birmingham) Ltd,
and printed in Great Britain
by Butler & Tanner, Frome
for David & Charles (Publishers) Limited
Brunel House   Newton Abbot   Devon

Published in the United States of America
by David & Charles Inc
North Pomfret   Vermont 05053   USA

CONTENTS

Publisher's note: In view of the complexities of the area, particularly in respect of ownerships, line openings and closures, and changes of station names, the maps must be regarded as timeless and not representative of a particular period of time except where specifically dated.

Holloway Bank *Having just emerged from Gasworks and Copenhagen Tunnels, Henry Oakley pilots 4-4-2 No 251, on the 'Plant Centenarian' special in September 1953, up Holloway Bank at the start of the climb that will extend to Potters Bar. Special trains were early features of the Great Northern main line; in the year after its opening, special trains were run for visitors from the Midlands and the North to the Great Exhibition of 1851. Brian Morrison*

Kings Cross Suburban *Typical of the age of steam suburban railways is 0-6-2T No 69513 leaving Kings Cross in 1955 with a Hatfield train. Some of these N2 tanks were built with small chimneys and condensing gear to enable them to work through the tunnels of the City 'Widened' Lines to Moorgate, the platform on the rising connection from which can be seen behind the train. P. H. Wells*

1
SETTING THE SCENE

*Commuter – one who spends his life
in riding to and from his wife*

In 1979, 766,000 BR and LT commuters made the daily journey to and from home, some from places as far distant as Bournemouth and Norwich. The typical London railway passenger, even on the Underground system, spends his journey reading, working, or just sleeping, and few ever think of the development of the system on which they ride. It seems as if the network has always been of its present shape and size and came into existence fully developed. A moment's thought indicates that this cannot be so as the railway system was constructed for particular reasons and changed in response to demands for passenger and freight traffic. Indeed, it must always be changing, and any account of it must freeze its development at a particular period; this book deals with the situation as it is in the early 1980s.

Rather than divide the area by line and route which would result in repetition, both in text and photographs, each chapter is devoted to particular aspects of London's railways in narrative and pictorial form. For those who wish to follow-up particular items, a bibliography is provided. As an introduction, this chapter portrays the general background, against which the following chapters can develop their particular themes.

Geography

London is located in a basin formed by the Chiltern Hills to its north and by the North Downs to its south. Across this basin from west to east flows the Thames which has cut a number of gravel terraces in the soft rocks of the basin. At the end of the dip slopes of the Chilterns lies a clay plateau from which extend long fingers of high ground. Perhaps the best known of these are the 'Northern Heights' of Hornsey, Finchley and Hampstead which descend steeply to the clay plain north of the Thames terraces. Between the terraces south of the river and the North Downs is an area of

gravel-capped hills with intervening clay vales, the hills broadly extending from Blackheath through Herne Hill to Wimbledon Common. The gravel terraces are more extensive north of the river, providing the site of the City and the West End, but run continuously from Staines to the Laindon Hills.

The complications of this physical geography are twofold. First, it is immediately apparent that a train from any of the London termini is faced with a climb to leave the London Basin. The most obvious examples of this are the lines from the Northern termini of Kings Cross, St Pancras and Euston. The line runs roughly northwards from Kings Cross avoiding the Northern Heights so far as it can, by passing to the east of Stroud Green where it is in cutting, but still climbing until it reaches Potters Bar. The St Pancras and Euston lines set off northward but are soon deflected to the west to avoid the Northern Heights. Until Hampstead both are parallel, but then their routes diverge, the St Pancras line to reach the River Lea north of Harpenden to cross the Chilterns and the Euston line to use the Tring Gap for the same purpose.

The second effect of the physical geography was on settlement patterns in London. Before the installation of main drainage in the latter part of the nineteenth century, the subsoil dictated which areas would develop. Gravel subsoil is free-draining whereas clay is impervious. Under these conditions gravel areas were the first to develop and the first to be served by railway. Population and housing growth were other important factors here and will be mentioned later.

London Defined

There are as many definitions of London as the purposes for which they are required. Administratively Greater London was defined in 1963, but to adopt this as the area to be covered by this book would produce odd results – for example, the Watford dc electric services beyond Hatch End would be excluded. With this in mind the area has been defined in transport terms. While it is shown in the map, the area has been defined

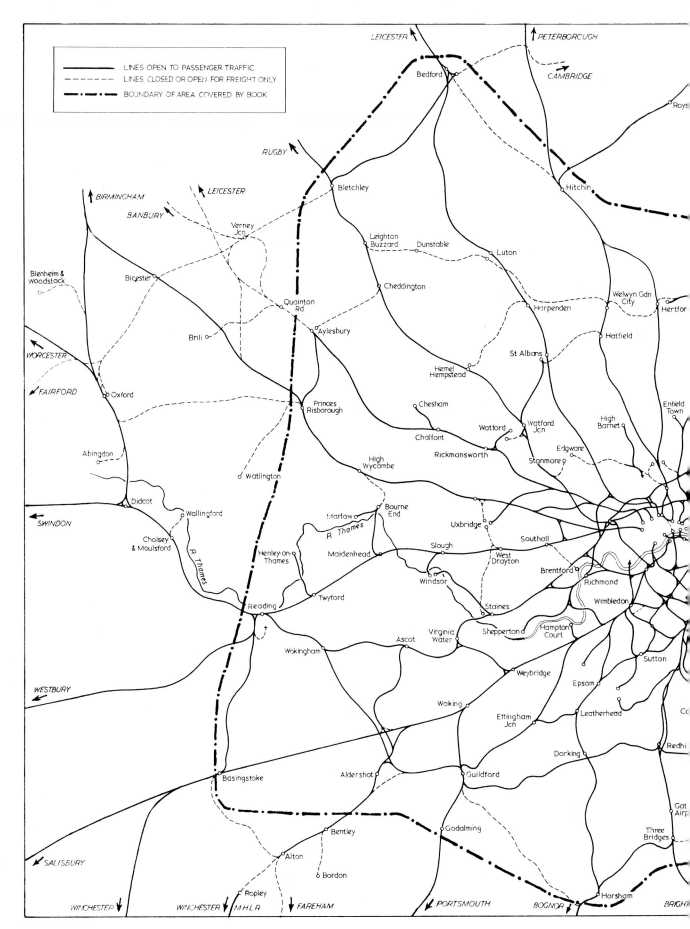

Railways in the Greater London area.

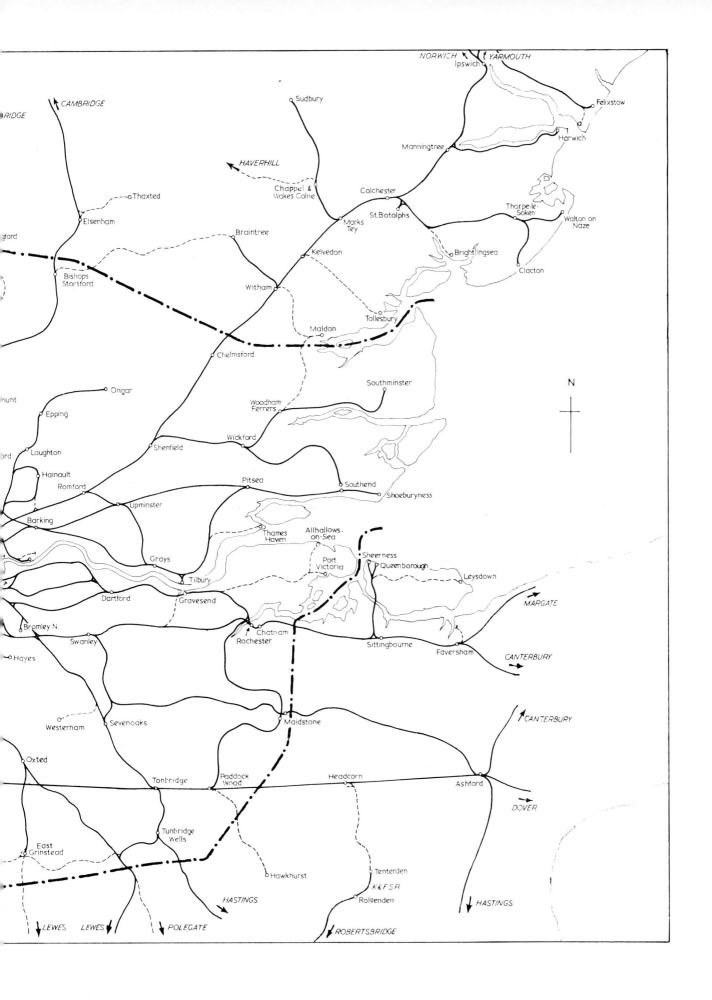

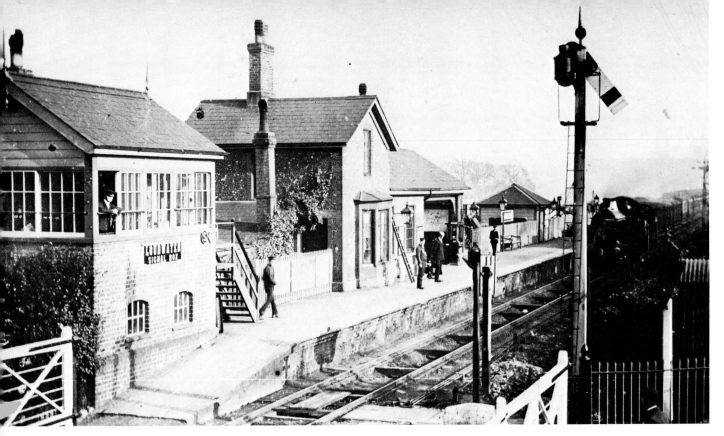

Loudwater *Loudwater station was sited on part of the Wycombe Railway of 1854 which ran from Maidenhead to High Wycombe. A subsequent extension to Aylesbury in 1863 enabled a through service to be operated from Maidenhead but this was cut back to High Wycombe in 1969. Final closure for Loudwater came with the section north of Bourne End in the next year, leaving the service to Marlow, which reverses at Bourne End.* High Wycombe Central Library

Vauxhall *The decline of main line steam is exemplified by Bulleid Pacific No 34013 at Vauxhall with a parcels train on 6 July 1967. Shorn of its Okehampton nameplate and shield this locomotive and its remaining sisters would be withdrawn, and Nine Elms locomotive depot closed, on the introduction of the Bournemouth electrification four days later.* North Western Museum of Science & Industry

by the terminus of the outer-suburban service on each of the lines into London. Inevitably, objections can be made to these boundaries. London's influence does not for example suddenly begin at Tonbridge but rather gradually increases along the former SER main line. Nonetheless, an arbitrary element cannot be avoided whenever boundaries are drawn. However, the influence of locations outside this immediate area is such that reference is made to ultimate destinations in the chapter on main lines.

London's Growth

In 1831 urban London covered only 18 square miles and contained 1.7 million people. In 1977 the GLC area had grown to 618 square miles with a population of 7.0 million. Behind these bare statistics lies a complex story of movements in population, in no small measure influenced by the development of the railway system and in turn having an influence on it.

Nevertheless, certain stages in urban growth can be distinguished. The first stage is old London, based upon the 'City' – that is the City of London – and Westminster, which was the limit of built-up London in the 1830s at the dawn of the Railway Age. By the turn of the century, the built-up area extended about as far as eight miles from Charing Cross and in the remaining years development pushed further out in the country, although it was by no means continuous. The inter-war years saw considerable infilling of the area and its expansion into the counties of Middlesex and Surrey,

Chesham *Although the Metropolitan opened its line to Chesham in 1889, it was generally worked as a branch from Chalfont after the extension to Aylesbury opened in 1892. In this 1955 view GCR Robinson 4-4-2T No 67416 fitted for push and pull working heads a three coach set of Metropolitan stock dating from 1898.*
Alan J. Willmott

Rayners Lane *Early days on the Metropolitan are apparent in this 1922 picture of Rayners Lane, which opened as a halt in 1906 on the Uxbridge branch. The junction beyond the bridge and the line to the right dates from the District Railway's 1910 extension from South Harrow. Housing development and consequent traffic growth led to a rebuilt station.* National Railway Museum

greatly encouraged by an alliance of speculative builders and electric railways. World War II called a halt to the process, and post-War 'Green Belt' legislation limited any further outward extension of London. Development beyond the 'Green Belt' since then has greatly increased long-distance commuting whilst at the same time decreasing the population of the inner suburbs. Indeed this movement was officially encouraged with the development of 'New Towns' such as Basildon, Hemel Hempstead and Crawley. Although it was intended that their inhabitants should find work in the towns, some prefer to commute to jobs in London, to increase the daily tide.

The real contribution of railways to London's growth was the separation of office and home that they

Waddon Marsh *In 1929 0-4-2T No 627 is seen propelling a Wimbledon train along that part of the LBSCR branch from West Croydon which is built on the former course of the Surrey Iron Railway, near Waddon Marsh. Freight was important in this area, notably the ¾ mile siding to Waddon Flour Mills and sidings for the gas works and two electricity generating stations.* Lens of Sutton

Thundersley *In 1956 ex-LTSR 4-4-2T No 41966 was restored as No 80* Thundersley *to mark the Centenary of the opening of the line to Southend. Built in 1909 by Robert Stephenson it was exhibited at the Imperial International Exhibition at the White City in that year, where, temporarily named* Southend-on-Sea, *it gained a gold medal.* Brian Morrison

made possible. 'Living above the shop' was an everyday occurrence in early Victorian days as the only form of transport was the horse. By combining frequent services and cheap fares, the railways made it possible for City workers to live in such places as New Southgate, Palmers Green, and Walthamstow. Yet in providing these facilities, the companies had to provide locomotives and rolling stock for use perhaps twice a day. As traffic grew, more facilities had to be provided, which encouraged more traffic, which required more facilities and so on. The *Sorcerer's Apprentice* nature of this task became apparent to Lord Colville, Chairman of the Great Northern, in 1882. 'Towns', he observed 'were springing up within two or three miles of Kings Cross as fast as people could build them'. The number of daily season ticket holders had increased by over 3,000 in two years, and to cater for present and future traffic the company had to carry out a programme of widenings between Kings Cross and Potters Bar. No wonder the company's historian, Grinling, was to refer to 'The Suburban Incubus'.

The Pattern of Railway Development

London's first conventional railway, the London & Greenwich, was opened in 1836 and, until 1849 the

Marlborough Road *The Metropolitan ambitions to trunk status started with the opening of the line from Baker Street to Swiss Cottage in 1868. Marlborough Road opened with this line to serve the northern part of St Johns Wood. The extension of the Bakerloo tube in 1939, with its own station at St Johns Wood, caused the station's closure in the same year. Now a restaurant, dinner can be taken where once tickets were purchased.* London Transport Executive

Harpenden *This unlikely combination of 4-4-0T and a former Pullman coach was introduced on the Midland line from Harpenden to Hemel Hempstead on 2 April 1906. Stabled at St Albans it worked first to Luton before returning to Harpenden to work branch services from the bay at the north end of the down fast platform.* Colourviews

same pattern of a line extending from a London terminus into the country was repeated, albeit lines such as the London & Birmingham and the Great Western were of greater national importance. Nevertheless, the pattern remained one of individual isolated lines with no links between them. This linking process began in 1849 with the opening of the connection between the London & Blackwall at Stepney and the Eastern Counties Railway at Bow. It was continued by a line from the London & Birmingham at Camden to Bow and another from Willesden to Kew. The 1850s and 1860s saw a continuation of these linking lines, notably the West London Extension and the Tottenham & Hampstead Junction and the establishment of a complex network in South London as the LBSCR, LCDR and SER developed separate City and West End terminals. The 1860s also saw the development of the Metropolitan and Metropolitan District railways, the first stage of the Underground network, which by 1875 had developed into today's Circle Line except for the section between Mansion House and Liverpool Street. This served most of the main line terminals and enabled passengers to avoid the busy streets of mid-Victorian London. Lines had also pushed out to suburban termini such as Chingford, Edgware and Crystal Palace. By 1875 the main pattern of the network was complete and only some infilling remained. Thus the Bromley North line opened in 1878, the LTSR direct route to Southend was opened in 1888, and the Bexleyheath line in 1895. The major development in the last quarter of the century was the completion of the Circle, expansion of the District westwards to Ealing and Hounslow, and the stage-by-stage opening of the Metropolitan Railway until it ultimately reached Verney Junction and Brill, with the GCR extending southwards to it from the Midlands.

Borough Market Junction *One of the busiest signalboxes in London, Borough Market Junction, controlled the lines to Cannon Street and Charing Cross. The 35 miniature lever electro-mechanical frame controlled over 1,000 trains a day, about 100 of them in the busiest hour. As trains destined for Cannon Street conflicted with those from Charing Cross, timetables maximised trains through the junction by planning parallel moves.* E. Wilmshurst

Development from 1900 until 1924 was largely concentrated on the establishment of a deep-level 'tube' system beneath Central London. While this era can be said to have begun with the opening of the City & South London Railway in 1890, it really came to life in the first ten years of the century, inspired by the American C. T. Yerkes. By 1910 four 'tubes' were in operation across Central London apart from the CSLR. The 1920s and 1930s were spent in extending them into the suburbs and welding them into one system,

15

especially after the formation of London Transport in 1933.

World War II marked high water for the railway system. Some services were withdrawn, never to return, while competition from car and bus after the war led to reduced rail traffic and some service withdrawals as a consequence in the 1950s and 1960s. Although electrification of lines has taken place in that time, the only new construction was the Victoria line, opened from Walthamstow to Victoria in 1969 (extended to Brixton in 1971), the Jubilee Line between Baker Street and Charing Cross in 1979, and the extension of the Piccadilly line to Heathrow Airport.

Competition from Tram and Bus

Railways took up their suburban task from around 1860 and until the end of the century were fairly secure from any competition. As the new century wore on the effect of tram and bus competition began to increase, and it would be as well briefly to review the developments which had led to this.

The bus dates from 1829, the year in which George Shillibeer started a service from Paddington to Bank. Although Shillibeer was financially unsuccessful, other operators were more soundly based and by 1839 horse bus routes were in operation along all the main routes leading out from London. As the railway system

Ayot *Ayot was the first passing place out of Welwyn Garden City on the branch to Luton and, until its destruction by fire in 1948, the first station. Ivatt Class J52 0-6-0ST No 1247 restored to Great Northern Railway livery, is seen on the South Bedfordshire Locomotive Club* Lea Flyer *special passing Ayot on 16 September, 1961.* P. Waylett

High Wycombe *In order to free itself of dependence on the Metropolitan Railway for its approach to London, the Great Central joined the Great Western in the construction of a joint line. High Wycombe was the terminus for the suburban services to Marylebone and Paddington which began on 2 April 1906, a day when the town's Chamber of Commerce gave a lunch for both companies. Here 4-4-2T No 359, built the previous year, stands in High Wycombe with the first train.* High Wycombe Central Library

developed in the 1840s and 1850s it brought more people into London and so stimulated the demand for buses, but generally the journey to work for those few who undertook it was by bus. Until the formation of the London General Omnibus Company in 1855, the industry had been comprised of individual garages with small fleets, which the General rapidly set about acquiring. By the end of the 1850s traffic congestion led to the construction of underground railways and this, together with the new suburban lines, meant that bus journeys remained static in the 1860s while train journeys increased rapidly. The bus held its own for short distances, but longer-distance traffic went by train, a pattern which held good until around 1900 with the bus concentrated in central London where it was free of tram and railway competition. The development of the motor bus in the 1900s, with its large carrying capacity and an ability to cover greater distances, led to a boom in 1905 yet the excesses of competition which this and similar incidents showed gradually brought co-ordination of London's transport.

Trams generally were introduced in London from 1870. Although a considerable network was soon constructed in the inner suburbs, the tramway system was not allowed to penetrate the central area, in the belief that trams would increase its congestion. By offering low fares trams rapidly built up considerable traffic, partly from those who had not until then used public transport. While these horse tramways offered competition to the railway in that area of operation, it was in the twentieth century that their effect was really to be felt. The London County Council had been established in 1889, and as a means of social reform began to acquire horse tramway systems from 1891. The principal acquisition was the 48 miles of tramway south of the river in 1898 which it determined to operate itself. In the first decade of the century the Council began the task of organising the hitherto separate lines into a unified system and electrifying them. At the same time it developed a cheap fares policy including workmen's tickets for early morning travellers. This movement encouraged the poorer-paid to move out to better accommodation in the suburbs where the LCC was active in the construction of housing. With the predominant part of its system south of the Thames, it was there that the principal effects of tramway competition were felt.

This concentration into larger operating units such as the LCC paved the way for the establishment of the London Passenger Transport Board in 1933. This had responsibility for bus, tram and tube services, and followed a policy of co-ordination between its various forms of transport. The services of the main line railways were included in a common pool of receipts

and the stage was set for the policy which has been followed ever since. It still contains one flaw. There is no overall authority in charge of all forms of passenger transport in the London area because the BR services are influenced by factors other than London's interests. Co-ordination is by agreement, not imposed by an authority.

Beyond the London Suburbs

Much of this introductory analysis has been taken up with a discussion of the development of London and the immediate suburbs. Yet the boundaries of this book as they have been drawn encompass a wide area stretching from Southend to Reading and from Hitchin to Three Bridges.

It is generally true to say that although the influence of London has always been felt in this area the period since World War I has seen a great strengthening of that influence, particularly with the rise of commuting over longer distances in the last 20 years. Places such as Amersham have ceded their country market town role to that of dormitory for London.

What this means for railway development is that the area has been traversed by main lines from the Capital, which have had objectives beyond it. However, these lines have acquired the additional purpose of catering for commuters. By contrast, local lines and branches in the area were provided for local objectives and have been closed from the effects of road competition, a common enough theme elsewhere. The line from Hatfield to Dunstable, for example, was promoted by local interests in order to provide Luton with railway facilities. The subsequent entry of the Midland Railway into the town provided better facilities and the line from Hatfield expired in 1965. The consequent effect of this process can be seen on the railway map of the area today; the main lines radiate from London like the spokes of a wheel, few branches remain to join them.

Railway Influence on London

As the railway network grew up, the nature of the service that was provided had considerable influence on the particular area it served. Indeed the status that was bestowed upon an area in Victorian times can continue to this day. As an example, Richmond is generally considered a 'desirable' area whilst Tottenham does not have the same social status. But Richmond was already established by the time the railway arrived in 1846, and developed as a high-class suburb where inhabitants could not be expected to favour a sudden influx of the 'lower orders' except as day trippers. Indeed it would not be in the LSWR's financial interests to encourage

them – prosperous commuters could pay higher fares. So the LSWR kept control of all railway approaches and followed a policy of high fares and low volume. By contrast Tottenham, although it existed as a town when the railway came in 1840, was overwhelmed by the construction of terraced houses in the 1870s and 1880s. Of a standard pattern with little garden space, they were built on a grid-iron street layout at a density of up to forty an acre. Here the Great Eastern had determined to develop an intensive service with cheap fares, the reverse of the LSWR policy at Richmond, from around 1870. The combination of cheap housing and cheap transport enabled a migration of lower-income workers from crowded areas such as Hackney. Of course, other influences were at work in forming the status of both places, notably the pattern of land ownership and the provision of other forms of transport such as the tram and the bus, but the railway played a significant part and was in turn affected by the status it had helped create.

Function of Railways

In the London area the railway is called upon to perform a number of different functions. The first role that can be distinguished for passenger traffic is long-distance travel to and from the capital, the original reason for the construction of the main lines. The second is shorter-distance traffic to the suburbs and to towns in the South East. This is principally associated with the journey to work but pleasure journeys for such purposes as shopping and entertainment are also included within this group. 'A day out' by train, particularly to the seaside, is nowadays much less common than it was, as the private car has taken over the function. The third role is movement within Central London, a task almost exclusively undertaken by the Underground system.

A similar long-distance role is discernible in the freight system where goods are consigned to or dispatched from London. The second role is really a specialised version of the first, serving the Port of London. Although today this largely means Tilbury, in the past there was a complex network to serve the docks and Thames wharves. Thirdly, the large number of railway routes to the Capital meant that a considerable interchange of freight traffic developed across London. The last is local traffic within the conurbation.

While all London's railways undertook these functions, the emphasis on each varied between the lines. Obviously some railways were specially constructed for one function; the Baker Street & Waterloo for example only provided for passenger traffic in Central London, and the Angerstein Wharf line was built solely to reach the Thames. Some, such as the LNWR and the GWR, considered that the development of suburban traffic would use track capacity needed for main line services and made no conscious effort to develop it. By contrast the GER, originally obliged to run workmen's trains for those displaced by the extension to Liverpool Street, developed them far beyond the statutory minimum with the result that its new terminus was dominated by the commuter. Even so, the GER and the LTSR saw some pleasure traffic to London's resort of Southend but for the family holiday in the West Country, Waterloo and Paddington provided many extra trains with the inevitable queues to wait for them. Long trains of coal rumbled down lines such as the Midland, milk was brought in from the West by the LSWR, and vegetables from East Anglia by the GER.

From this it can be seen that there is no typical London railway. Each undertook different tasks and these tasks changed as time passed. The result was a system with considerable variety and interest. Some lines have now passed and can only be recalled through books such as this. Demolition and rebuilding slowly change the face of what remains, but the best way to understand the system is to go and look at it with a discerning eye and an enquiring mind. Under these circumstances much will be revealed.

Willesden *Willesden Shed was the principal freight depot for the former LNWR lines in London. Of straight and roundhouse type, it was located on the down side of the line, close to Willesden yard. Some of its allocation can be seen in this 1964 picture with Class 5MT, 8F and BR Standard types evident. Closed in 1965, its electric depot successor still undertakes the maintenance function.* Hugh Ballantyne

Battersea *Battersea, on the West London Extension Railway, saw a variety of passenger services in its life from 1863 to 1940. This view shows a former LNWR 'Coal Tank' in 1933 on the service from Willesden (Main Line) to Clapham Junction. This last remnant of LNWR services to Waterloo and Herne Hill ceased in 1940.* H. C. Casserley

2
IN THE BEGINNING

It would be wrong to claim that the origins of railways were to be found in London. Indeed, the prehistory of railways in Britain goes back to at least 1605, when Sir Francis Willougby built a waggonway to take his coal from Wollaton near Nottingham to the Trent. Tramroads were in use in Shropshire, Northumberland and Durham by 1800 when the capital was railless. Yet there are five instances where developments in London took the story of railways one step further forwards.

In chronological order of operation they are the Surrey Iron Railway, Richard Trevithick's trials in Euston Square, the London & Greenwich Railway, the London & Croydon Railway and the London & Blackwall Railway. The Surrey Iron Railway, authorised in 1801, was the first public railway and London's first railway; Trevithick's trials in 1808 helped in the development of the high-pressure steam engine; the London & Greenwich was the precursor of London's railway system; the London & Croydon and the London & Blackwall were two examples of alternative systems of motive power, the former atmospheric propulsion and the latter cable operation, and both in the end came to naught.

Surrey Iron Railway

In the gradual evolution of railways, one of the steps was the horse tramway as feeder to a canal. Here the canal was the principal form of transport and the railway was incidental to it. In the evolutionary process the Surrey Iron Railway was the first to be promoted purely as a railway and not as an adjunct to a canal.

It arose from the need to provide a safer means of communication between London and Portsmouth. The Napoleonic Wars had emphasised the danger to shipping of sailing through the Straits of Dover in order to reach London, a danger which could be avoided if they put into Portsmouth. Schemes to realise the link by tramroad or canal were advanced. In 1799 construction of a horse tramway from London to Portsmouth was countered by a proposal for a canal between Wandsworth and Croydon. Difficulties with water

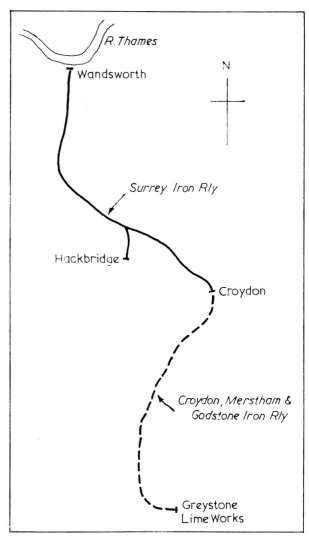

The Surrey Iron Railway and the Croydon, Merstham & Godstone Railway.

supply meant the only practical course would be to canalise the River Wandle, but the interference this would have caused with the works on the river made it impractical. Accordingly, plans were changed to the construction of a railway which could form the first stage to Portsmouth.

A survey was undertaken of the necessary works and

a Bill introduced into Parliament, which ultimately resulted in an Act on 21 May 1801 incorporating the Surrey Iron Railway. This was to run from a dock alongside the Thames at Wandsworth to Croydon, with a branch from Mitcham to Hackbridge. The company lost no time; a meeting held at the Spread Eagle Inn, Wandsworth on 4 June appointed officers and resolved to advertise for tenders to undertake the work. By 27 July the contract for building the dock was let and on 9 January 1802 it was completed and opened.

By this time work on the railway was well advanced. Although the line was not formally opened throughout until 26 July 1803, there is evidence that parts of it were in use before then. It seems that the branch to Hackbridge did not open until 1804. With the first stage in hand thoughts turned to extensions towards Portsmouth, and another meeting at the Spread Eagle Inn on 3 June 1802 resolved to survey from Croydon to Reigate, a proposal which culminated in the Croydon, Merstham & Godstone Iron Railway Act of 17 May 1803. As well as the main line, this authorised a branch from Merstham to Godstone. Plans continued to circulate for extensions towards Central London and Portsmouth, but Napoleon's defeat at Trafalgar in 1805

Wharncliffe Viaduct *To enable the Great Western Railway to cross the valley of the Brent at Hanwell, Brunel built an eight arch brick viaduct which became known as the Wharncliffe Viaduct in tribute to Lord Wharncliffe's assistance to the Company as chairman of the House of Lords committee on its Bill. His armorial bearing the motto* Avito Viret Honore *can be seen on the right hand pier.* R. Davies

reduced the need for an overland route between London and Portsmouth. This left the Surrey Iron and Croydon, Merstham & Godstone with a purely local role. Indeed, the latter company did not construct the whole line authorised by the Act. Only the portion from its junction with the Surrey Iron at Croydon to Merstham was built and opened in 1805. However, the Croydon Canal built a link to the Croydon, Merstham & Godstone from its terminal basin in Croydon. By use of the Croydon Canal traffic could be carried to the Grand Surrey Canal and thence the Thames.

Ideas continued to circulate to develop the two railways. Plans to reach Portsmouth by means of canal in 1810 and 1812 did not materialise. William James took an interest in 1818, 1822 and 1823, proposing a railway from Central London to join the older lines and to convert them to locomotive operation. Indeed, their absorption into a larger plan would have been the only way to ensure their continuance. Traffic on the Surrey Iron Railway was light and shareholders' dividends were small and rare, none being paid after 1825. The position was the same on the Croydon, Merstham & Godstone, although the use of Merstham lime in major building works in London ensured some activity in the twenty years until 1833. It seems that two companies let the collection of tolls on their railways.

Both railways were worked on similar principles to a canal in that the company did not convey traffic, but merely made its tracks available to anybody who wanted to use them on payment of the appropriate toll. The line was double with each track being used for one direction, although crossovers were provided at intervals, and horses provided the means of traction. The four-wheel waggons were generally of about 3¼ tons in weight when loaded and about 5ft wide, 8ft long and 2ft deep.

Merstham *Almost buried in the grass near the* Jolliffe Arms *at Merstham, this picture shows some remains of the Croydon Merstham & Godstone Iron Railway. Its 3ft fish-belly cast iron rails are clearly apparent, resting on stone blocks, and set at a gauge between 4ft 1in and 4ft 2in. The plateway nature of the line can be seen from the flanges on the rails which were inside the wheels of the vehicles.*
London Borough of Croydon

The Surrey Iron Railway followed the River Wandle at a ruling gradient of 1 in 120 crossing the river twice on wooden bridges. These gentle gradients were not found on the single line onwards to Merstham, where cuttings and embankments were necessary as the line climbed towards the gap in the North Downs.

The track of the Surrey Iron line was L-section cast-iron rail in 3ft 2in lengths fixed by iron spikes at each end into wooden inserts in the top of stone sleeper blocks. The rail flange, which guided the flat-tyred wheels of the waggons, was higher in the middle than at the ends to give greater strength where it was suspended between the stone blocks. The blocks were set in a gravel foundation which between the rails was compacted by the horses hauling the waggons. Arrangements on the Croydon, Merstham & Godstone line were generally similar, and the gauge of both lines was approximately 4ft 1in.

The poor financial results of both lines have already been mentioned, principally because of the lack of traffic. Indeed, the Act of abandonment of the Surrey Iron Railway recorded that 'the traffic along the said line has ever since the completion thereof been very small, and has of late years been diminishing'. As contemporary records of both companies are few it is difficult to assess the amounts of traffic carried. The principal traffic on the Croydon, Merstham & Godstone must have been lime from its upper terminus, and references have been made to a return traffic in manure. Certainly the toll sheet of the Surrey Iron Railway that survives itemises lime and all manures, coal and dung separately, which indicates these were expected to be the principal traffics on the line. Industry was concentrated in the Wandle valley, some 38 factories in 1805, and it was expected that the Surrey Iron Railway would obtain valuable business from them. Whether the works continued to use existing forms of transport after the opening is difficult to tell. What is certain is that they did not make great use of the railway. The conclusion that remains is that the two railways were promoted as part of a trunk line and once that plan failed, the local traffic that they could attract was very limited. Under these circumstances, closure was inevitable.

The end of the railways came from 1837. The London & Brighton (L&B) took over parts of the Croydon, Merstham & Godstone (CM&G) for its own route but, this so injured the older company that the L&B was required to purchase the whole of its route. Once achieved, all that remained was for the CM&G to be dissolved on 1 July 1839. The Surrey Iron Railway became enmeshed in an ultimately unsuccessful scheme for the London & Brighton to use it as a means of reaching the London & South Western Railway

Camden Bank *On the opening of the London & Birmingham Railway the 1 in 77 of Camden Bank was thought too steep for locomotive operation. Trains were consequently hauled up the bank by cable from 1837 to 1844 and this view of Camden shows the two chimneys of the fixed engines which could draw trains up the distance of rather more than a mile in between three and five minutes.*
Elton Collection

terminus at Waterloo. The SIR Dissolution Act was passed on 3 August 1846, traffic ceased on 31 August and in the two years the Act had allowed, the company was wound up.

Trevithick's Trials

Richard Trevithick was born on 13 April 1771 near Carn Brea in Cornwall and at the age of 19 entered local employment as a mining engineer. Water had long been a problem in the mines and unless it was raised to the surface, it would eventually flood them. The cost of drainage was great and the need to find a more efficient method led to Thomas Newcomen's invention in 1708 of an atmospheric engine. If steam is admitted to a cylinder and then condensed by a jet of water, a partial vacuum is obtained. Atmospheric pressure will force a piston at the top of the cylinder down as air moves to fill the vacuum. If steam is re-admitted, it destroys the vacuum and a counterweight can restore the piston to its position at the top of the cylinder ready to start again. The objection to Newcomen's engine was the waste of energy inherent in alternately heating and

cooling the cylinder. In 1765 James Watt overcame this problem by provision of a separate condenser which remained permanently cool whilst the cylinder could be kept permanently hot. Steam could be drawn from the cylinder into the condenser as it was required. Although first patented in 1769, it was not until after it was extended in 1775 that production began in earnest. The engines were limited to a to-and-fro motion, and Watt invented a number of devices in the 1780s to produce a rotary movement.

By sealing the top of the cylinder, Watt was able to create a vacuum on each side of the piston. This enabled the steam to provide power on both the upward and downward strokes of the piston instead of just on the downward as in the Newcomen engine. However, Watt's engine used steam at little higher pressure than the atmosphere, as he thought the use of higher pressure steam dangerous and its application to locomotion frivolous. It was left to Trevithick to develop locomotive engines which because of the high pressure could be smaller and lighter. He started by making a model in 1797 but the expiration of Watt's patent in 1800 became the spur for development. In 1801 Trevithick had built a steam road carriage at Camborne; a second in 1803 had been demonstrated in London. The poor state of the roads told against these carriages so he turned to 'tramroads' whose more regular surface enabled a locomotive to make better progress. After the construction of Trevithick's first locomotive at Coalbrookdale in 1803 his second and more famous engine entered service in 1804 on the Penydarren tramway in South Wales; a year later came the construction of his railway locomotive at Newcastle-upon-Tyne. It was not until 1808, at the age of 37, that he returned to locomotives and the *Catch-me-who-can*.

The origin of this locomotive appears to be a wager. Certainly the episode starts with a report in *The Times* in 1808 that a 'Steam Engine' was being prepared to run against any horse in the October meeting at Newmarket and that Trevithick had been asked to exhibit the engine prior to this. Its maximum speed was quoted as 20mph 'and its slowest rate will never be less than 15 miles'. Subsequent newspaper reports added that the locomotive weighed eight tons and would be 'exhibited to the public in the fields adjoining the Bedford Nursery, near Tottenham-court-road'. The exhibition was due to commence at 11.00am on Tuesday, 19 July 1808, but 'the ground under the Railway, on which it was to run, being too soft and spongy, requiring additional support of timber' the opening was postponed until the following Monday. Trevithick had found this problem in trial running, when the locomotive broke a number of the rails, and had to re-lay the track before trials commenced.

23

Richard Trevithick's Railroad Euston Square 1809

'Catch-me-who-can' *Richard Trevithick's* Catch-me-who-can *was successfully displayed on a circular track near the Euston Road in 1808 and this is an artist's impression of the scene. For a fee of one shilling, the curious could obtain admission to the enclosure behind the palisade to stare whilst the brave might have ridden on the engine.* Colourviews

Tickets of admission to the enclosure were advertised as being available in all the coffee houses in London and at the Orange Tree, New Road, St Pancras. The admission cards featured a drawing of the locomotive above which was printed 'Trevithick's Portable Steam Engine *Catch-me-who-can*' and below it 'Mechanical Power Subduing Animal Speed'. This was a clear reference to the wager against horses, and there are a number of other contemporary references to this contest. Although the precise date when the public exhibition began is not available, the wager was advertised for Wednesday and Thursday 21 and 22 September. The locomotive was to run at its London site for 24 hours from 2.00pm Wednesday against any horse in the country. During that time it was calculated it would run at least 240 miles. No reports can be found of the actual trial, so further details are tantalisingly unavailable.

The exact site of the trials is difficult to specify. All accounts are agreed that it was to the south of the New Road (now the Euston Road), east of Tottenham Court Road, west of the Bedford Nurseries (about where Gordon Street is today) and north of the boundary of the Southampton Estate (which can be taken to be Torrington Place). In 1808 the area where University College stands was not built upon and it seems that this is the likely site. In any event a plaque on the wall of University College in Gower Street marks the event. The locomotive appears to have had four wheels with the motion transmitted to the rear pair and to be a simple design based on an earlier dredger engine.

Neither coupled nor geared, the smooth wheels ran on smooth rails which were probably of plate section as used on tramways at that time. The fragmentary evidence of operation is contradictory. One source refers to a carriage being propelled by the locomotive while another states that the public could ride on the locomotive if they were bold enough or be content merely to watch.

Again, the date when the exhibition was closed to the public is unknown. No doubt the novelty value of the locomotive would decline and this would be reflected in the admission fees which would not pay the running expenses. Perhaps, more importantly, Trevithick would feel that the exhibition had accomplished its purpose; the railway locomotive had been demonstrated to a wider audience in London than it would have been at Penydarren or Newcastle. It had been shown to work and Trevithick moved on to fresh subjects. With Andrew Vivian, he had patented the high-pressure steam engine for stationary and loco-motive use in 1802. By 1807 he had a one-fifth share in the patent with three others holding the balance, but it appears he sold his interest around September 1808 to Messrs Haynes & Douglas, cotton merchants of Tottenham Court Road. Whilst motives are difficult to establish so much later, it does not seem impossible that Haynes & Douglas may have gained their initial interest from the exhibition near their premises and Trevithick, finding a buyer, was happy to part with his share of an idea he had brought to fruition.

The development of the railway locomotive then passed into the hands of others, notably the colliery engineers William Hedley and George Stephenson. However, it was not until 1829 when Stephenson's *Rocket* won the Rainhill Trials on the Liverpool & Manchester Railway, that the railway locomotive really came into its own and the Railway Age began. By then Trevithick had been occupied on other matters for 21 years. He returned to locomotive matters in 1831 when he patented a boiler and superheater, but two years later he died at the age of 62. He had played a major role in the development of the railway locomotive and the trials of 1808 had played their part in that.

London & Greenwich

Although the Surrey Iron Railway was London's first, it was the London & Greenwich which set the pattern that suburban railways were to follow in the London area. It was promoted in 1832, after the Liverpool & Manchester had proved the practicality of railways, to connect London with Greenwich as the first stage of a line into North Kent, Dover and the Continent. From a terminus on the south side of London Bridge, which

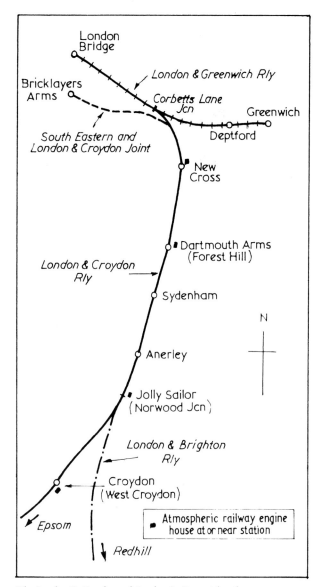

The London & Croydon and London & Greenwich railways.

had been re-opened in 1831 after Rennie's rebuilding, it was to run through Deptford to Greenwich.

It was to traverse an area of market gardens and small houses intersected by lanes, drainage ditches and the Surrey Canal. To avoid level-crossings the railway had to be above or below ground level, and the high water table in the area decided the matter in favour of a viaduct, 3¾ miles and 878 arches long. To turn the viaduct to good use the company intended to build houses in the arches, and some were actually built at Deptford. Alas, the idea did not appeal, and most of the arches were let for commercial use, a state of affairs which continues today. To give access to the arches a boulevard was built on one side of the viaduct, while on the other a second could be used by pedestrians on payment of a toll, to take a direct line to Deptford but at a cheaper fare than the train. In time the boulevards

Corbetts Lane *This view of the London & Greenwich crossing Corbetts Lane emphasises the low-lying land the line traversed which required the construction of the viaduct. The brick construction of the viaduct is apparent as are some of the gas lamps which illuminated its whole length. Along it runs a train of first or second class coaches whilst behind it are masts of ships in the docks.*
Greater London Council

enabled some widening of the viaduct to be undertaken without the need to purchase land. The company produced gas and this was used in the early days to illuminate the viaduct. Other notable engineering works were the skew bridge over the Surrey Canal, the bridge over Deptford High Street supported by fluted iron columns, and the lifting bridge over Deptford Creek.

The line was opened from Deptford to Spa Road in February 1836, extended to a temporary terminus near London Bridge in October and was ceremonially opened from London Bridge on 14 December 1836. It took a further two years for the remaining section from Deptford to Greenwich to be opened, and even then it was to a temporary station. The line made inroads into coach and omnibus traffic but had little effect on the river steamers. It did not carry goods, so local passengers were its main traffic, supplemented from 1837 by the carriage of mails. Services were good as trains ran at 15-minute intervals on weekdays from 08.00 to 22.00, with a journey time of 12 minutes. Fares were high, more to recoup the high cost of construction than to reflect the price passengers were prepared to pay. Attempts were made to increase excursion traffic but ultimately the company proved unremunerative. To improve matters, an extension to Gravesend and Dover was proposed in 1838 but the

opposition to the intended crossing of Greenwich Park killed the idea.

However Parliament, whilst refusing the extension, indicated that it would require other companies whose plans it was considering to use the Greenwich line to reach the London terminus. So from 1839 the London & Croydon's trains were fed on to the Greenwich at Corbetts Lane junction, 1¾ miles from London Bridge. The Croydon's trains were joined from 1841 by the London & Brighton's and from 1842 the South Eastern; both of these companies made use of the Croydon to reach London. To provide the extra capacity for these trains the Greenwich obtained powers in 1840 for two extra tracks to be built over the southern boulevard and to pay for it charged its three tenants 4½d [2p] per passenger. The Croydon and South Eastern were so incensed by the charge that they built and opened a line from a ½-mile short of Corbetts Lane to a new terminus at Bricklayers Arms. Opened on 1 May 1844, its location was not quite the 'Grand West End Terminus' it was claimed, but it served its purpose. Deprived of traffic, the Greenwich agreed to lease its undertaking to the South Eastern. Confirmed by Parliament in 1845, the Greenwich gave up running trains. Until absorbed by the Southern Railway in 1923, its main business was to receive the rent from the South Eastern and declare a dividend for its shareholders.

The junction at Corbetts Lane can claim to be the site of the earliest of signal boxes. 'In consequent of the trains (London & Croydon) having to pass along the Greenwich railway . . ., the utmost care and vigilance are required to prevent collision with the Greenwich trains. A signal-house is, however, placed at the junction; and by judicious arrangements, accidents . . .

seldom occur.' The arrangements were red discs worked by a pointsman from a cabin. When raised at right angles to the track, a disc indicated 'stop' and if parallel to the track, 'proceed'. At night a red light meant 'stop' and white 'proceed'.

Some idea of operations can be found from a study of the accounts of the London & Greenwich for 1839. Receipts were roundly £55,000 and expenditure £33,000 giving a surplus of £22,000 for the year. The majority of receipts came from passengers, although £3,500 was derived from a toll of 3d [1p] for each passenger in the Croydon's trains that used the Greenwich line in the period from 5 June. Curiously enough, the Greenwich company's fares nominally comprised two elements, a charge for haulage of 9d [4p] first-class, 5d [2p] second-class and 3d [1p] third-class and a toll of 3d [1p] irrespective of class. An average fare of 8d [3p] from the 1.5 million passengers indicates that the majority travelled second-class, a state of affairs supported by contemporary reports. First-class coaches comprised three compartments, second-class were in one compartment and third-class open.

Approximately one-third of expenditure was on the locomotives and their crews. Five of the locomotives were four-wheeled and the remaining four six-wheeled. There were eight drivers and eight firemen. Under the arches at Deptford station was the repair workshop and here three 'coke and water fillers', four cleaners, four fitters, one millwright, five smiths, two boilermakers, one joiner and four carpenters were employed. Further major items of expenditure were the maintenance of the tracks, the wages of the 22 policemen who were employed, rates, taxes and duty and staff salaries.

As the century wore on, the original viaduct saw successive widenings. In 1842 the first widening over the southern boulevard brought an additional two tracks from Corbetts Lane Junction for the South Eastern, Brighton and Croydon companies. Then in 1849 the opening of the line to Gravesend via Blackheath brought an additional track from North Kent East Junction to Corbetts Lane Junction and two additional tracks from there to London Bridge on the site of the northern boulevard. Next in 1866 the South London line of the LBSCR provided three more tracks on the south side of the viaduct from a quarter-mile

London Bridge *By 1866 traffic at London Bridge had been increased by the opening of the SER extension to Charing Cross in 1864 and to Cannon Street in 1866. To cater for it, a new signalling system was provided by Saxby & Farmer which comprised two signalboxes AB and CD, erected over the approach tracks, with semaphore signals on their roofs.* Ann Ronan Picture Library

north of Corbetts Lane Junction. The final widening came in 1901 on the north side of the viaduct by the SER; three tracks were provided south of Spa Road and two onto London Bridge. So there were eventually no less than eleven tracks between London Bridge and Spa Road, built piecemeal over nearly 70 years.

London & Croydon

This railway was authorised in June 1835 to run from a junction with the London & Greenwich Railway at Corbetts Lane to Croydon, a distance of 8¾ miles. The company's station at London Bridge was necessarily adjacent to the London & Greenwich terminus, for it used that company's tracks for the first 1¾ miles to Corbetts Lane where it gained its own metals. Although it diverged on the south side of the viaduct at Corbetts Lane, its station at London Bridge was to the north. The inconvenience of the consequent need to cross the Greenwich led the two railways to exchange station sites in 1844.

The line's principal fame was the atmospheric experiment which started in 1844. By that time the Croydon was used by trains of the London & Brighton and South Eastern from a junction at Jolly Sailor, today's Norwood Junction, so arrangements had to be made to provide a separate track for the atmospheric trains. From London Bridge to Corbetts Lane the Greenwich viaduct was to be widened on its south side to provide an additional track for the Croydon; from Corbetts Lane to Jolly Sailor the Croydon would provide an extra track to the east of its existing lines, and from Jolly Sailor to the terminus one of its existing two tracks would be converted for atmospheric working.

During the passage of the Croydon's Act through Parliament much had been made of the New Cross incline, a gradient of 1 in 100 for nearly 2¾ miles. Regarded as steep at the time, it caused considerable difficulty to locomotives which had to be assisted on the climb. At the same time, Jacob and Joseph Samuda were looking around for a company to demonstrate the atmospheric system that they had developed with their partner Samuel Clegg. An approach by the Samuda brothers to the Croydon in August 1840 came to nothing, but by 1844 with its tracks being used not only by the Brighton but also the South Eastern, the Croydon's suburban service was not as fast and frequent as it desired. In part, its answer was to join with the South Eastern in the building of Bricklayers Arms station to be free of the congestion and high tolls of the Greenwich. Once the Croydon was able to run into it, the service was increased, accommodation improved and lower fares charged to Bricklayers Arms. In the expectation of further traffic and to retaliate

against a projected London & South Western Railway branch, the Croydon decided to extend for 8½ miles to Epsom. If this extension were continued into London by a third independent track, it would provide a good test for the atmospheric system, which the Croydon intended to use on a line to Chatham with which it was associated. The atmospheric system would help to overcome the difficulties of the New Cross incline, and a third track would leave the existing two free for the main-line services of the Brighton and South Eastern.

In principle, the system was based upon the pressure of the earth's atmosphere. In application, a cast-iron tube was laid in short lengths between the rails, spiked to the sleepers. Each tube had a slot about 2in wide at the top, set within a valve seating of 7in. A leather valve was bolted to an iron rib cast on one side of the seating and iron plates attached to the top of it made it rest on the other. These plates prevented the leather from being forced down into the tube and as they were only 8in long, enabled the valve to be opened in short lengths.

Under some coaches was a piston which snugly fitted the diameter of the tube. When the piston was in the tube, the arm connecting it to the coach passed through the valve. Stationary engines provided power for pumps to produce a vacuum in the tube ahead of the piston. The higher pressure behind the piston drove it forward, as the air sought to fill the vacuum, and the piston hauled the coach to which it was attached. As the piston travelled along, so the arm opened and closed the valve on the tube.

Construction began in October 1844 on the five-mile section from Croydon to Dartmouth Arms (today's Forest Hill) with intermediate stations at Sydenham, Anerley and Jolly Sailor. Because the additional third track was on the east side of the existing Croydon lines, a timber viaduct with approach gradients of 1 in 50 was necessary to carry the atmospheric line over the Brighton line at Jolly Sailor. Engine houses were built in a Gothic style at Croydon, Norwood and Dartmouth Arms. The first trial trip was held on 22 August 1845 when 60mph was attained and in September 70mph was reached by a train of six coaches. On 20 October a special train was run for the guests of the Directors. After lunch at London Bridge, a special train left at 2.00pm for Forest Hill, where a piston carriage was substituted for the locomotive, and the five miles to Croydon were covered in 8¾ minutes with a maximum speed of 52mph.

Work continued on the engine houses which were to have two 50hp low-pressure beam engines with 40in cylinders, to be run in tandem or separately, with a smaller engine for pumping water. Forest Hill as the principal passing station was to have two more engines to speed up trains and assist trains up the New Cross

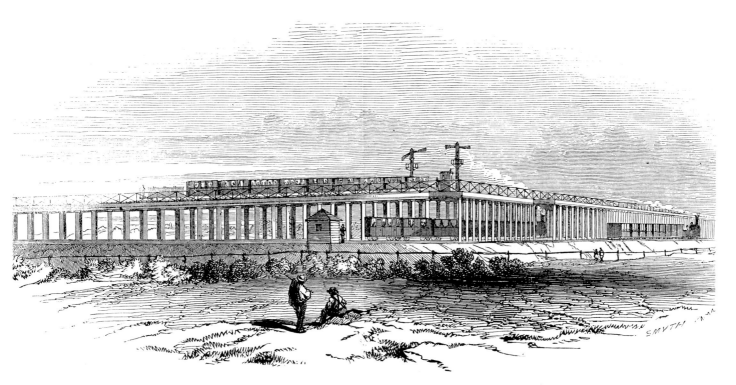

incline. Two engines were to be installed at New Cross and one at London Bridge. Each engine house had a siding for coal trucks but as the Act stipulated no smoke was to be made, coke was first used. Later anthracite and even coal were burned. The engine houses were connected by electric telegraph.

The Board of Trade had given permission to open Forest Hill to Croydon in November 1845, but the company preferred to wait to open the whole line. The earthwork for the third line was almost finished to New Cross and representations were made to the Greenwich to hurry up the widening of the viaduct. However, in the New Year opinions changed and the line opened on 19 January. Breakages in both engines at Croydon forced steam-haulage for the next two days, and even when atmospheric working was then resumed the engines continued to cause problems. By March when a new timetable with 32 trains a day was introduced, matters improved, and it was reported in May that the additional track to New Cross would be ready for traffic in June, although the second pair of engines for Forest Hill were unlikely to be ready. May brought a further improvement in the timetable and in the first two weeks passengers were some 9,000 above the same period in 1845.

But problems began to occur with the leakage of the valve caused partly by its design and partly by the sealing compound. Not only the extension to Epsom, but the completion of the main project were now thrown into doubt. Uncertain of which way to proceed, the company backed both forms of power.

Norwood Junction *In order to enable its trains to cross the London & Brighton and South Eastern Railways without a break in the atmospheric pipe, the London & Croydon had to build this wooden viaduct, near today's Norwood Junction station. It carried a single line on gradients of 1 in 50 but abandonment of the atmospheric traction in 1847 in favour of locomotive operation, rendered it redundant.* Ann Ronan Picture Library

By August 1846 the tube had been extended to New Cross, the engines were being erected and completion to London Bridge seemed imminent. However, the previous month the Croydon and the Brighton were amalgamated as the London, Brighton & South Coast Railway (LBSCR) and the end of the atmospheric was in sight. Despite the suggestion that the project should be completed to give a full test to the atmospheric system, the LBSCR directors were not in favour. To them it was unreliable, unproven, non-standard and expensive. When they decided in December 1846 that the Epsom extension should be locomotive worked, it meant that the atmospheric line would be isolated by locomotive working.

On 14 January 1847 tests were held on the New Cross incline. The first train of four coaches travelled non-stop from New Cross to Croydon, 7½ miles at 36mph. Public working from Forest Hill to New Cross began around 27 February, using the second pair of engines at Forest Hill for uphill working and gravity for downhill. Alas, the incline proved too much for unaided atmospheric traction because the diameter of the tube was too small and the engines underpowered. With the imminent opening of the Croydon line, the

Rotherhithe *Marc Brunel's Thames Tunnel of 1843 was taken over by the East London Railway in 1865, used by its trains from 1869 and in 1876 formed part of a double-track railway linking the Great Eastern to the Brighton and the South Eastern. Used as a cross-London route for passenger and freight traffic, this joint line was vested in London Transport after nationalisation. A 'C' Stock motor car heads a train arriving at Rotherhithe at the south end of the tunnel.*
National Railway Museum

death knell sounded and the LBSCR ordered locomotive working to start from 4 May 1847.

London & Blackwall

Between London Bridge and Blackwall the River Thames takes two broad meanders. The river route is some 2½ miles longer than a direct land route to the North. When the East and West India Docks opened in the 1800s, the traffic between the City and Blackwall increased considerably. The East India Dock Road of 1810 provided road connection, but plans for a rail link did not culminate in an Act until 28 July 1836, when the Commercial Railway Company was authorised to construct a line from Minories to Brunswick Wharf,

Blackwall. Realising that a City terminus was essential, the company met with defeat in 1837 when it promoted a Bill to extend the line to Lime Street but was successful with a proposal to go to Fenchurch Street, authorised in 1839, at the same time changing the company's name to the London & Blackwall.

The delay in obtaining a City terminus meant that the line was opened from a temporary terminus at Minories to Blackwall on 6 July 1840 and the section into Fenchurch Street did not open until 2 August 1841. The line was built to a gauge of 5ft, used on the Eastern Counties Railway, and there were originally intermediate stations at Minories, Shadwell, Stepney, Limehouse, West India Docks and Poplar as well as the two termini. Cannon Street Road between Minories and Shadwell opened in August 1842. The line was carried on a brick viaduct from Fenchurch Street to West India Dock Road and then on embankment for just less than half a mile before running through a slight cutting to Blackwall. In the 3½-mile length, the line fell at an average gradient of 1 in 248 towards Blackwall, although there were three sections of ascending gradients and one level.

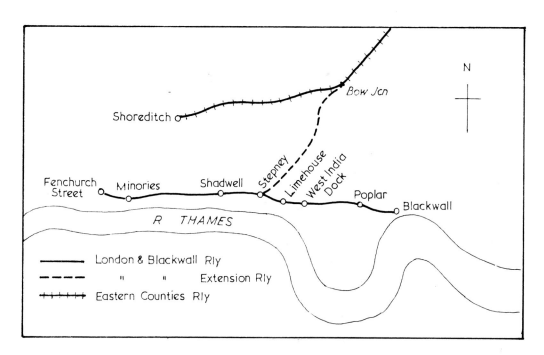

The London & Blackwall Railway.

However, it was the form of working that was the principal interest. As the line ran through a built-up area with closely-spaced intermediate stations, it was thought that locomotives could not be used. The low speeds necessary, the time taken by station stops and the danger of burning coke expelled in the exhaust were factors which were held against locomotive working. Operation by stationary engines and ropes was therefore introduced, although of a very distinctive style. Although there were two tracks, the 'North Line' and

Blackwall *Blackwall station was a structure of some architectural note sited on Brunswick Wharf alongside the Thames. Its cramped platforms and tracks are apparent in this 1936 view; three platforms serve two tracks, the shorter at one time being used by North London trains. In the last year of service trains ran at about fifteen minute intervals on weekdays to and from Fenchurch Street.*
London Borough of Tower Hamlets

Stratford *Stratford became a junction in 1840, when the Northern &
Eastern line to Broxbourne opened, and more than a century of change is
evident in this 1949 photograph. The original station is in the centre
behind the new signalbox whilst a goods train waits to join the GE main
line. Preparations for the new electric service are evident with the
platforms for interchange with the tube on the right.* British Rail

the 'South Line' were worked independently of each
other. The pairs of engines for hauling the ropes were
placed just short of the terminals. The more powerful
pair which drew trains up the gradient of the line
towards London, was placed under the railway at
Minories station, whilst the down pair was housed in a
special building at Blackwall. In addition to these
engines for normal use, a pair of extra engines of equal
power was provided at each end of the ropeway.

The rope, of 5¾in circumference, ran over sheaves
fixed in the centre of the tracks between the engines at
each end of the line. The length of each rope was twice
the distance between the engines, so that as it was

unwinding from the drum at one end it was winding
onto the drum at the other. Trains arrived or departed
from Fenchurch Street or Blackwall by their own
momentum or by gravity.

Whilst the precise method of operation varied during
the time the line was rope worked, an outline
description will illustrate the principles. As has been
mentioned, each line was separately worked but the
cycle of operations would be identical. A train leaving
Blackwall would comprise four coaches and would run
out of the terminus by gravity to the start of the rope to
which it would be attached. Simultaneously, a coach
would be attached to the rope at each of the intermediate stations. When all was ready, the engineman at
the Minories station was informed by telegraph and he
would wind in the cable. This would haul all the
coaches towards the Minories and as each arrived there,
the guards who accompanied each coach would
disconnect it from the rope and allow it to run into

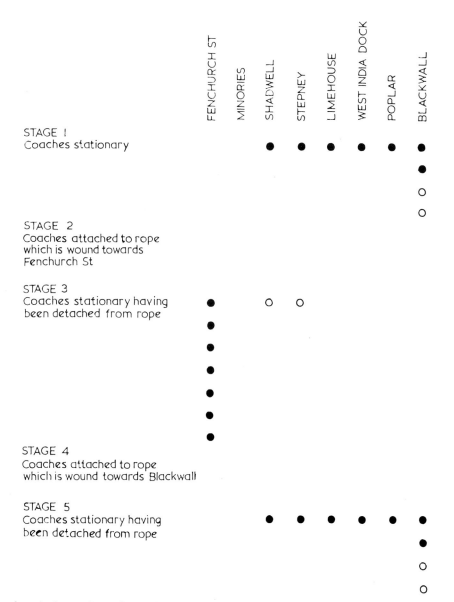

Diagram of operation of rope haulage on the London & Blackwall Railway. Each spot or circle represents a coach at different stages in the cycle of rope travel. A passenger from one intermediate station to another has to travel to the terminus and change.

Fenchurch Street with the momentum it had acquired from the rope. The only exception was that two of the coaches from Blackwall had been detached and brought to a stand at Stepney and Shadwell respectively. Now seven coaches stood at Fenchurch Street (one from each intermediate station and two from Blackwall), one at Shadwell and one at Stepney. Once loaded the seven coaches left Fenchurch Street by gravity to run to Minories where they were attached to the cable. The two coaches at Shadwell and Stepney were also attached to the cable and it hauled all nine coaches towards Blackwall. Of the seven that left Minories, one was detached at each station leaving two to run to Blackwall where they joined the two coaches which had run direct from Shadwell and Stepney. These four coaches destined

for Blackwall had, of course, run from the end of the rope into the terminus by their own momentum. With four coaches at Blackwall and one at each intermediate station, the cycle was complete and could begin again.

The service was advertised in 1843 as running every fifteen minutes from 08.00 until 21.45 but on Sundays services were suspended from 10.45 until 13.00 so as not to interfere with Church services. Speeds from 20mph to 30mph were achieved and carryings were good, 1.782m passengers travelling in the last six months of 1846. Problems occurred with breakage of the hemp cable; wire cable was later substituted and proved more satisfactory. The major problem for passengers was the need to make a journey between intermediate stations via the termini.

Carriages were of three types. The first-class of four compartments held forty, the mixed had two central first-class compartments each capable of holding ten, flanked by end third-class compartments for twenty and the third-class with four compartments held about seventy in all. All carriages had two lever brakes and were painted dark blue with the company's arms on the panels.

The London & Blackwall was self-contained, which facilitated its novel method of operation, but the formation of the London & Blackwall Extension Railway Company in 1845 to build a link from Stepney to Bow on the Eastern Counties Railway ended its isolation. Operation by locomotives was incompatible with cable traction and furthermore the Eastern Counties was being converted to 4ft 8½in gauge. So from 15 February 1849 the London & Blackwall changed to orthodox locomotive operation on the standard gauge in preparation for the opening of this new link on 2 April 1849. This change was marked by the construction of an iron roof on the original line alongside Limehouse Basin to prevent damage to sailing ships by sparks from locomotives.

This link to Bow and subsequent connections to the North London and London Tilbury & Southend Railways meant that the Blackwall service became less and less important at Fenchurch Street. Although leased by the Great Eastern Railway from 1865, the London &

Stepney Junction *At Stepney Junction the original London & Blackwall line of 1840 branched to the right whilst the 1849 link to the Eastern Counties swung left. The Blackwall line platforms became disused upon the withdrawal of the Blackwall service in 1926 and although the signalbox stood until 1961, all that remains today is the curved platforms to be served by trains on the former LTSR system.* London Borough of Tower Hamlets

Blackwall company survived until the railway grouping of 1923. Blackwall services lasted three years longer. 4 May 1926 saw their permanent withdrawal in the face of bus and tram competition.

The decline of traditional work in the Docks in the 1970s led to the establishment of the London Docklands Development Corporation, with the objective of bringing new life to the area. As part of its plan for improved transport links, a light railway has been proposed to link the City with the Isle of Dogs. This would use part of the London & Blackwall as well as the North London route to the docks, and bring back passengers over the defunct part of the L&B after some 60 years!

34

3
TERMINI

London's 15 main line termini provide a rich inheritance, both from their historical significance to the development of the Capital and in their widely varying architectural contribution. The majority of these stations, although modernised to suit the needs of today, retain a lot of atmosphere from the past, and, while the locomotives and trains may have altered, much of the flavour of the age of steam can still be found.

London's main line termini are unique to the extent that such a large number of separate stations was provided. This reflects the importance of London as the focal point of the railway network, and the spirit of competition between the major companies when the trunk routes were being laid down.

Euston *A terminus of considerable interest and variety, the departure side of old Euston was starting point for much of Britain's industrial heartland and countryside of Northern England, Wales and Western Scotland. Here, Royal Scot 4-6-0 No 46153 The Royal Dragoon waits on 14 June 1954 with the inaugural 16.55 express to Liverpool.* Brian Morrison

The development of London's termini is a fascinating story in its own right but it is not the intention to duplicate here work which has been thoroughly undertaken elsewhere. (See, for example, *London's Termini*, Alan A. Jackson. David & Charles 1969). It is simply enough to provide the key opening dates and closures, where applicable, which are summarised in Table 1 at the end of this chapter. However, it will be seen that the provision of London's termini spanned some 63 years from the opening of the first part of London Bridge by the London & Greenwich Railway in 1836 to the final addition of Marylebone by the Great Central in 1899.

It is difficult now to imagine London without access to the trunk routes which the termini provide. The 1830s brought the first four, London Bridge, Euston, Nine Elms (later Waterloo) and the first Paddington station. Euston and Paddington were to become the most important in terms of major trunk routes, between them serving much of the North and West of England. The southern termini have always been more important for the development of local and suburban services, although Waterloo competed with Paddington to serve the South West as well as Hampshire and Dorset before being run down, gaining 'The Withered Arm', and losing the celebrated Atlantic Coast Express.

The 1840s produced just two more termini, both of which were to bring the railway into the City. Within a matter of days in July 1840 the London & Blackwall opened its Minories terminus, the line being extended in the following year to Fenchurch Street, while the Eastern Counties opened Bishopsgate. Under the Great Eastern, services from both termini to the East were to become linked, although it was not until 1874 that the extension to Liverpool Street was completed. The two could not be more contrasting. Fenchurch Street was small, cramped, and provided intensive suburban services, first to Blackwall and later Tilbury and Southend, accommodating also NLR and GER trains. Liverpool Street became the chief City terminus with both the extensive Great Eastern suburban services and trunk routes serving East Anglia and the Continent via Harwich. In common each has however floods of office workers to and from the City, which ebb and flow at the morning and evening peak hours, with periods of relative tranquillity between.

On 7 August 1850 the Great Northern Railway began operating from a temporary terminus at Maiden Lane, opening Kings Cross two years later, to provide the East Coast competitor to the London & North Western Railway from Euston and many of the great annals of railway history to follow from these two remarkable companies. The 1850s also laid the foundations for the opening of Victoria in the early 1860s. Like Liverpool Street's relationship to the City, Victoria was ideally situated for the West End while also becoming focal point for services to the Continent via Dover and Folkestone. A station which boasted both the Golden Arrow and the Brighton Belle could not fail to arouse the interest of railway enthusiast, historian or traveller.

The 1860s brought the final rash of openings with no less than six new stations, excluding Victoria which had earlier origins at Wandsworth and Pimlico. Four of these were to serve the south and south eastern areas. The first, Blackfriars and Ludgate Hill, brought the London Chatham & Dover Railway closer to the City; the other two, Charing Cross and Cannon Street, provided West End and City termini for the South Eastern Railway. Ludgate Hill, an inadequate station for peak use and partly superseded with the opening of Holborn Viaduct in 1874, was closed in 1929. The other two stations were later additions of established companies seeking their own freehold tenure in London. Broad Street enabled LNWR and North London Railway services to reach their own City terminus adjacent to Liverpool Street, and St Pancras gave the Midland its London foothold after years of struggle to obtain adequate running powers over competitors' lines, first to Euston via Rugby and then to Kings Cross by way of Bedford and Hitchin.

Although Liverpool Street (1874) and Blackfriars (1886) opened later, they had their origins in earlier stations, leaving only Holborn Viaduct (1874) and Marylebone (1899) to complete the picture. Of all the London termini, Marylebone was probably the least justified on traffic grounds. As with the Midland's London extension, this was a scheme by a Northern-based company to thrust southwards to London. It was closely associated with the northward expansion of the Metropolitan Railway and other schemes being promoted by its Chairman, Sir Edward Watkin, who controlled several related interests, which could have provided a direct link to the Continent via a Channel Tunnel. In the event the grand terminus scheme for Marylebone never exceeded the present four platform faces, and it is surprising that services have not been diverted elsewhere.

Serving the East

Fenchurch Street:

This is a remarkable little station of four platforms, which despite the overhead wires associated with electrification of Tilbury and Southend services from 1961/2, still retains much of the atmosphere of the age of steam. Opened in 1841, it was the first City terminus. The present station façade dates from 1853,

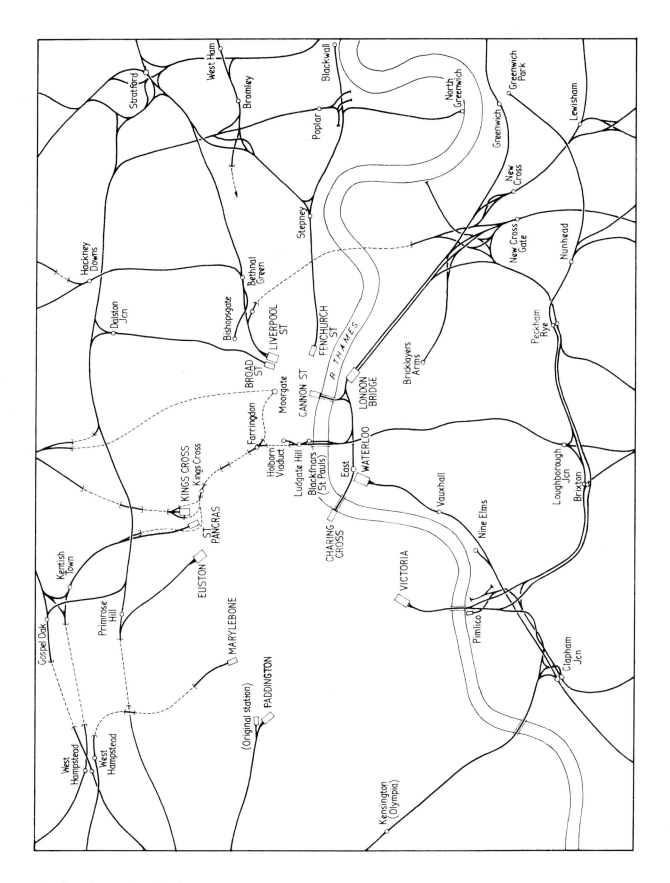

Main line railways in Central London.

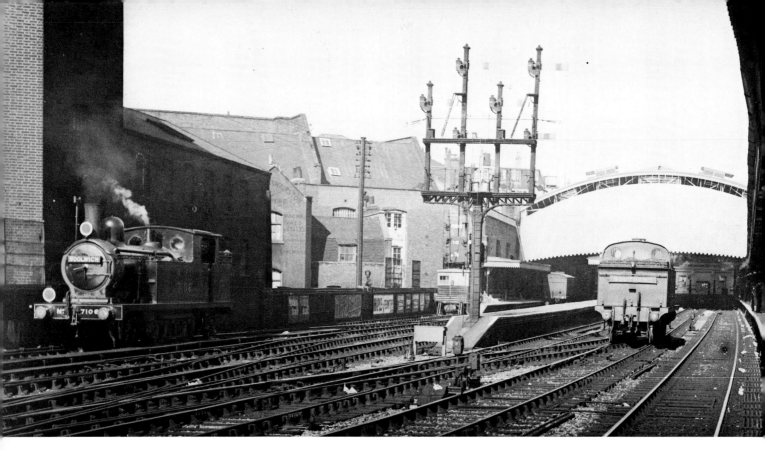

Fenchurch Street *Opened by the London & Blackwall Railway in 1841, Fenchurch Street was the City's first terminus. This 1926 view shows the station before remodelling in 1935, with an ex-GER 2-4-2T awaiting a duty to North Woolwich and a 'Tilbury tank' in the station.* H. C. Casserley

but the track layout was remodelled in 1935 and again simplified in association with electrification. The London & Blackwall, which built the station, was founded upon the then busy river steamer traffic, but the longer term future for the station was ensured by its use first by the North London Railway from 1850 and then by the Eastern Counties Railway in 1854. The present Tilbury and Southend services were established in the mid-1850s from a joint scheme by the London & Blackwall and Eastern Counties Railways which formed the London Tilbury & Southend Railway. The GER gained a further interest in the use of the terminus for its suburban services by leasing the L&B from 1 January 1866. Blackwall services were withdrawn in 1926. GER services ran from Fenchurch Street to North Woolwich until 1940, over the Epping branch until 1947 and the Shenfield line to 1949. The Midland influence was introduced on the LTSR when its services reached Barking via the Tottenham & Forest Gate Railway in 1894, the Midland taking over the LTSR from 1912. So it was that the former 'Tilbury tanks' were superseded by Stanier and BR Standard 2-6-4Ts which saw out the intensive steam suburban service until replaced by the present electric units.

Liverpool Street:
Whatever the future of this splendid structure, Liverpool Street remains one of the busiest and architecturally interesting main line stations in London. Opened in 1874/5, this City terminus of the GER was necessitated by the inconvenience for passengers of the original terminus at Bishopsgate.

In addition to the suburban network developed by the GER, the terminus provides main line services to East Anglia and Essex, including Continental boat trains via Harwich. In steam days, the station was often gloomy and clouded by smoke and was associated with the pant of Westinghouse brake pumps fitted to the suburban tank locomotives.

The cavernous atmosphere of the west side of the station was partly created by its situation below ground level, overshadowed by Broad Street station on the viaduct above. The heavy ironwork and brickwork, flanked at the rear by the Great Eastern Hotel, adds to this atmosphere which, even with the demise of steam, provides the Victorian flavour of so much of the terminus. Any redevelopment will preserve the train shed which has been the subject of considerable activity by conservationists.

The eastern side, platforms 11–18, was opened in 1894 and usually accommodates Shenfield and Southend services. Naturally, the later construction of this part of the station gives it a lighter, less heavy atmosphere.

The mixture of electric and diesel operation provides an added interest, which is enhanced from time to time by the activities of Stratford diesel depot which maintains a long tradition of individuality in the locomotives it operates.

To the North and West

Euston:

The intrusion of the London & Birmingham Railway in 1837 to the then fashionable squares and terraces on the northern fringe of London must have come as something of a shock, since at that time rail travel was still in comparative infancy. From its beginning as a train shed at the foot of Camden Bank was to develop a sprawling, untidy layout of fifteen platforms set back off Euston Road behind the Euston Hotel and the grand Doric portico which beckoned the way to the station and the Great Hall of 1849. Sadly, as Euston expanded to meet the growing demands of the LNWR, the original L&B station was gradually swallowed up, although the hotel, Doric arch and the Great Hall survived until swept away in the reconstruction of the station opened in October 1968.

The old station, however, could not fail to arouse affection and an exit from the Underground came up onto the passenger concourse on the arrival side, affording the first view of steam in platforms 1 and 2. The central part of the station, built around the original terminus, was used by Watford electric services, local and parcels trains, and the western platforms were for departures.

The new Euston, while causing the loss of much of historical significance, brought considerable improvements to passenger amenities associated with electrification of the West Coast route to Scotland. The concourse has the atmosphere of an airline terminal, light, attractive and warm, a fitting start or end to a journey on the 'Premier Line'.

Broad Street:

In its present form, Broad Street is doomed. Bereft of all but a small portion of its former overall roof

Liverpool Street *Liverpool Street opened in 1874 as an extension from Bishopsgate and has since become one of London's busiest termini. Two class B1 4-6-0 Nos 61286 and 61203 stand with the impressive trainshed in the background and the platforms of Broad Street on the viaduct behind.* C. R. L. Coles

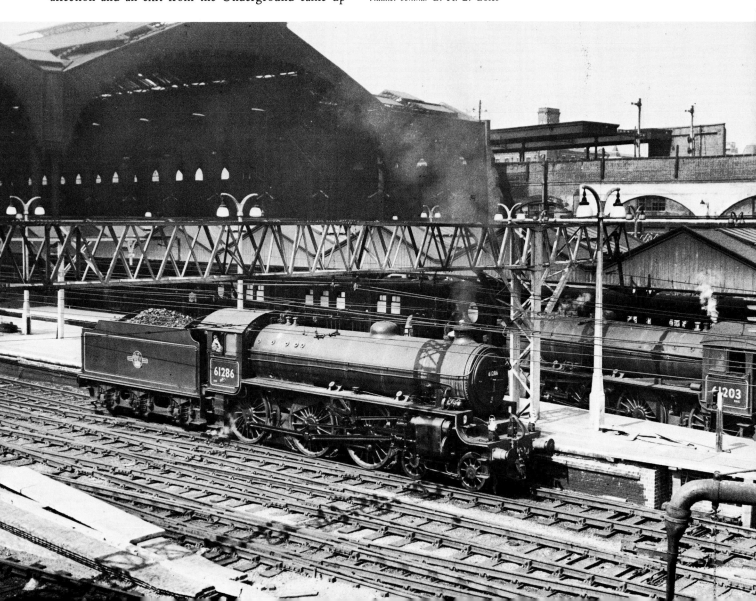

and with much of its platform capacity no longer in use, it is now only a matter of time before its ultimate closure and absorption into a redeveloped Liverpool Street.

Broad Street opened in 1865 as a means of obtaining more direct access to the City for LNWR and North London Railway services than previously possible via Fenchurch Street. Broad Street in its heyday at the turn of the century was very busy, accommodating suburban services from the LNWR main line, from Poplar and Bow, Richmond and Kew Bridge, the 'Outer Circle' via Kensington (Addison Road) and NLR services from the GNR 'Northern Heights' stations via the Canonbury Curve. Now used only by Richmond and Watford trains, the facilities are run-down and depressing; even at peak hours the station is eerily quiet despite efforts to promote the cross-London Broad Street to Richmond route.

Apart from a brief 'City to City' service to Birmingham and Wolverhampton, Broad Street's services have always been suburban in character. The arrival of competing bus and tram services at the turn of the century was countered by electrification but continued reduction in traffic flows between NLR stations and the City, partly due to competition from the Underground, eventually caused the run-down station of today, a depressing memorial to the effect of competition which has been difficult to stem despite extensive publicity campaigns.

Kings Cross:
Completed in 1852, Lewis Cubitt's multi-arched train shed replaced a temporary structure at Maiden Lane opened in 1850. Kings Cross provided the start of competition to serve Scotland and enabled London to be linked by rail to many principal destinations on the eastern side of the Pennines.

Euston *Reconstruction of Euston in the 1960s brought order from chaos for passengers but lost a station with much of historical importance. Here Jubilee 4-6-0 No 45593 Kholapur, since preserved, stands at Platform 1 in 1951 having arrived with a train from Blackpool. Note the semaphore ground signal controlling the crossover between the tracks of Platforms 1 and 2. Brian Morrison*

Owing to expansion of suburban services during the latter years of the nineteenth century, various additions were required. These included provision for services over the Metropolitan Railway's City Widened lines, introduced in 1863 at York Road for southbound trains and, from 1878, by a northbound platform on the Hotel Curve which was notorious for smoke, slipping and stalling in the restricted tunnel which led to the platform. A new suburban station was added on the west side in 1875 and this was further extended in 1895 and again in 1924.

The station was shared until 1868 by the Midland, which then transferred its facilities to St Pancras. Suburban services reached their peak at the beginning of the twentieth century, and after 1939 services over the Edgware, Barnet and Alexandra Palace lines were either transferred to London Transport or closed. The opening of the Piccadilly line extension to Cockfosters in the early 1930s also led to loss of suburban patronage while the Victoria line, opened in 1969, further affected suburban travel patterns.

The station has been tastefully modernised in conjunction with the GN suburban electrification project, and a travel centre, shops and concourse added onto the Euston Road frontage. With the opening in 1976 of the Finsbury Park to Moorgate route, transferred from London Transport, GN services over the Widened lines were withdrawn, but much of historical interest remains to compete with cleanliness of today's suburban electrics and the speed of the Inter-City 125s.

Kings Cross *Parcels, newspapers and mails have been a traditional aspect of London's main line termini. Immortalised by the documentary film* Night Mail *of 1936, showing the work of the Euston – Glasgow overnight mail express, the picture depicts an East Coast equivalent being loaded at platform 10, Kings Cross on a winter's evening in 1947.* C. R. L. Coles

St Pancras:
The magnificent gothic façade of St Pancras station commands the eastern end of Euston Road and over-looks its plainer neighbour, Kings Cross. Opened in 1868, the frontage building was a hotel until 1935 and is now offices.

The interior of the station is a lofty reminder of dramatic Victorian engineering at its finest, Barlow's single span overall roof matching the best of modern work. This masterpiece of glass and steel covers a station which caters now for inter-city services to Leicester, Nottingham and Sheffield, in addition to the St Albans, Luton and Bedford electric suburban services. In the past, of course, destinations also included Manchester and Liverpool and the most picturesque of the three routes to Scotland, the Settle & Carlisle. Although the Thames-Clyde Express may be no longer, the Scottish run is still possible, but only for the more venturesome train-changers wishing to take an alternative to the Electric Scots.

Entrance to the station is either from the wide sweeping ramped cab approach or by quaint 'typically Midland' steps from Pancras Road. An alternative is

St Pancras *Modernisation has swept away much of the atmosphere but brought improvements for the passenger. St Pancras in 1956, however, retained many aspects of Midland origin, with a gantry of lower quadrant signals and two massive signalboxes. In front of the station signalbox is the wagon hoist which gave access to the warehouse below the terminus.* A. R. Brown

St Pancras *The Midland Pullman unit stands quietly in Platform 6, waiting to form the 18.10 service to Manchester Central on 15 October 1965. The picture does justice to Barlow's magnificent single span roof at St Pancras, setting a scene which seems so familiar yet strangely dated. Note the parcels vans on the right.* North Western Museum of Science & Industry

from the Underground by steps to two entrances at the back of the passenger concourse. The booking hall is an impressive focal point of interest, its brickwork and ornate woodwork being of a quality worthy of permanent preservation. Unseen below, the cellars, formerly used for beer traffic from Burton, were reached by a wagon hoist at the end of platforms 5/6.

Marylebone:
Saturday 3 September 1966 was a sad day for railway enthusiasts and historians alike, for it spelt the end of the former Great Central main line to London after a mere 67 years. The last main line to be built, it was the first to close, although Marylebone has survived as the terminus for truncated services to Aylesbury and Banbury.

Marylebone itself is a quiet station, shyly hidden behind 222 Marylebone Road, headquarters offices of the British Railways Board and previously the Great Central Hotel. It never achieved the grandeur planned by the GCR, remaining a modest, but interesting, structure of four platform faces, a rather unlikely

Marylebone *Until the final withdrawal of main line trains in 1966, Marylebone had a surprising variety of main line and suburban services for a station of its size. BR standard 2-6-4T No 80139 is half hidden in shadow after arrival with a mixed set of suburban stock. St Marylebone Society and Westminster City Libraries*

terminal for The Master Cutler or The South Yorkshireman.

Yet it had considerable excitement and contrast. The peak hours were of interest for the busy movements of suburban trains, while services to the East Midlands and to Manchester resulted in an interesting mixture of main line motive power.

After years of LNER and Eastern Region supremacy and a brief period of Western Region control, it was left to the LMR to run down and supervise the eventual closure, the honours falling to Stanier Class 5 No 44984 to haul the final scheduled services over the former GCR London Extension route.

Today Marylebone attracts custom for its real ale at the restored station bar, while the insignia GCR still beckons the passenger through the iron gates to the concourse.

Paddington:

This masterpiece of a station holds romance not only for its historical associations but for the memories of glorious holidays in the sun, care of The Cornish Riviera Limited, for this was a fitting entrance to the 'Great Way West'.

Along with London Bridge, Euston and Nine Elms, the GWR was an early arrival in London, the original Paddington, opened in 1838, being on the site of the parcels depot west of Bishop's bridge, to the north-west of the present station which opened in 1854. Brunel, whose broad gauge began the long tradition of Great Western individuality, gave his company a splendid London terminus which is still today a building of much character and architectural merit, retaining a good deal of former GWR flavour.

Paddington can be viewed from several angles. Perhaps the most pleasing is the approach from Praed Street, past the Great Western Royal Hotel down the ramp to the cab road. High up on the station offices, completed in 1933, the GWR insignia affords the passenger a welcome, while that company's coat of arms still adorns the entrance canopy. Beyond are the trains, still attractive, although no longer in characteristic chocolate-and-cream or having the lure of steam, but nevertheless offering the comfort and speed of the Inter-City 125s. Another way in is from Eastbourne Terrace onto Platform 1. Entrance from LT's Circle or Bakerloo lines will bring the traveller up steps onto 'The Lawn', while access can also be obtained via the Hammersmith & City line platforms from Paddington (Suburban). A good view of the station is afforded from the footbridge linking the platforms at the country end, although Paddington's jewel has to be the view across the transept from the balcony above Platform 1.

Although the classic GW locomotive designs of the King or Castle may be no more, Brunel would surely be pleased with his station's present use, which remains the undisputed gateway to the West.

Waterloo:

The first terminus at Nine Elms gave the London & Southampton Railway the springboard from which its successor, Waterloo, was successfully to project the LSWR.

Opened in 1848, ten years after Nine Elms, the original station at Waterloo expanded piecemeal, becoming the central portion with additions of 1860 on the north-west side and a link to the South Eastern in 1864. Further extensions, 'Cyprus' in 1878 and 'Khartoum' in 1885, resulted in an unsatisfactory muddle, even worse than that at Euston.

Rebuilding became necessary and began in 1900, although not completed until 1922. The concourse is ranged in a curve at the head of the platforms and station facilities are in the frontage block which sweeps around the concourse. Until completion of Euston, this was London's most modern terminal building.

The station was never ideally situated for the West End or City, always having the great divide of the Thames. However, it is an impressive structure when approached by steps through the Victory Arch (the LSWR War Memorial) or from the footway over York Road, onto the back of the concourse on the 'Windsor side'. Other entrances from Waterloo Road are less than impressive, although the pedestrian link to Waterloo East, the former connection to the SER, is of interest.

Today the station has an air of sterility, the bulk of its services being quiet and clean electrics. Class 33s, 47s, 50s and 73s on the remaining locomotive-hauled services to Weymouth, Salisbury and Exeter fail to arouse interest in quite the same way as the Bulleid Pacific, Lord Nelson, King Arthur and various other steam locomotive classes which they replaced.

Nevertheless, the 21 platforms provide a substantial range of activities, the widely varying types of passenger matching the variety of traffic and the areas served. Although in recent years it has lost the 'battle of the West' to the GWR route, the spirit of the LSWR still lives on in the scale of operations which Waterloo provides.

South of London

Apart from the LSWR at Waterloo, whose prime objectives were south-west and west, the remaining termini which serve the South of England are associated with three major companies, the London, Brighton & South Coast Railway (formed in 1846 by an amalgamation between the London & Croydon and London & Brighton companies) the South Eastern Railway and the London Chatham & Dover Railway. Operations were considerably simplified when the latter two companies came into joint working arrangements under the South Eastern & Chatham Railway Managing Committee in 1899.

To summarise, London Bridge became terminal for LBSCR and SER trains, Charing Cross was an SER extension to obtain better access to the West End and Cannon Street provided the SER with a City terminal. Victoria gave the LBSCR and the LCDR a West End terminal while Blackfriars, Ludgate Hill and Holborn Viaduct were LCDR termini serving the City.

London Bridge:

This is London's oldest terminus, opened in 1836 by the London & Greenwich Railway. Expansion was to occur

London Bridge *The busy and complex approach to this, London's oldest terminus, is exemplified by this view of London Bridge in about 1910. Apart from the pointwork, signals and elevated signalbox, the picture shows the terminal's locomotive servicing sidings, a feature common to most of London's termini in the steam era.* Pamlin Prints

quickly. In 1839 the London & Croydon Railway opened a separate terminal at London Bridge and ran over the London & Greenwich to Corbetts Lane, Bermondsey, before turning south through New Cross to West Croydon. Two other companies were also interested in reaching London Bridge, the South Eastern Railway, by extending the L&CR through Coulsdon and Redhill before turning east to Tonbridge, Ashford and Folkestone to Dover, and the London & Brighton Railway, which was to share the route to Redhill and then continue southwards to Brighton. The schemes were linked by Parliamentary insistence, ownership of the line from Norwood (where the L&BR and SER diverged from the L&CR to Redhill, whence the SER swung eastwards) being 45% to L&BR and 55% to SER. This was to be the cause of constant conflict eventually resulting in the LBSCR opening in 1899 its own diversionary route, the 'Quarry Line', avoiding SER metals.

The L&BR commenced operations in 1841 and the SER in the following year. A new station was necessary at London Bridge to house the four companies and this opened in 1844, when the London & Greenwich exchanged stations with the London & Croydon. However, the former whose tracks the others were obliged to use, raised its tolls, which led to the L&CR and the SER jointly opening a new 'Grand West End Terminus' at Bricklayers Arms to avoid running over the Greenwich metals. Although never successful for passenger traffic, closing in 1852, the

objective of overcoming the London & Greenwich tolls was successfully achieved, the site becoming an extensive freight depot and locomotive shed.

The L&GR and the L&CR had been small, pioneering concerns whose livelihood became dependent upon the activities of the larger main line companies which used their metals. Amalgamation was only a matter of time. The SER moved first, leasing the L&GR in 1845, but the L&BR secured the L&CR in the following year to form the LBSCR.

The original station was now too small and in 1850 the SER partitioned its portion of the station, the SER building a new terminus on the north side of the site and paving the way to the SER's subsequent extension to Charing Cross and Cannon Street. The LBSCR followed suit with extended facilities on its side.

The dust had hardly settled on this new arrangement when, to meet expanding service commitments and a need to get closer to the City and West End, the SER proceeded with its extension to Charing Cross, requiring conversion of its terminal into a through station. This it completed in 1864. Further traffic increases resulted in modifications to track and signal-

London Bridge *The approaches to the southern termini are complex, as depicted in this 1961 aerial view of London Bridge and Cannon Street. The 'Brighton' and 'South Eastern' sides of London Bridge and their approach lines are in the top of the picture while the triangular junction and bridge to Cannon Street dominates the still busy upper Pool of London.* Aerofilms Limited

ling by the LBSCR in the late 1870s and a reconstruction of the SER facilities again in the mid-1890s. A final modification was made with the completion in 1902 of four new terminal platforms on the site of the former SER continental goods depot which it had established between its 'through' station and the LBSCR terminal when constructing the Charing Cross line. This brought London Bridge to a total of 21 platforms approached by no less than eleven tracks over the viaduct from Bermondsey. The L&GR would have been surprised to see into what its original viaduct had

grown, although the company lingered on until 1923 mainly for the collection of rents.

The unplanned growth of the station was unsatisfactory and led to BR reconstructing the station which was completed in 1978. Although the footbridge connecting both parts of the station succeeds in uniting it, the origins of both parts are still recognisable.

Charing Cross:
The SER-inspired Charing Cross Railway Company completed the extension from London Bridge across the Thames to its new West End terminus in 1864. This short extension was constructed at high cost and with some difficulty but gave the SER an excellent frontage on to the Strand at street level, although the remainder of the extension was on bridge or viaduct.

The station originally had a single-span overall roof similar to that at Cannon Street. Due to structural weakness, this collapsed in 1905 during maintenance work. As a result, the train shed was re-roofed with the present ridge-and-furrow type which gives the station a light and modern appearance.

Despite its cramped nature, the SER used the station for boat train services, although after several periods of transfer to Victoria, these were moved permanently by the SECR to Victoria in 1920.

Until the end of steam in 1961, the mixture of suburban electric services and Kent Coast and (until 1958) Hastings line steam services gave Charing Cross a lot of interest. This was no better seen than from the steps of the Victory Arch at Waterloo as West Country or Schools class locomotives and trains rounded the final curve from Waterloo East to cross Hungerford Bridge with a rumble and trail of white smoke, coming to rest at the concourse where so many continental journeys had ended.

Cannon Street:

In an effort to match the competition from its rival the LCDR, the SER crossed the Thames by a branch from the Charing Cross extension to a City terminus at Cannon Street, opened in 1866.

From the outset, the practice was to run most trains, including Continental services, from Charing Cross in and out of Cannon Street. These trains were initially well-used for local travel until the District Railway opened along the Embankment. Continental services were finally withdrawn from Cannon Street in 1914, apart from a brief spell to relieve Victoria in the mid-1930s.

The overall roof was badly damaged in 1941 during an air raid and the glass was later removed, but it was not until early 1959 that the roof was finally dismantled during the rebuilding, leaving only the massive side walls.

Steam operation ended in 1959, and today the station deals only with weekday commuter services. From the river or the incoming train the outline of the traditional terminus is seen, whereas from the road or Underground it appears as a modern station of the 1960s.

Charing Cross *Opened in 1864 by the South Eastern Railway to serve the West End, Charing Cross has an extensive mixture of suburban and main line services to Kent and Sussex. Schools class 4-4-0 No 30912* Downside *awaits departure in 1951 with a train for Hastings.* P. H. Wells

Charing Cross *A complication in SECR working into London until the 1920s was the fact that most Kent Coast trains called at both Cannon Street and Charing Cross, entailing reversal at the former, and complicated engine movements. This view of the Charing Cross approaches before the first world war shows the array of running and shunting signals necessary for engine release and shunting moves*

Victoria:

Opened between 1860 and 1862, this was the culmination of earlier LBSCR and LCDR moves to reach the West End across the Thames. It was to develop into essentially three stations in one, the LBSCR, when rebuilding its station between 1901 and 1908, providing two end-to-end stations, enabling maximum capacity to be obtained from the platforms, while the LCDR station adjacent became established for Continental traffic. The LCDR station was also shared by GWR trains from 1863 until 1915. Other cross-London services operated for several years from the Midland, GNR and the LNWR, but all regular cross-London services into Victoria were withdrawn by 1917.

The approaches to Victoria are extremely complicated and cross the river by the Grosvenor Bridge. The LCDR route approaches from the south east by way of Brixton, while the Brighton line comes via Streatham and Balham, through Clapham Junction, thence crossing the LSWR main line to reach Victoria.

Until 1923/4 and the common management of the Southern Railway, the two stations were physically isolated, but in 1925 the linking of the two concourses was undertaken. The Chatham side is of interest for its Continental services, concentrated at Victoria by the SECR in 1920. Although the Golden Arrow and the Night Ferry have gone, the concourse still throngs with foreign tongues when Victoria provides the first welcome to visitors arriving by train from the Channel ports, or by air via Gatwick.

Another aspect of Victoria which has also gone forever, but which gave the station a special interest, was the Pullman services. Many trains contained a Pullman Car, while the Golden Arrow and the Brighton Belle were the chief all-Pullman trains. Other termini also provided such facilities, Kings Cross offering the Yorkshire Pullman and the Tees-Tyne Pullman, Liverpool Street the Eastern Belle and Waterloo the Bournemouth Belle, these being just a sample from the many others, while in diesel days the Midland Pullman and Western Pullman operated from

VICTORIA · STATION
PIMLICO · 6 · 12 · 01

H. Penton

St Pancras and Paddington; the Manchester Pullman runs with electric locomotive traction from Euston. Sadly, apart from the latter, these and other similar trains are now only memories, as the standard of Inter-City has been brought up to those similarly provided by Pullman trains.

With suburban electrification by the LBSCR and the Southern Railway, Victoria continues to attract the daily surges of commuters at the morning and evening peak hours, especially from services on the Brighton side. The bulk of main line steam operation from the terminal ceased with the Kent Coast electrification in 1959/60 and with it much of the remaining character of the train services was lost, although it was not until 1963 that steam finally succumbed on services to Oxted, Uckfield and East Grinstead.

Blackfriars, Ludgate Hill and Holborn Viaduct:
The LCDR began using temporary accommodation at Victoria in 1860, but not content to remain excluded from serving the City, set about establishing cross-London services by linking up with the Metropolitan at Farringdon and incorporating City terminal facilities.

This it achieved by diverging from its Victoria route

Victoria Victoria has always been a station of contrasts with its continental services, lines to the Sussex and Kent Coasts and extensive suburban services. This line drawing of the station in 1901 shows its external bustle and the range of signs for destinations served. Upheaval is about to take place again with extensive redevelopment to meet the needs of the 1980s. Elton Collection

at Herne Hill, opening a terminus on the South Bank, which it called Blackfriars, in June 1864. This substantial station remained in use for passengers until 1885, when like Bishopsgate and Bricklayers Arms it was converted to a freight terminal. Blackfriars became a through station in December 1864, when the first Blackfriars railway bridge was opened, and trains terminated at a temporary station on the north bank of the Thames until Ludgate Hill was opened in the following year. The junction with the Metropolitan was opened in January 1866 and Ludgate Hill then also became a through station. In May 1886 a second bridge across the Thames gave access to the LCDR terminal which it called St Paul's, renamed Blackfriars in 1937. This was to share in continental traffic, immortalised in stone plaques naming destinations; these plaques have been preserved in the rebuilt station.

49

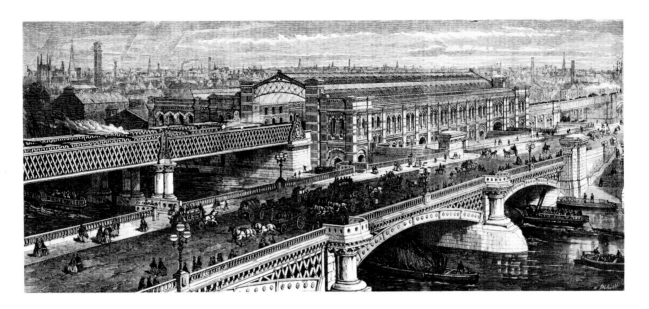

Blackfriars *The London Chatham & Dover Railway, in providing access to the City and a cross-London link to the Metropolitan, opened this 'temporary' terminus in 1864 on the South Bank which it called Blackfriars. This soon became a through station and remained in passenger use until 1885 when it was converted to a goods terminal.* Mary Evans Picture Library

Cannon Street *The former overall roof of this terminus is well illustrated in this lithograph of Cannon Street in SER days. How many of today's City commuters who use its present facilities during the rush hours would be aware of its history or the Continental services which once used its platforms?* Museum of London

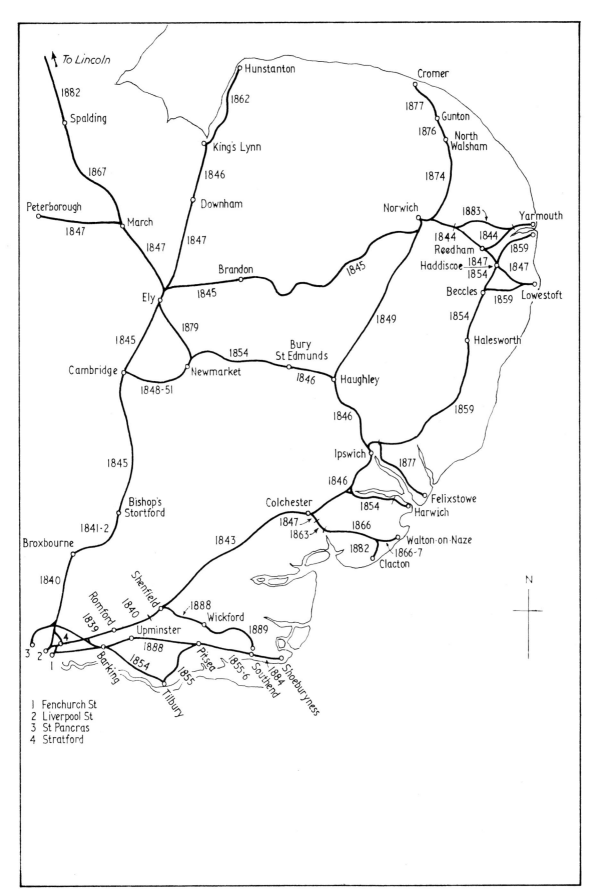

Rail development in East Anglia.

Brentwood Bank *Battle of Britain Class No 34057 Biggin Hill,
temporarily loaned to the Eastern Region, descends Brentwood Bank in
1951 with an up-Norwich express. A newly introduced electric train
follows on the left.* C. R. L. Coles

Liverpool Street, with Norwich and King's Lynn
predominating.

Until the end of steam operation, these were
fascinating main lines, the use of Britannia Pacifics on
the top link runs providing a fitting swansong. Now
there remains little to capture the imagination, neither
Bethnal Green nor Brentwood Banks providing too
much difficulty, while Stratford is only a shadow of its
previous complexity. Nevertheless, the combination of
speed and the flavour of the past, still makes a journey
from Liverpool Street or Fenchurch Street an interesting
experience.

Competing Northwards

Main line services from Euston, Kings Cross, St Pancras
or Marylebone in the area covered by this book were
not the complex but compact structure of those to East

Anglia. Rather, these had common factors at their
southern ends, both geographically and in the traffic
they carried. First, they were all main lines with
objectives principally in the Midlands or North of
England and Scotland. Second, they each had to cross
the Chiltern barrier and Northern Heights. Third,
suburban services were never so well developed, the
main line services being generally more important than
the suburban facilities provided.

The LNWR:
The London & Birmingham Railway, opened throughout in 1838, was the first to traverse the Chiltern Hills.
With the formation of the LNWR in 1846, Euston was
destined to serve much of the industrial West Midlands,
the Potteries, factory towns and cities of Lancashire as
well as North Wales, Cumbria and Western Scotland.
With destinations throughout much of Britain's
industrial heartland, the LNWR surely earned its self-
styled title of the 'Premier Line'.

South of Rugby, no major main line diverged from
the trunk route, junctions being made with only minor
branches or secondary cross-country lines. Watford's
interest was as northern terminus of the LNWR 'New
Line', the DC suburban electric services from Euston

As a result of congestion and inconvenience at Ludgate Hill, Holborn Viaduct was opened in 1874, Ludgate Hill finally closing in 1929. Today, Blackfriars and Holborn Viaduct have the buildings of the twentieth century and the echoes of the nineteenth. Closed at weekends, with little use on weekdays outside peak hours, they never have the bustle of other termini.

Holborn Viaduct has lost an island platform and its overall roof, Blackfriars the western of its two bridges, while there is virtually no trace of Ludgate Hill. In 1969, the once busy cross-London freight link, on which Snow Hill was located under Holborn Viaduct until shut in 1916, was closed, bringing to an end this interesting inter-regional facility.

TABLE 1: LONDON TERMINI, SHOWING OPENING DATES AND ORIGINS

LONDON BRIDGE	14 December 1836	London & Greenwich Railway
LONDON BRIDGE	5 June 1839	London & Croydon Railway
Bricklayers Arms	1 May 1844 – January 1852	South Eastern Railway
EUSTON	20 July 1837	London & Birmingham Railway
FENCHURCH STREET	2 August 1841	London & Blackwall Railway
Minories	6 July 1840 – 24 October 1853	London & Blackwall Railway
WATERLOO	11 July 1848	London & South Western Railway
Nine Elms	21 May 1838 – 11 July 1848	London & Southampton Railway
KINGS CROSS	14 October 1852	Great Northern Railway
Maiden Lane	7 August 1850 – 1852	Great Northern Railway
PADDINGTON	16 January 1854	Great Western Railway
Paddington (original station)	4 June 1838 – 29 May 1854	Great Western Railway
VICTORIA (Brighton side)	1 October 1860	Victoria Station & Pimlico Railway
VICTORIA (Chatham side)	25 August 1862	Victoria Station & Pimlico Railway
Wandsworth Common	1 December 1856 – June 1858	West End & Crystal Palace Railway
Pimlico	29 March 1858 – 1860	West End & Crystal Palace Railway
CHARING CROSS	11 January 1864	South Eastern Railway
Ludgate Hill	1 June 1865 –3 March 1929	London Chatham & Dover Railway
BROAD STREET	1 November 1865	North London Railway
CANNON STREET	1 September 1866	South Eastern Railway
ST PANCRAS	1 October 1868	Midland Railway
LIVERPOOL STREET	2 February 1874	Great Eastern Railway
Bishopsgate	1 July 1840 – 1 November 1875	Eastern Counties Railway
HOLBORN VIADUCT	2 March 1874	London Chatham & Dover Railway
BLACKFRIARS (St Paul's)	10 May 1886	London Chatham & Dover Railway
Blackfriars	1 June 1864 – 1 October 1885	London Chatham & Dover Railway
MARYLEBONE	15 March 1899	Great Central Railway

Stations in lower case, apart from Ludgate Hill, have been related to the current main line station to which they were linked.

(Table reproduced by kind permission of Mr Alan A. Jackson based upon his book *London's Termini*, David & Charles 1969)

4
MAIN LINES

The main line approaches to London are closely associated with the termini which they serve. London has a range of trunk lines, from relatively short-haul routes to the Channel ports and south and east coast resorts, to the medium- and long-distance services which are characteristic of those to the West of England and Wales, the Midlands and the North.

Much of the background history of the main lines has already been outlined in the previous chapter; it is the purpose here to detail something of the individual characteristics and atmosphere of each route and its relation to other lines in addition to expanding upon its history where appropriate. While the sections incorporate aspects from the steam age, the modern railways of today, based on Inter-City and with electrification and HSTs, are carrying the railways into new opportunities and development.

Eastern Approaches

The main line approaches to Liverpool Street are dominated by Bethnal Green Bank, Stratford and the tower blocks of London's East End. The spine of the GER main line today is the route through Stratford, Shenfield and Colchester, giving access to East Anglia and the Essex Coast resorts. At Bethnal Green, the main line to Cambridge and North Norfolk diverges by the 'cut-off' route opened in 1872, through Hackney Downs to rejoin the original Lea Valley line from Stratford at Coppermill Junction.

The first section, opened in 1839 by the Eastern Counties Railway, ran from a temporary terminus at Mile End to Romford. The following year saw extensions to Shoreditch (renamed Bishopsgate in 1846) and Brentwood, as well as the opening of the first stage of the Northern & Eastern Railway from Stratford to Broxbourne. The future importance of Stratford as a railway junction thus was secured by this early connection.

Expansion of the two primary routes continued piecemeal, Bishop's Stortford being reached in 1842 and Colchester in the following year. The Cambridge line was first to Norwich, by completion of several sections in 1845 through Cambridge and Ely and thence onwards to Yarmouth, having been opened from Norwich in the previous year. Meanwhile, the route via Ipswich was opened to Haughley in 1846 and throughout to Norwich in 1849.

In the early years, services via Cambridge were favoured for Norwich but from the formation of the GER in 1862 neither Cambridge nor Ipswich was predominant. From 1888, however, the Ipswich route was chosen as the main route for Norwich, which with its other traffic makes it still the more important today.

The most important subsequent expansions were to King's Lynn from Ely in 1847 and to Harwich in 1854, although Parkeston Quay was not opened until 1882. Lowestoft (1859), Hunstanton (1862), Walton-on-the-Naze (1867), Felixstowe and Cromer (1877), Clacton (1882) and Southend (1889) were the other principal objectives of the main line network served by Liverpool Street after its opening in 1874/5.

From 1892 until World War I trains ran from Liverpool Street to York using the Great Northern & Great Eastern Joint Line from March to Doncaster via Lincoln. Two other interesting aspects of Liverpool Street's main line operations are Continental services via Parkeston Quay and the highly seasonal traffic to the popular east coast holiday resorts, now sadly much diminished.

In addition to suburban services to Fenchurch Street, the GER also used St Pancras from 1870 until 1922 as a 'West End' terminal primarily serving Cambridge and Norwich, for Royal trains to Wolferton, and Newmarket race specials. Competition for Southend links Liverpool Street with Fenchurch Street, both routes of which could have been secured by the GER if the LTSR had not been incorporated into the Midland system from 1912.

Electrification of services to Southend (both routes), Walton-on-the-Naze and Clacton and rationalisation or closure of other links means that Norwich, Harwich, King's Lynn and Lowestoft provide the remaining principal main line locomotive-hauled services from

Baker Street. A train of 1938 tube stock, now the oldest on LT, waits to leave for Watford on the through Bakerloo Line service which ran over LMR tracks northwards from Queens Park. After being cut to peak hours only, the through workings were discontinued north of Stonebridge Park in 1982. London Transport Executive

London Transport does not often have to contend with snow but this 1973 tube stock train of the Piccadilly Line, built for use with the opening of the Heathrow extension, enters Oakwood depot after a moderate fall. London Transport Executive

Overleaf: A panoramic view north-westward from the roof of Harrow-on-the-Hill station, Metropolitan Line. North- and southbound Baker Street–Uxbridge trains, formed of A60/62 stock, pass each other. On the extreme left are the two tracks used by BR DMUs on the Marylebone–Aylesbury service. London Transport Executive

Until completion of electrification from Rickmansworth to Amersham in 1961 Metropolitan services to Aylesbury were electric locomotive hauled between London and Rickmansworth, with steam traction onwards. In 1958 Metropolitan locomotive No 5 *John Hampden* draws to a stop at Moor Park on an Aylesbury–Baker Street working. G. M. Kichenside

A feature of the 1938 surface stock, originally classified as O and P, and the cars which formed the post second world war R stock, was the flared lower edge to the body sides, clearly seen in this view of a COP train on District Line service at Turnham Green. Here there are four tracks with the Piccadilly Line in the centre, but this section originally belonged to the London & South Western Railway. London Transport Executive

Camden Bank *An interesting practice, now much diminished because of more efficient utilisation, was the movement of empty coaching stock between terminus and carriage sidings. Here, Class 5 4-6-0 No 44771 climbs Camden Bank with empties on 14 June 1954.* Brian Morrison

covered by this book is no less dramatic or interesting. The start from Kings Cross is through the notoriously slippery Gas Works and Copenhagen Tunnels, which sometimes defeated heavy steam-hauled trains in their smoky environs. Like Euston, such complications, which brought out the full skills of the engine crews in coaxing their smoking giants through such difficulties, is hardly noticeable today with modern traction.

At Belle Isle, between Gas Works and Copenhagen Tunnels, restricted views of the 'throat' to Kings Cross Goods and Top Shed could be seen on the west side, a location overlooked by the North London line passing overhead. Thence onwards, the beat of the Pacific at the head would be gradually increasing with rising speed as Finsbury Park was passed, a complex arrangement of lines to accommodate with minimal crossing the Canonbury link to the NLR and the former GN Northern Heights branches which, until 1970, curved away to the north west, as well as linking into the yards and sidings of the area. Today Finsbury Park diesel depot, which closed in 1981 following the run-down of

locomotive-hauled trains as a result of HST and emus, can be seen on the west side, while since 1976 GN suburban electrics have run to Moorgate via the former GN & City line.

Before Harringay the line crosses the Tottenham & Hampstead line, linked by a single-track spur, and then passes Ferme Park carriage sidings, once a busy marshalling yard, on the left and Hornsey electric multiple-unit depot behind sidings on the right. As Wood Green is approached, carriage sidings and sheds parallel the up side, while fine views of Alexandra Palace, commanding the suburbs of North London, can be seen to the left.

The express then passes Wood Green at speed, the station being opened in 1859 and since 1871 junction

61

Watford Tunnels *The speed and power of Coronation class 4-6-2 No 46245* City of London *is captured as it bursts out of Watford tunnel disrupting the tranquil sunlight.* Real Photographs Co Ltd

Hatfield *This early view shows Hatfield with its partial overall roof spanning the up-slow line. In its heyday, Hatfield was a busy junction, with branches to St Albans, Hertford and Dunstable. It would be interesting to know how the platform staff would have reacted to today's ER High Speed Trains!* Neil Jenkins collection

MAIN LINES

for a branch to Enfield. In 1918 this branch was extended into the 'Hertford Loop' which rejoins the main line at Langley Junction, Stevenage, and in the past provided relief to the main line for the two-track section between New Barnet and Potters Bar.

Tunnels pierce the high ground of the flanks of Muswell Hill between Wood Green and New Southgate and at Oakleigh Park. After avoiding the high ground of Barnet to the west, the line passes through Hadley Wood tunnels, which was a popular place to watch main line steam at full stretch. At last through Potters Bar Tunnel, brief respite was to be had for steam-hauled expresses through Hatfield, junction for St Albans (1865–1951), Hertford (1858–1951) and Dunstable (1860–1965). The Hertford and Dunstable branches paralleled the main line before diverging east and west beyond Welwyn Garden City.

Now entering the eastern extremities of the Chilterns the line crosses Digswell Viaduct, a fine structure of 40 arches, before plunging into Welwyn Tunnels. The train then passes through Knebworth and the Hertford Loop trails in from the south at Langley Junction, with the site of Langley Watertroughs just beyond.

At Hitchin the steam locomotive shed and yard nestled between the main line and a low outcrop of chalk on the up side, marking the start of the somewhat gentler stretch through Huntingdon to Peterborough and beyond. Hitchin is junction for the GN route to Cambridge (opened for local trains between Cambridge and Hitchin in 1852 and for through services from Kings Cross in 1866) taken by the Cambridge Buffet Expresses before preference was given to Liverpool Street in the late 1970s. On the down side a small diesel depot was built to replace the steam locomotive shed, although this has now closed. This depot was adjacent to the former Midland goods depot at the end of the branch from Bedford (1857–1962), used by Midland trains to Kings Cross until transferred to St Pancras in 1868.

The Midland:
London's third route to Scotland, the Midland from St Pancras, has a gentler start, the terminus and approaches being elevated above the natural relief of the area so as to have sufficient height to bridge the Regent's Canal. The immediate approaches to St Pancras were flanked on the down side by extensive freight yards, both at Somers Town, adjacent to St Pancras, and just north of the Regent's Canal. To the east the view was dominated by the GN Kings Cross goods depot and Top Shed. Panoramic views of the whole complex could be seen from the North London line which crosses the main lines and to which freight spurs were provided.

At St Paul's Road Junction just north of the NLR viaduct, the Midland link to the Widened lines from Moorgate joins, over which the first passenger services to London via St Albans commenced from 13 July 1868. The line, now in cutting or short tunnel, then starts its wide westward sweep through the inner suburbs of Kentish Town before entering the tunnels under Haverstock Hill.

Kentish Town was a mecca for watching steam. Until January 1981 junction for Barking services, a seat at the end of the up-main platform provided a marvellous range of services and motive power. Perhaps most impressive were the expresses, particularly northbound, spuming steam and smoke with an exploding sensation as they passed beneath Junction Road bridge, those southbound at speed vibrating the platform, combining with the rush of wind and roar of the wheels and rails. Local and semi-fast suburban trains called from time to time interspersed by terminating movements of the Barking line service. On the freight relief lines (now the main line with St Pancras remodelling), freight trains, parcels and empty coaching stock passed while a progression of light engine movements to and from Kentish Town locomotive depot, generally using the 'Barking' platforms, completed the variety.

With more yards on the down side, the Barking line then curved away to the north-east at Engine Shed Junction, to the rear of Kentish Town locomotive shed. After passing beneath the Broad Street to Richmond line, a freight spur from the Barking line trails in at Carlton Road Junction. Through Haverstock Hill Tunnels, the line emerges at West Hampstead, again crossing beneath the Richmond line, with the Metropolitan and Marylebone lines close by to the south. A major transport interchange has been proposed for this location, incorporating a terminal for re-activated Southern Region services via Snow Hill, but it is doubtful whether this would ever prove economic.

At Cricklewood extensive marshalling yards and carriage sidings are on both sides of the line. The former steam locomotive shed was on the west side where the triangular link from Acton Wells Junction brought extensive inter-regional freight traffic. Shortly after Hendon, the freight relief lines cross the main lines and down slow to join the slow lines at Silk Stream Junction.

The route crosses the former GN Edgware branch (1867–1939) at Mill Hill; as St Albans is approached the ex-GN branch from Hatfield (1865–1951) passes beneath.

As the train strides northwards, Harpenden is the next station of note, although no longer junction for the Midland branch to Hemel Hempstead (1877–1947). The line then crosses the Chilterns with the GN branch from Welwyn approaching from the south-east passing beneath the main line at East Hyde to run parallel with

63

Silk Stream Junction *The complex track arrangement of the Midland main line in the London area begins at Silk Stream Junction where the freight relief lines cross the fast lines and the down slow. With the junction signalbox in the background, 2-6-4T No 42178 takes the up-slow on a local service in March 1957.* Alan A. Jackson

it to Luton (Bute Street). This line is still used for freight traffic onwards from Luton to Dunstable.

As at Bletchley, the Midland approach to Bedford is festooned by brick kilns and old workings. The Bedford to Bletchley line is crossed at Kempston and the run into Bedford station was past the locomotive depot on the left and yards to the right, behind which the Hitchin branch came in to join at Bedford Midland station. An ornate, typically Midland structure, Midland Station was replaced by a better sited station to the north in 1978.

The GCR:

The Marylebone line is closely associated with the Metropolitan 'main line' from Baker Street, which was administered for many years by the Metropolitan & Great Central Joint Committee.

Drawing out of Marylebone, only traces can be found today of the GCR goods depot which was on the west side. The line then passes almost immediately into a long shallow tunnel which takes the route beneath the hallowed turf of Lords Cricket Ground with a brief glimpse of the western portals of Primrose Hill Tunnels and South Hampstead Station where the route crosses the LNWR line to Euston. Emerging at Canfield Place, the route then curves sharply westwards, rising to meet the Metropolitan which it parallels to Neasden, crossing the Broad Street to Richmond line at Kilburn. At Neasden both the Metropolitan and the GCR lines are bridged by the Midland route from Acton Wells to Cricklewood from which a spur trails in past the former site of Neasden locomotive shed.

Neasden South Junction is the point of divergence of the link to the GW & GC Joint Line at Northolt, which formed part of the GW Birmingham Direct Line. On the up side the main Neasden LT depot covers a large area, of interest in the past for the Metropolitan steam locomotive shed, while extensive marshalling yards were on the down side. Facilities for football traffic at Wembley Park serve Wembley Stadium, although from 1923–1968 the Stadium was directly linked from Marylebone by a loop from the Northolt line. Wembley Complex also serves the Stadium area today, while Wembley Central is the nearest station on the Euston line.

The LNWR line is crossed again at Northwick Park, an interesting location in the past for observing trains over both lines, before making junction with the Metropolitan at Harrow South Junction where the Metropolitan & GC Joint line commenced.

Harrow-on-the-Hill, rebuilt and expanded to the present six platforms between 1938 and 1948, is also junction for the Metropolitan branch to Uxbridge, opened in 1904. Before completion of the quadrupling in 1962, all GC and Metropolitan trains ran on the same pair of tracks to Watford South Junction, a bottleneck relieved by the quadrupling just prior to the run-down of the GC line freight and main line traffic.

At Watford South Junction, the Metropolitan and LNER joint branch, opened in 1925, diverges to Watford, having crossed the LNWR Rickmansworth branch (1862–1952) at Croxley Moor. The climb into the Chilterns then begins in earnest, passing a number of picturesque stations and the Chesham branch, opened from Chalfont in 1889.

Aylesbury is terminus of the present diesel multiple-unit services from Marylebone. Here the Princes Risborough branch, opened in 1863 as part of the Wycombe Railway, joins from the south, and the route is then through Quainton Road. This is now occupied by the Quainton Railway Society; it was formerly junction for the Brill Branch (1872–1935) and point of commencement of the GC route northwards while the Metropolitan diverged to terminate on the LNWR Oxford to Cambridge line at Verney Junction (1868–1936).

From Neasden South Junction, the Northolt line travels almost due west past Wembley Complex, serving Wembley Stadium and Exhibition Centre, crossing the LNWR main line just north of Wembley Central and the Piccadilly line beyond Sudbury.

At Northolt, junction is made with the GW line from Old Oak Common, built as a joint enterprise with the GCR and administered from Northolt to Ashendon Junction by the GW & GC Joint Committee. Opened for passengers between Neasden and High Wycombe in 1906, GW services reached Aynho Junction in 1910 and provided a more direct GW line to Birmingham than via Oxford.

Since 1947 Central Line tube services have run to Greenford and were extended to West Ruislip in the following year, paralleling the main line on the down side. Between Ruislip Gardens and West Ruislip,

Harrow-on-the-Hill *Robinson Class C4 Atlantic No 6090 draws into Harrow-on-the-Hill in the mid-1930s with a train from Leicester. The picture shows Harrow (Met) as it was until rebuilt by London Transport in 1938/9, although it was not until 1948 that the platform capacity was increased from four to six. Main line steam continued to call at Harrow with services to and from the Midlands until their withdrawal in 1966. Rev. Charles Praeger*

Central Line car sheds are located, and the line crosses over the Metropolitan Uxbridge branch.

Approaching Denham, which had been the objective of the Central Line until stopped by World War II and the Green Belt which followed, the line crosses both the Grand Union Canal and the River Colne to where a triangle junction was made with a branch to Uxbridge High Street (1907–1939). Now climbing into the Chilterns, junction was made also with the Wycombe Railway from Maidenhead (1854–1970) at High Wycombe, much of the Wycombe Railway being incorporated into the new route across the Chilterns to Princes Risborough.

Until the run-down of services using the line in the late 1960s, Princes Risborough was a busy junction station with branches to Aylesbury (1863), Oxford (1864–1963) and Watlington (1872–1957). The GW main line then crosses the Vale of Aylesbury, bridging the LNWR Oxford to Cambridge line at Bicester and rejoining the Oxford to Birmingham route at Aynho junction. Meanwhile, the GC rejoined its main line by a link between Ashendon and Grendon Underwood Junctions, opened in 1905, which crossed the Brill branch at Wotton.

Into the Sunset

The GWR:

Formerly in the charge of Star, Castle, or Western, but now most probably an HST, a journey from Paddington still retains something of the individualistic atmosphere of its originating company, the GWR.

The immediate approaches are today dominated by the Westway road and the former goods facilities on the site of the first Paddington Station are no longer rail-served. At Westbourne Park the London Transport Hammersmith & City line curves away to the south-west, but little of interest now remains of the once-busy yards and sidings which paralleled the main line to Old Oak Common. Approaching Old Oak Common the line passes beneath the West London line, from which a spur trails in from North Pole Junction, and the main carriage sidings and Old Oak Common diesel depot occupy a large site on the north side of the line.

The Birmingham route diverges to the north-west and the main line crosses over the former GW Ealing & Shepherds Bush line. Then the North & South Western Junction Railway crosses, with a link from Acton Wells Junction used by inter-regional freight workings. The extensive Acton marshalling yards are on the north side as Acton Main Line station is passed.

Ealing Broadway is a suburban interchange of some importance, where the Ealing & Shepherds Bush curves in from North Acton. Although never used as intended

by the GW, which built it to serve a proposed suburban terminus at Shepherds Bush, the line assumed far greater importance for LT's Central Line services which were extended from Wood Lane in 1920. The Piccadilly line tube route to Rayners Lane also crosses together with the District Line branch, opened in 1879, which shares the Ealing Broadway terminal with the Central Line. Ealing Broadway is additionally terminus for the diesel shuttle service to Greenford, a line opened in 1904 which makes a triangular junction between West Ealing and Hanwell.

The line then crosses the Brent Valley by means of the Wharncliffe Viaduct, immortalised in J. C. Bourne's lithographic portraits of early GW scenes, to approach Southall, junction of the branch to Brentford Dock (1860–1942, but still open in part for freight). Here, Southall locomotive depot, now used for DMU stabling, provided some interest along with the yards and sidings of the West London industrial estates through Hayes to West Drayton.

West Drayton was junction for two branches, to Uxbridge Vine Street (1856–1962) and Staines West (1885–1965). Separate schemes were mooted to extend the Vine Street line, first to Rickmansworth to join the LNWR branch from Watford and then to the GW & GC at Denham. Although the latter was built, the link in Uxbridge between High Street and Vine Street stations was never completed.

The route taken by the main line avoided the Royal Estate at Windsor, but Slough became junction for the short GW branch to Windsor & Eton, opened in 1849. A five-road engine shed stood on the Windsor edge of the triangle formed by the branch with the main line.

Trains then carry on westwards, hugging the Bath road and the Thames Valley, avoiding the higher land of Burnham Beeches and the Chilterns to the north. Maidenhead, junction for Bourne End (opened 1854) and Marlow (opened 1873), and Twyford for Henley-on-Thames (opened in 1857) are the only other points of real interest until the Southern line from Waterloo approaches from the south-east as the train draws in towards Reading. The final half-mile overlooks the site of the former Southern locomotive shed, goods yards and station adjacent to Reading General opening the way to the real West beyond.

The LSWR:

The backbone of the former LSWR lines is to Bournemouth, which incorporates the London & Southampton route, through Clapham Junction, Wimbledon, Weybridge, and Woking, where the route to Guildford and Portsmouth diverges, and beyond to Basingstoke where the West of England line leaves.

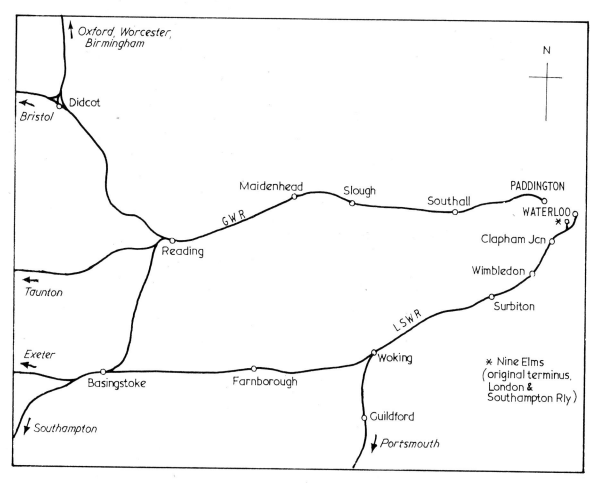

Routes to the West.

Sonning Cutting *The prime of GW motive power, King class 4-6-0 No 6028* King Henry II, *renamed* King George VI *in 1937, takes a down Cheltenham express through the Sonning Cutting, epitomising GW main line running in the London area.* Real Photographs Co. Ltd.

Providing the last main line steam in London, lingering until 1967, Waterloo like Paddington is synonymous with holidays in the West Country accompanied by suitcases, sandwiches and endless patience for the long journey ahead with the family. Fathers with a railway interest and sons of a similar disposition were at an advantage, for there was much to watch out for.

Leaving behind the busy platforms of Waterloo, the first elevated section affords brief glimpses of the Houses of Parliament across the river before the train accelerates through Vauxhall. Often an M7 0-4-4T and train of tank wagons would be unloading milk here for the depot opposite the station.

Nine Elms goods, the original terminus of the London & Southampton before the extension to Waterloo in 1848, was located on the up side between the main line and the river. The extensive Nine Elms locomotive depot occupied the south side in the area now devoted to part of the new Covent Garden Market, sadly not even rail-served.

The mile stretch from Queenstown Road Battersea to

Clapham Junction is a veritable maze of lines and junctions. The Victoria to Brixton line crosses overhead while the Brighton route to Streatham merges at Pouparts Junction before swinging away again at Clapham Junction. A brief glimpse of Stewarts Lane locomotive shed can be seen to the south, just before passing Queenstown Road.

At Latchmere Junction, links fan out from the West London Extension line to permit through running to Victoria (the route once taken by GW suburban trains), Brixton, Streatham or Barnes, these routes being mainly used by inter-regional freight trains and some Midlands to south coast passenger services.

On the main line at Wimbledon the East Putney line, opened in 1889 and now used by LT District Line services, comes in from the north. On the opposite side the Tooting, Merton & Wimbledon line, opened in 1868, curves in from Streatham. A loop, closed in 1929, was effected to the south through Merton Abbey, although the Wimbledon to Merton Park section remains open as part of the ex-LBSCR Wimbledon to West Croydon branch opened in 1855. Shortly afterwards the Wimbledon & Sutton Line, opened in 1929/30 by the SR, also diverges sharply to the south.

At Raynes Park the line to Epsom, opened in 1859, swings away southwards, another line interfacing with LBSCR territory, while at New Malden the Kingston loop, opened in 1869, leaves to serve the town which successfully fought to keep the railway away and then regretted it when Surbiton was served so well. West of

Wimbledon *In the South West London suburbs, Wimbledon is a focal point for branches to Streatham, West Croydon and Sutton in addition to LT District line trains and local services on the main line. King Arthur Class 4-6-0 No 777 Sir Lamiel eases cautiously past Wimbledon D signalbox which has been shored up for removal in connection with the reconstruction of the station in 1929. H. C. Casserley*

Surbiton the line to Hampton Court, opened in 1849, branches northwards from the route and shortly afterwards to the south the 'New' Guildford line, opened in 1885, branches also.

Like the Hampton Court branch, the link to Virginia Water, which leaves the main line just after Weybridge, was also an early branch, opened in 1848 to Chertsey. This was extended in 1866 to Virginia Water to join the Staines to Wokingham line.

Woking is the busy junction between the original Southampton route and the Portsmouth line, opened throughout in 1859 after much trauma with the LBSCR, but not gaining today's importance until after electrification in 1937.

Guildford on the Portsmouth line was reached in 1845 by the Guildford Junction Railway. In 1849 it became a junction with the opening of the LSWR line to Farnham and the arrival of the Reading Guildford & Reigate line, which from 1852 became part of the South Eastern Railway. The line was also extended to Godalming although another ten years was to pass before completion southwards.

Beyond Woking the main line continues to Basingstoke. At Pirbright Junction the line via Aldershot opened in 1870 to Farnham and Alton diverges on the south side. Aldershot still has the remains of the once-extensive system of lines that served the army installations in that town. The SER line from Ash Junction to Reading passes under the main line east of Farnborough, as does the single electrified line from Aldershot and Frimley to Ascot – this latter facility was opened between Ascot and Sturt Lane Junction on the main line in 1878, and to Ash Vale to link with the line from Pirbright Junction to Alton in the following year.

Basingstoke remains of interest for the junction with the Berks & Hants line which reached the town from Reading in 1848 and is heavily used for cross-country workings. For two brief periods, 1901–17 and 1924–32, Basingstoke was also junction for the Basingstoke & Alton Light Railway. The locomotive depot and yard occupied a site at the north-west end of the station, and after closure of the GW shed in 1950 serviced most locomotives working in the area.

After Worting Junction near Battledown, the original Southampton line continues to Winchester while the West of England main line swings away westwards towards Salisbury, being opened to Andover in 1854 and finally reaching Exeter in 1860.

A Day by the Sea

The LBSCR:
Brighton was the central objective in Sussex and was reached from London Bridge by the London &

Brighton in 1841. After its merger with the London & Croydon to form the London Brighton & South Coast Railway in 1846, development of its services from London Bridge resulted in a link to Victoria in 1860, with portions for both termini splitting at East Croydon, today one of London's key suburban railway centres.

The initial route to Victoria, over which the LCDR obtained running powers, was via the West End of London & Crystal Palace Railway which the LBSCR absorbed in 1859. However, in 1862 the LBSCR opened the present main line route, which diverges from the London Bridge line just south of Norwood Junction, to run via Streatham to rejoin the WE&CPR at Balham.

Both routes to East Croydon are fascinating, the London Bridge line being steeped in the history of the London & Croydon and dominated by the approach from New Cross, with its maze of tracks and junctions to South Bermondsey where it parallels the South Eastern across the impressive eleven track viaduct to London Bridge. After New Cross, the route is crossed by the truncated portion of the former LCDR Greenwich Park branch (1871–1917) and the 'Catford Loop' (opened 1892). At Sydenham, the Crystal Palace line (opened 1854) curves away westwards and the LCDR main line (opened 1863) emerges from the eastern end of Penge Tunnel. The approach to Norwood Junction is historic because of the junction made with the LBSCR line to Pimlico, opened in 1857, together with the original LCDR Victoria line (opened 1858) which joins the LBSCR at Bromley Junction.

South of Norwood Junction station is a further web of tracks which provide the ultimate in flexibility for train routing. Basically, the original London & Croydon route to West Croydon curves away westwards while the Victoria direct line swings in from Selhurst to join the London Bridge line at Windmill Bridge Junction. Spurs permit through movements between Norwood and Selhurst (opened 1862) and West Croydon and Selhurst (opened 1865, supplemented by a second spur in the twentieth century).

From Victoria the LBSCR main line rises to cross the Thames by the Grosvenor Bridge and then swings west, crossing the LSWR main line to Clapham Junction, where it turns away southwards. At Balham the WE&CPR continues eastwards, while the main line again turns south to Streatham, where it passes beneath the Peckham to Mitcham line. Through Selhurst, the line crosses the West Croydon branch to join the London Bridge route at Windmill Bridge Junction and thence to East Croydon. From 1868 to 1871 and again from 1886 to 1890 a short branch from the main line served Croydon Central, which was mainly used as a

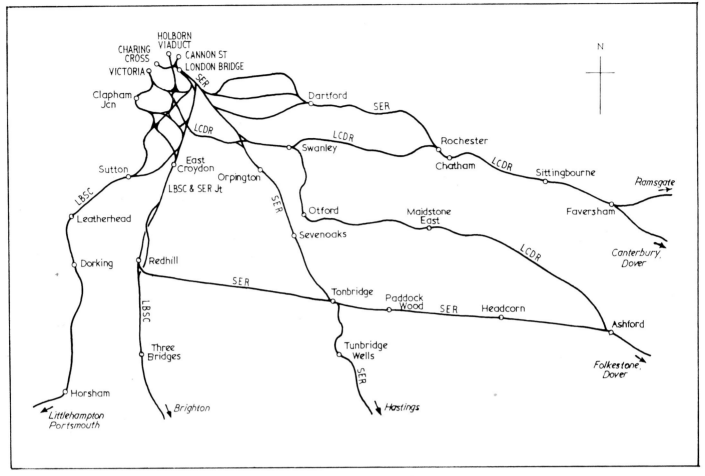

Routes to the South and South-East.

terminus for cross-London trains from Willesden and Liverpool Street.

At South Croydon a branch to East Grinstead, built partly as a joint line with the SER, was opened in 1884. Then two SER branches diverge at Purley, that to Caterham being opened in 1856, the cause of much friction between the LBSCR and the SER, and to Tattenham Corner opened between 1897 and 1901.

Redhill is junction for the original SER main line to Dover, opened in stages between 1842 and 1844, and with the opening of the Reading Guildford & Reigate Railway in 1849 provided the potential for cross-country main line running to the Channel ports, although reversal is necessary at Redhill.

The coast served by the LBSCR was from Portsmouth in the west to Hastings in the east with Brighton about centrally placed, forming an inverted 'T' shape to the system. Bognor, Littlehampton, Worthing, Newhaven and Eastbourne were to become important south coast resorts served between these points, with Dorking, Horsham, Redhill, Three Bridges, Haywards Heath and Lewes the key inland towns served by the main lines.

The coastal line from Brighton to Portsmouth was completed in 1847, but with competition from the LSWR this route to Portsmouth from London was too circuitous. The result was the 'Mid Sussex Line', although completion was haphazard. The London & Croydon was extended from West Croydon to Epsom in 1847 and extension from Epsom to Leatherhead continued by means of a joint LBSCR and LSWR scheme completed in 1859. In the same year the section from Horsham, which had been served since 1848 by a branch from the 'main line' at Three Bridges, to Petworth was opened, the latter itself becoming a branch in 1863 with the opening of the line from Hardham Junction to Arundel Junction to link into the coastal line. The final section between Leatherhead and Horsham was completed four years later in 1867. The Littlehampton branch was opened in 1863 and the Bognor branch in the following year while, until its closure in 1963, the Hayling Island branch could be reached by changing at Havant.

The coastal line eastwards from Brighton to Hastings was opened in 1846, with the link from Keymer Junction to Lewes opening in the following year. In 1868 the line from Tunbridge Wells also reached

Lewes. Newhaven was linked by a branch from Southerham Junction in 1847, and gradually developed for LBSCR Continental services via Dieppe. Eastbourne was reached similarly by a branch from Polegate in 1849.

The SER & LCDR:

Main line services to the Kent Coast developed from conflict between the SER and the LCDR, centred around the objective of Dover and its potential continental traffic.

The first route to Dover was the SER via Redhill and Ashford, completed throughout in 1844, and as already noted was closely associated with the LBSCR Brighton line. Hastings was reached by the SER branch from Ashford opened in 1851, which joined the LBSCR coast line at Bopeep Junction, and itself a further source of conflict with the LBSCR. The origins of the present Hastings main line stemmed from 1845 with the opening of a branch from Tonbridge to Tunbridge

Selhurst/Norwood *The London Bridge to Croydon line makes a series of complex junctions south of Norwood Junction. Class 33/0 No 33 048 passes Selhurst Yards with a special from Brighton to Clapham Junction on 6 April 1978. The skyline shows the impressive office centre of Croydon and a connection to the Streatham and Victoria line crosses the bridge.* Brian Morrison

Wells, the section from Tunbridge Wells to Bopeep Junction being completed in 1852.

Margate was first served by a SER branch from Ashford, opened in 1846 by way of Canterbury (West) and Ramsgate (Town) to Margate (Sands). By the opening of its line via Lewisham and Dartford to Gravesend, and the absorption of the Thames and Medway Canal's railway, the SER was enabled to serve Rochester in 1849. At this point further extension was prevented by national financial crises which resulted in suspension of new projects and led the way to competition from the LCDR.

Extension was effected by the East Kent Railway,

71

East Croydon *This view of East Croydon in 1968 shows the busy goods yard at that time and part of the extensive station complex. East Croydon is a key interchange for the Victoria and London Bridge lines and marks the fringe of the inner suburban network to the north and the outer suburban and main lines to the south.* E. Wilmshurst

whose line from Strood to Faversham was opened in 1858 on course for Canterbury. Although this at first appeared to be a purely local affair that would be absorbed eventually into the SER, the EKR obtained powers for an extension from Canterbury to Dover and, after failing to achieve running powers over the SER North Kent line, obtained sanction for its own route from Strood to St Mary Cray and thence over the Mid Kent to Bromley and the WE&CPR to Victoria. In 1859 the EKR changed its name to the LCDR. The section from Faversham to Canterbury (East) opened in 1860 enabling LCDR trains to operate from Victoria to Canterbury and its trunk line to Dover was completed in the following year.

As a result of LCDR competition, the SER opened its cut-off line from St John's to Tonbridge in 1868, crossing the LCDR at Chislehurst. Links between the two lines were established in 1902 and 1904 as one of the first improvements of the SECR following merged operations in 1899. Meanwhile, the LCDR increased its competition by opening from Faversham to Ramsgate Harbour in stages by 1863.

Swanley to Sevenoaks was opened as a branch from

the LCDR in 1862, and in 1874 a branch to Maidstone East from Otford was completed, this reaching Ashford in 1884 providing a third 'relief' main line to Dover in later years.

For most of the Nineteenth Century, the over-provision of competing routes was wasteful, but the fusion of the two companies under a Managing Committee of the SECR in 1899 brought rapid improvements. Apart from opening-up commuter traffic on the main line routes to London, the Kent Coast lines became firmly established for Continental traffic at Dover and Folkestone, between 1876 and 1901 from Queenborough to Flushing also, and for holiday traffic to the resorts on the Thanet coast.

The big difference between the lines south of London and those north of the Thames, with the exception of those from Liverpool Street, was the degree of electrification. Fenchurch Street, Euston, Kings Cross and St Pancras electric services are much later BR projects. The southern schemes began as suburban electrification by the LBSCR and the LSWR and extended in due course to third-rail main line electrification by the Southern Railway, continued by BR Southern Region.

The Brighton line was the first treated with full electric services at the beginning of 1933. Electric services to Sevenoaks via Orpington and St Mary Cray were introduced in early 1935. The LBSCR route to Hastings was finished later that year, including the Keymer Junction to Lewes line and the Seaford and Eastbourne branches.

In 1937 the Portsmouth line was electrified from Waterloo together with associated services to Alton and Staines via Virginia Water. Results were again impressive. In the following year Victoria to Portsmouth services were electrified together with the Three Bridges to Horsham branch, the coastal line from West Worthing to Havant and the Bognor and Littlehampton branches. In 1939 electric service to Reading, Gillingham, and Maidstone were further extensions completed, but other extensions planned were halted by World War II. It remained for BR to complete the electrification or dieselisation of the rest of the main line networks.

Diesel-electric multiple-units replaced steam workings on the Tunbridge Wells and Hastings Line in 1957/8 together with Hastings to Ashford, and services in the Southampton area. The Kent Coast electrification from Gillingham to Ramsgate and Faversham to Dover was completed in 1959, including the Sheerness branch. Phase II of the Kent Coast electrification extended electric services in 1961/62 from Sevenoaks to Dover and Ramsgate, from Maidstone East to Ashford and Maidstone West to Paddock Wood, from Ashford to Minster and over the Folkestone Harbour branch. The present main line electric network was completed in 1967 with electrification to Bournemouth.

The rapid withdrawal of steam workings in the late 1950s and early 1960s brought to an end the interesting mix of motive power, but the use of electric locomotives and later electro-diesels retained some variety. These are enhanced by continuing inter-

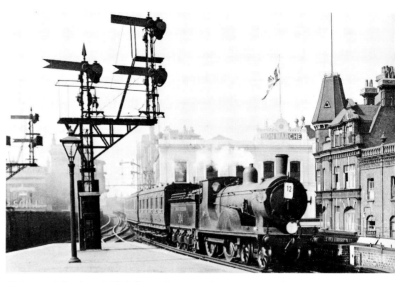

Brixton *A Southern 4-4-0 drifts into Brixton with an express via the Catford Loop on 28 March 1928, the picture being a delightful period piece with gas lamp and lower quadrant signals.* H. C. Casserley

regional traffic which bring diesel workings from other parts of the system into the 'electric' area, while Waterloo retains its diesel haulage on the remaining West of England trains and some locomotive-hauled trains can still be seen at Victoria and London Bridge.

Orpington Junction *One of the first acts of the working arrangements between the SER and the LCDR companies after their fusion in 1899 into the SECR was to build links between their separate lines at Petts Wood. On 20 July 1929 a boat train for Dover negotiates Orpington Junction in the charge of King Arthur class No 769 Sir Balan.* H. C. Casserley

5
FOR BUSINESS

Apart from freight, the use of London's railways for business purposes can be broadly divided into two types of passenger traffic. Commuter travel forms a very substantial part of London's railway business, imposing its own patterns of heavy peaks while, being at the nub of the system, there are many important 'Inter-city' business links from London to the key provincial cities. It is with the former that this chapter is mainly concerned.

Suburban and local passenger travel is not entirely concerned with the trunk arteries into the centre, although these are of most significance. London's railway history has seen interesting cross- and round-London services, and remnants of these still remain, while there are also some useful branch and local

services. In addition, the chapter recalls the once numerous special services to the Kent countryside which took hop-pickers to the Garden of England from the inner suburbs of South and East London.

Suburban arteries and byways

All thriving business and commercial centres need good and efficient transport links if they are to develop. The sheer scale and growth of London has meant that the infrastructure necessary to provide the peak services to transport the workforce daily to and from employment in London is out of all proportion to anything needed

Great Eastern and London, Tilbury & Southend suburban lines.

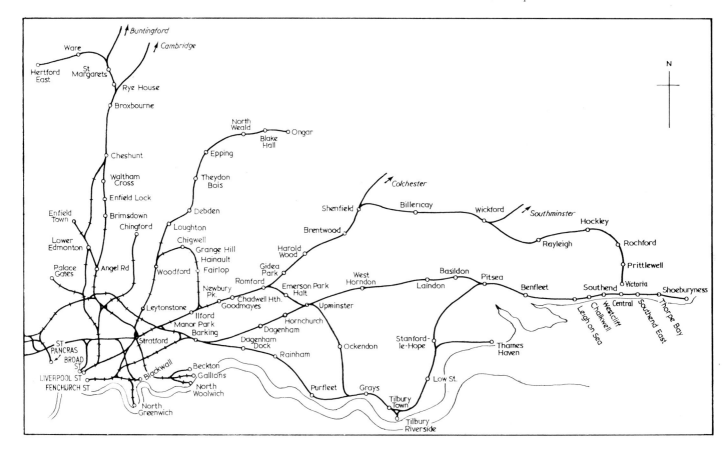

elsewhere. Thus, when dealing with 'commuter' problems generally, the predominant part of BR's commuter traffic is in London and the South East, imposing a special burden on rail facilities and difficulties of peak costs.

As a result of the proximity of Underground services and the geographical development of London, the major flows of traffic are now mainly from east and north-east London and from south of the Thames. Services north and west of London have never seen the same kinds of passenger flows, and it is interesting to contrast the resulting impact upon the termini and lines serving these areas.

The GER & LTSR lines:
Liverpool Street remains today one of the busiest of London's termini, serving the large suburban area created by the GER. Heavy commuter flows still emanate from the Romford and Lea Valley lines, although services over the Loughton and East London branches have been transferred to LT, while the links to the Docklands via Stratford were more of local significance.

The once extensive suburban services into Fenchurch Street from the GER lines ceased finally with the withdrawal of trains from the Shenfield line in 1949, leaving the present services to Tilbury and Southend.

Barking *The line opened to Tilbury in 1854 via Stratford and Barking. At the turn of the century, commuter traffic increased rapidly and what had become the LTSR main line was quadrupled from Bromley to Barking. District Railway electric trains were extended in 1908, the year in which this photograph of Barking was taken, soon after completion of the widening.* The Museum of London

These are chiefly of an outer suburban nature, since the inner suburban traffic was taken-over almost entirely by the extension of the District electric trains to Barking in 1908 and Upminster in 1932. The line is well placed to carry commuters from locations like Benfleet, Westcliff, Southend and Thorpe Bay to the City. Electrification in the early 1960s increased the attraction of these dormitory towns and localities facing onto the north bank of the Thames Estuary. The early importance of the London & Blackwall, on which Fenchurch Street was founded, faded as the more important Dockland traffic moved downstream as local road competition grew, and passenger services were withdrawn in 1926.

The development of Basildon as a New Town in the 1950s gave potential new traffic, but it was not until 1974 that a long promised new station was provided to serve it. The link from Tilbury to Pitsea, the original Southend route, is now mainly of strategic importance for industrial purposes, the Thames Haven branch

Low Street *The original route to Southend was via Tilbury, opened 1854–6. This was shortened in 1888 by the opening of the direct line through Upminster and the original section between Tilbury and Pitsea lost its strategic importance. Ex-LTSR 0-6-2T No 41986 calls at Low Street on 19 September 1956 with a train for Thames Haven.*
H. C. Casserley

serving the oil refinery, while the Tilbury line itself generates local travel related to the Docks and associated Thameside industries, notably the Ford motor works at Dagenham. The 'direct' line between Barking and Pitsea through Upminster was opened in 1888 and significantly cut the distance and journey time to Southend.

Built by the LTSR as a useful cross-link for Tilbury traffic, the Romford to Grays line now operates as two separate units on either side of Upminster. The Grays-Upminster section (opened 1892) was included in the electrification of the former LTSR lines, although the Romford – Upminster line (opened 1893) remains a dmu shuttle service and has survived two closure attempts.

From 1939 when services were cut back from the City, until January 1981 when they were transferred to Gospel Oak, Kentish Town was the London end of lines which linked into the LTSR at Barking. Opened in two stages, the first section was built by the Tottenham & Hampstead Junction Railway and opened from Tottenham Hale to Highgate Road in 1868. Initially operated by the GER, the service was taken-over by the Midland in 1870/1 after a new spur was laid from Kentish Town. A connection towards the north was opened from Junction Road Junction to Carlton Road Junction in 1883, used mainly for freight, but the pre-1981 pattern was established in 1900 by the opening of a curve from Engine Shed Junction, Kentish Town,

to join the 1883 link at Highgate Road (Low Level) enabling trains to reach Kentish Town. In 1894, the Tottenham & Forest Gate Railway was opened from South Tottenham to join the original LTSR main line at Woodgrange Park with a connection towards East Ham (closed 1958). The MR extended some trains to East Ham and commenced through services to Southend and boat trains to Tilbury, and it was through this influence that it came to take-over the LTSR in 1912.

East of Stratford on the former ECR main line suburban traffic was slow to develop, but during the latter years of the nineteenth century housing and industrial growth in the inner suburban area gradually led to an outward spread of the eastern perimeter of London, Ilford and Seven Kings being the first affected at the turn of the century. In 1910 Gidea Park was opened to serve a new estate and the result was the expansion of Romford also – development continued around Romford until the late 1950s. Quadrupling took place in stages, reaching Shenfield by 1934, which remains the extremity of the main suburban services.

In the Lea Valley, the first branch was opened in 1849 from Angel Road through Lower Edmonton to Enfield. However, it was not until 1870 that the branch from Lea Bridge to Walthamstow was opened, the extension to Chingford following three years later although the projected link to High Beach did not materialise.

In 1872 the line from Bethnal Green was opened to Lower Edmonton (High Level) via Hackney Downs and Stoke Newington, this then becoming the principal route to Enfield Town. Part of the original Enfield branch from Angel Road to Lower Edmonton (Low Level) was thereafter used only by a few trains until 1939, and was closed entirely in 1964.

A branch from Seven Sisters to Palace Gates, projected in part to tap the Alexandra Palace traffic, was opened in 1878 and plans were to connect it to the GN Alexandra Palace branch, but this was not pursued. During World War II, the line was heavily used as a diversionary freight route for trains via the Hertford Loop. While the branch enjoyed services to Liverpool Street for many years, in its latter form trains ran primarily to North Woolwich using the 1880 curve connecting Seven Sisters and South Tottenham where they gained the Lea Valley line to Stratford and thence to North Woolwich. The branch was closed in 1963. Although the services were run down before their withdrawal, an end-to-end trip over the route was a fascinating experience because of the many junctions traversed, the interesting views afforded of the Stratford area, the complicated lineside connections, and scenes in the docklands.

Bethnal Green *The GER operated the most intensive steam service possible from its suburban catchment areas into Liverpool Street which, on introduction in 1920, was called the 'Jazz' service. This view shows Class N7/5 No 69669 on 4 June 1958 calling at Bethnal Green with the 18.27 local service to Enfield Town. Electric services were introduced in 1960.* Brian Morrison

North Woolwich *Workaday London is caught in this setting of a typical docklands suburban train of quint-art stock departing from North Woolwich on 30 January 1960 in the charge of class N7/3 0-6-2T No 69718.* T. Wright

An additional effect of the opening of the Hackney Downs line was the diversion of most trains using the Lea Valley to run via Clapton, thus relieving Stratford and slightly shortening the route. Even today the section from Stratford to Coppermill Junction has little passenger traffic potential, mainly crossing the Hackney Marshes and being flanked by Temple Mills marshalling yard.

The remaining part of the ex-GER system in this area was the Churchbury (later Southbury) Loop from Bury Street Junction to Cheshunt. Although opened in 1891, local road competition caused withdrawal of regular services in 1909 but the Loop was incorporated into the electrified system completed in November 1960.

North of Cheshunt, Bishop's Stortford and Hertford East (opened 1843) are important outer suburban centres, but the Buntingford branch (1863–1964) remained a rural operation to the end.

The area between the Lea Valley and Romford lines was served by the GER Loughton branch opened in 1856. Extension to Ongar through Epping was achieved in 1865, while in 1903 the Fairlop Loop was opened from a triangular junction between Ilford and Seven Kings to Woodford. As with the other GER suburban branches, initial development was slow, but during the twentieth century there has been rapid growth. These branches were incorporated, with the initial exception of the Epping-Ongar section, into LT's Central line by 1949. To serve housing develop-

Epping GER tank No 1041, complete with 'Liverpool Street' destination board, stands at the entrance to the yard of the then rural Epping station in 1902. LT Central Line trains reached Epping in 1949 but the service to Ongar remained steam hauled until 1957. British Rail

ment along the Eastern Avenue, a new tube link from Leytonstone to Newbury Park was opened in 1947, and part of the former loop line south of Newbury Park was closed.

Railways to the Docklands areas via the North Woolwich line and its branches, together with those to Blackwall and North Greenwich, were mainly of local importance for moving the workforce to the docks from nearby communities, dealt with in Chapter 10. Of related interest, however, is the sparse dmu service from North Woolwich, although now cut back to Stratford, through Lea Bridge to Tottenham Hale, making interchange with the Victoria Line, and the daily service to Camden Road. The latter service, introduced in May 1979 with GLC support, resulted in re-introduction of passenger services over the NLR between Dalston Junction and Victoria Park, thus gaining the North Woolwich line via Channelsea Junction. A new interchange station with the District line has been opened at

West Ham, together with various other improvements.

Electrification of the GER suburban network had been mooted as early as the turn of the century as traffic peaked. However, the cost involved caused a reassessment and in 1920 the GER introduced as the solution what was probably the most intensive steam suburban service in the world which became known as the 'Jazz'. This name was derived by the yellow and blue stripes which were painted along the top of the coach sides to indicate first and second class. In 1925 new quintuplet articulated rolling stock was introduced, replacing ex-GER four-wheeled sets, which remained in use until 1960. 'Quad-arts' were introduced at about the same time on the ex-GN lines.

Electrification came slowly. The Loughton branches were transferred to LT between 1947 and 1949, and one of the last acts of the LNER was electrification to Shenfield, completed by BR in 1949. BR extended electric trains to Chelmsford and Southend in 1956, to Clacton and Walton-on-the-Naze in 1959, although not completing the whole scheme until 1963. In November 1960 electrification of the Hackney Downs lines was commissioned, with Enfield, Chingford, Bishop's Stortford and Hertford East all being converted from steam operation, but it was not until 1969 that the Lea Valley line between Cheshunt and

Coppermill Junction was completed. With dieselisation of main line services, this enabled steam to be eliminated at Liverpool Street in the Autumn of 1962.

To the 'Northern Heights' and Chilterns:
Suburban services on the ex-GNR lines were the most extensive of those serving the area north and west of London. These comprised services calling at local stations on the main line, including outer-suburban services to Royston, the Hertford Loop and the 'Northern Heights' branches to Edgware, High Barnet and Alexandra Palace. In addition to the use of Kings Cross suburban, some services ran over the Widened lines to Moorgate until all were transferred in 1976 to the former Great Northern & City line to Moorgate. Trains of the North London Railway also ran to various destinations via Canonbury, which in later years brought ex-LMSR locomotives to these routes, including 'Jinty' 0-6-0Ts. The remnants of these services were withdrawn from Broad Street in 1976. For several years in the late nineteenth and early twentieth centuries LCDR and SER trains also ran to GN destinations via the Snow Hill (Farringdon) link. At the peak of suburban travel over these lines in the early twentieth century Finsbury Park, never a hospitable station, became a key interchange for services to the

Dalston Western Junction *As part of general improvement of local services in North London, a North Woolwich to Camden Road service was introduced with GLC support. Here the 18.00 to North Woolwich passes Dalston Western Junction where the former NLR extension to Broad Street, opened in 1865, branches to the right. Broad Street is now used only by Richmond and Watford trains. R. Davies*

three termini, between the main line, the Edgware group of branches and Underground services.

The Edgware branch opened in 1867, with only Highgate and Finchley being at that time of any significance. High Barnet followed in 1872 and the short branch to Alexandra Palace from Highgate was opened with the Palace on 24 May 1873, initially bringing great crowds. However, the branch followed the fluctuating fortunes of the Palace, which was destroyed by fire on 9 June 1873, and was closed and re-opened no less than eight times between 1873 and 1898 to close completely in 1954. LT take-over of part of these lines is dealt with in Chapter 8.

Development around the stations on the main line took the built-up area to New Barnet by World War I but the catchment area suffered significant competition with the opening of the Piccadilly line tube, the absorption of the Barnet line into the Northern line and the development of competing bus services. Outer

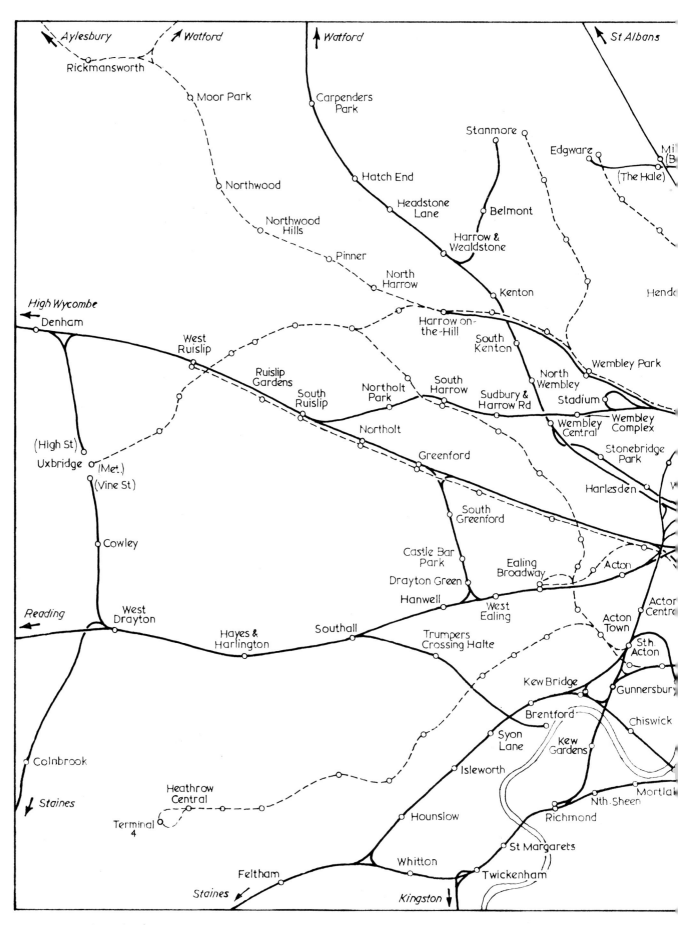

Suburban lines to the North and West.

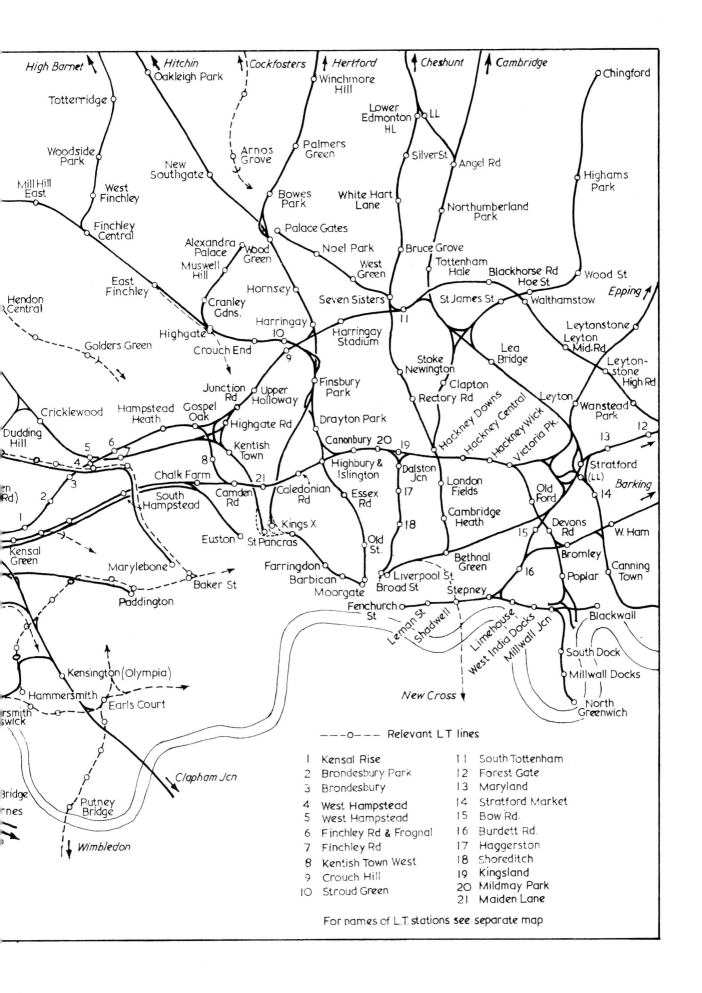

High Barnet ↑   *Hitchin*   ↑ *Cockfosters*   ↑ *Hertford*   ↑ *Cheshunt*   ↑ *Cambridge*   Chingford

Oakleigh Park
Totteridge
Woodside Park
Mill Hill East
West Finchley
Finchley Central
New Southgate
Arnos Grove
Palmers Green
Winchmore Hill
Lower Edmonton HL
LL
Silver St
Angel Rd
Highams Park
Hendon Central
Golders Green
East Finchley
Alexandra Palace
Muswell Hill
Wood Green
Bowes Park
White Hart Lane
Noel Park
West Green
Bruce Grove
Tottenham Hale
Northumberland Park
Blackhorse Rd
Hoe St
Wood St
Epping ↑
Cricklewood
Hampstead Heath
Gospel Oak
Junction Rd
Upper Holloway
Highgate
Crouch End
Harringay
Crouch Hill
Stroud Green
Hornsey
Harringay Stadium
Seven Sisters
St James St
Walthamstow
Leytonstone
Leyton Mid. Rd
Leytonstone High Rd
Dudding Hill
Kensal Green
Marylebone
Paddington
Baker St
Chalk Farm
South Hampstead
Camden Rd
Caledonian Rd
Kings X
St Pancras
Euston
Kentish Town
Highgate Rd
Drayton Park
Canonbury
Highbury & Islington
Dalston Jcn
London Fields
Cambridge Heath
Old Ford
Devons Rd
Bromley
Poplar
W. Ham
Canning Town
Essex Rd
Old St.
Farringdon
Barbican
Moorgate
Liverpool St
Broad St
Stepney
Fenchurch St
Leman St
Shadwell
Limehouse
West India Docks
Millwall Jcn
Blackwall
South Dock
Millwall Docks
North Greenwich
Stoke Newington
Clapton
Rectory Rd
Hackney Downs
Hackney Central
Hackney Wick
Victoria Pk.
Leyton
Wanstead Park
Lea Bridge
Stratford (LL)
Barking
Bethnal Green
Bow Rd.
Burdett Rd.
Haggerston
Shoreditch
Kingsland
Mildmay Park
Maiden Lane
Kensington (Olympia)
Hammersmith
Earls Court
Putney Bridge
Clapham Jcn
Wimbledon

- - -o- - - Relevant LT lines

1	Kensal Rise	11	South Tottenham
2	Brondesbury Park	12	Forest Gate
3	Brondesbury	13	Maryland
4	West Hampstead	14	Stratford Market
5	West Hampstead	15	Bow Rd.
6	Finchley Rd & Frognal	16	Burdett Rd.
7	Finchley Rd	17	Haggerston
8	Kentish Town West	18	Shoreditch
9	Crouch Hill	19	Kingsland
10	Stroud Green	20	Mildmay Park
		21	Maiden Lane

For names of L.T. stations **see** separate map

suburban expansion subsequently occurred chiefly at Potters Bar, Hatfield, Welwyn Garden City and Stevenage. Branch services to St Albans, Luton and Dunstable and Hertford were all withdrawn by 1965. The GN served Enfield by a branch in 1871 which was extended to Cuffley in 1910 and Langley Junction, to form the 'Hertford Loop' in 1918.

In BR days, with much reduced inner suburban traffic, improvements could be concentrated on the expanding outer suburban potential. Diesel multiple-units and diesels replaced steam working between 1958 and 1962, but despite the use of some BR standard suburban coaching stock on locomotive-hauled peak-hour services, ageing Gresley 'Quad-arts', gas-lit stations and semaphore signalling were still much in evidence. After considerable delay, electrification of the GN suburban network was authorised in 1971 and new trains were introduced between 1976 and 1978 to Moorgate and Kings Cross, and those over the Widened lines withdrawn.

Midland suburban services initially served the main line and the T&HJ very well, but by World War I competition from trams, buses and tubes resulted in the loss of much traffic. As a result services stagnated and it was not until 1960 when dmus were introduced that there was significant improvement. The Midland route remained the last major main line into London to be operated primarily by traditional methods, retaining semaphore signalling and largely unremodelled track-work, but the Bedford electrification, completed in

Holborn Viaduct Low Level (Snow Hill) *The line leading up from the former Snow Hill station and the 'Widened' Lines is graphically illustrated in this picture showing its relation to Holborn Viaduct main line station, partly built over the connection.*
H. C. Casserley

Highgate *In 1880 Highgate was a fashionable suburb enjoying GNR services to Kings Cross (opened 1867), NLR trains to Broad Street (introduced 1875) and cross-London services to the LCDR and SER. In this view, an up NLR train pauses at Highgate in tranquil surroundings, not entirely dispelled today by the busy Archway Road.*
Haringey Public Libraries

1982 including services to Moorgate, can now provide the commuter with an adequate service and reconstructed operating facilities. The main beneficiaries are outer suburban travellers.

Travel patterns from Euston have been revolutionised since electrification of main line and suburban services in the 1960s and the concurrent development of Milton Keynes and Northampton. Inner suburban traffic was never great, although this was stimulated by the 'New Line' DC electric services in the early years of the twentieth century. In 1890 the Harrow & Wealdstone to Stanmore branch was opened, the only intermediate station at Belmont being added in 1932. Although the branch was mainly of local significance, it aided development of the area but was cut back to Belmont in 1952, to be closed to passengers entirely in 1964. Some local traffic was also generated with the opening of the Rickmansworth branch from Watford in 1862 (closed 1952), St Albans in 1858 and to Croxley Green in 1912. Until introduction of the interval Birmingham emu and improved Inter-City electric services, Rugby had only an indifferent steam service, with semi-fast trains, often in the charge of Patriot or Jubilee locomotives but more often Class 5s, although it now enjoys some commuter travel. However, Northampton, Milton Keynes, Bletchley and Leighton Buzzard generate significant outer suburban traffic with Tring, Berkhamsted and Hemel Hempstead the main intermediate stations.

Suburban facilities from Marylebone to Aylesbury are integrally linked to LT services on the Metropolitan line, and are all that remain of services previously operated further north on the ex-GC main line. However, Marylebone maintains a separate identity in its trains via Northolt to High Wycombe and Banbury over the former GW&GC Joint line. Whether in the charge of an attractive GC 4-4-2T around the turn of the century, or an L1, LMS or BR Standard 2-6-4T in the latter years, these workings were of some interest before the demise of steam. Requiring some smart turn-rounds, the peak hour at Marylebone in the 1950s, still with some lower quadrant signals, was worthy of observation. A vantage point near the entrance to the tunnel under Lords gave views of movements to and from the carriage sidings on the left (now Marylebone diesel depot), the entrance to the freight depot and locomotive servicing yard on the right and the approach layout to the station. Then and today outside the peak hours, particularly during dark winter evenings, Marylebone is a quiet, almost eerie, station with few travellers.

Before quadrupling of the main line north of Harrow at the end of the 1950s, steam trains ran through on what is now the LT local lines and offered a stopping service to Marylebone as well as the electric trains to

Farringdon *Fowler 2-6-2T No 40037, fitted with condensing apparatus for working over the 'Widened' Lines, climbs into Farringdon with a Moorgate service in June 1959. Note the link to the LT lines and the trolleybus crossing the bridge.* T. Wright

Camden *Local services from Euston were not greatly developed until the completion in 1922 of the LNWR 'New Line' for full electric services from Watford to both Euston and Broad Street and tube services via Queens Park. A former LNWR Oerlikon-equipped electric unit accelerates as it reaches the top of Camden Bank past Camden locomotive shed with a train for Watford on 9 June 1945.* H. C. Casserley

Baker Street and the City. Moor Park, prior to reconstruction, was little more than a wayside halt, set amongst the trees of the Moor Park Estate.

Today, the once attractive intermediate stations on the Northolt line are run down and little used, but West Ruislip and many of the stations to High

Wycombe remain interesting and useful facilities. Sadly, very few main line trains now use this route which, until rationalisation in the 1960s, was the principal WR line to Birmingham Snow Hill, a considerable variety of main line WR steam intermingling with those of the ER, which then operated on Marylebone line trains between freight and local services. Princes Risborough, once a busy junction, is now a depressing remnant of its former interest.

For a station of its size, local services form a comparatively minor part of Paddington's traffic. In common with the other main line stations, inner suburban traffic has declined significantly while long-distance commuter traffic has increased in recent years so that today even Didcot and Swindon with their HSTs see commuter travel. West of Ealing Broadway, with its Greenford link, many of the local stations to Reading produce comparatively small but useful traffic, much of which is local in nature to the industrial areas of Slough and the West London suburbs. The Windsor branch generates some further traffic, in addition to the Bourne End and Marlow line and the Henley branch. Unfortunately, West Drayton has lost its Staines and Uxbridge services. The branch from Southall to

Brentford has also closed to passengers, together with the link from Bourne End to High Wycombe which provided a useful cross-country facility from Maidenhead to Aylesbury via High Wycombe and Princes Risborough, in addition to other connections. Reading provides connections with local SR services, while the former GW link to Basingstoke also produces some London-bound passengers.

'Cross-Town' Services:

Outside the Southern Region, the ex-North London services from Broad Street to Richmond offer a handy but under used 'round London' suburban service, which has defied all efforts of the publicity men but still remains alive . . . just! Its stations, once attractive, substantial and ornate affairs (eg Highbury, Dalston Junction and Broad Street) languish in a general air redolant of decay and neglect. This was not always so. In the latter quarter of the nineteenth century, before the onslaught of competition from tube and bus services, the private car and changes in geographical and demographical factors, NLR services were heavily used and expanding, a satellite of the LNWR but with an independent streak of entrepreneurial flair to tap the developing suburban market. The golden years of the NLR saw its trains crossing from the Docklands area at Poplar, and from the City by at first Fenchurch Street and later Broad Street, through what has become the middle suburban zone of North and West London to Richmond in the south west. Services also penetrated into the GN and LNWR suburban area.

Uxbridge (Vine Street) *Single unit Gloucester RC & W Co W55024 draws out of Uxbridge (Vine Street) bound for West Drayton on 26 March 1962. 0-6-0PT No 9642 shunts wagons in the yard.* T. Wright

Kensington (Olympia) *Of little regular use today, apart from exhibition and special traffic, Kensington (Olympia) was an important link in the 'Middle' and 'Outer' Circle suburban services of the nineteenth century and their remnants which remained until 1940. Also used for summer holiday traffic, a Class K1 2-6-0 awaits departure with a train from Sheffield on 30 June 1956. E. Wilmshurst*

Traffic peaked at the turn of the century and then began to fall rapidly, only stemmed by electrification of the Broad Street to Kew Bridge and Richmond services in 1916, as part of the LNWR 'New Line' project completed in 1922. Although the LNWR Oerlikon-equipped units were replaced by BR Standard electric stock in the early 1960s, the BR stock rides poorly and the continuing threat of vandalism and general abuse results in an austere appearance – a railway almost under siege!

Willesden Junction suggests the potential of Finsbury Park but never apparently obtained it. Opened in 1866, it was at the confluence of the LNWR main line, the Hampstead Junction, the West London and the North & South Western Junction lines and both low- and high-level platforms were provided. The station was rebuilt in 1894, providing more convenient interchange facilities, but today only the Watford and Richmond lines connect, the main line platforms having been closed and demolished in 1962.

Trains continue to rattle relentlessly over the junctions to Gunnersbury and Richmond, the former once a substantial station offering useful interchange facilities, but today a mere island platform draughty and almost unprotected, where the District line services converge.

Round-London services have never been very successful, perhaps because of the generally excellent exchange facilities via the centre, or simply because there has never been the volumes of traffic wishing to make the cross-suburban journeys afforded. However, they did enjoy a brief interlude of comparative success before killed-off by competing road or Underground services. Kensington (Addison Road) featured largely in these schemes. Of course there were some inter-company services for several years in the nineteenth century using the East London, the LCDR cross-Thames and Snow Hill link and the West London line. Of these only the West London route remains in use for such purposes.

Kensington was strategically placed on the route which connected the LNWR main line at one end, with a link to the Hampstead Junction Railway at Mitre Bridge Junction, and the LSWR, LBSCR and the LCDR at Clapham Junction at the other. Intermediately, a spur connects with the GW main line at North Pole Junction, a link was made with the Ealing & Shepherds Bush and the Hammersmith & City in the vicinity of White City, the LSWR line from Richmond joined just north of Kensington and the District comes in from Earl's Court.

Between 1863 and 1915 a GWR Southall to Victoria service was operated and in 1872 trains began running between Moorgate and Mansion House, via the H&C and Kensington, these being known as the 'Middle Circle'. In the same year a Broad Street to Mansion House service, known as the 'Outer Circle', was inaugurated, both the 'Middle' and 'Outer' Circles extending services commenced several years previously. Other LNWR and LSWR round-London links were also introduced. At first these were well patronised for their connections to Central London and the City, but soon more direct links stole their franchise and they were gradually curtailed.

Electric trains commenced on the truncated 'Middle Circle' in 1906 and the 'Outer Circle', reduced to no more than a Willesden to Earl's Court service, was electrified in 1914. Some SR and LMSR passenger trains continued between Willesden and Clapham Junction but in 1940 all advertised passenger services were withdrawn. Since re-introduction of services in 1946, Kensington (Olympia), as it was renamed, has been

85

used only by LT exhibition trains, a service to Clapham Junction (unadvertised for many years), holiday and special train workings, latterly as a relief terminal during the reconstruction of Euston, and for motorail services.

Of little use but for purely local travel was the NSWJ branch from South Acton to Hammersmith & Chiswick, which carried passengers from 1858 until 1917.

To Southern Suburbs:
Many of the LSWR suburban services have been referred to in Chapter 4 as they relate to main line links to Waterloo. However, those lines north of the main line, serving the Thames Valley areas, are worthy of more detail.

In south-west London, Clapham Junction is one of the more complex track and station arrangements, opened in 1863 for interchange between the LSWR and LBSCR, although the bulk of travellers pass through its platforms rather than join or transfer trains at them. Clapham (actually in Battersea) achieved its junction status in 1846 when the Richmond branch was opened, being extended to Datchet two years later and reaching Windsor in 1849. In the same year as Windsor was served the Hounslow Loop was opened to Isleworth from Barnes, on the Richmond line, the loop being completed to Feltham Junction in 1850. Interesting features of both lines are the river crossings at Barnes and Richmond, which make attractive settings for the railway.

To the north, the potential for cross-links was realised by the North & South Western Junction line, which was opened in 1853 between Willesden and Old Kew Junction. North London Railway passenger trains used this route to reach Kew Bridge and by 1863 were running to Kingston, using curves at New Kew Junction and Barnes which had been opened in the previous year to avoid the reversals necessary since 1858 on the extension of services to Twickenham.

In order to avoid this circuitous route, the present line from South Acton Junction to a new terminus at Richmond, adjacent to the original station, was opened in 1869. NLR trains thereafter ran only to Richmond and Kew Bridge and the curve at Barnes was closed. The independent stations at Richmond were not united until rebuilt by the Southern Railway. District and Metropolitan Railway trains reached Richmond in 1877, in addition to GW trains, using the tracks of the LSWR branch opened in 1869 to Kensington (Addison Road). District trains joined at Studland Road Junction – the site of the junction can still be seen west of Hammersmith together with other remains – while Metropolitan and GW trains came via the H&C at

Grove Road Junction. Metropolitan and GW services were withdrawn in 1906 and 1910 respectively.

To the south, Kingston was missed by the main line and was first served in 1863 as a branch from Twickenham. Almost six years later the extension to the main line at Malden was opened creating the Kingston loop. This necessitated a new high-level station and both were rebuilt in the 1930s. The Shepperton branch was opened from Strawberry Hill in 1864. In the present triangle formed by the branch an electric multiple unit depot stands, this using the buildings of the converted Strawberry Hill locomotive shed, opened in 1897 and last used by steam in 1923.

In addition to Barnes and Richmond, the LSWR also bridged the Thames at Kingston (Kingston Loop), Kew (Gunnersbury and Kensington branch) and Putney (linking to the District at Putney Bridge). The Wimbledon to East Putney line remains BR signalled and maintained, although the trains are almost entirely LT District line services. SR services from Waterloo via Point Pleasant Junction were withdrawn in 1941 and the line is used almost solely now as a relief route and for empty stock workings.

These lines never carried intensive commuter traffic, the areas served being of lower density housing. However, they did stimulate development in the Thames Valley area and remain more useful for local purposes.

Of the complex southern suburban services throughout the remainder of South London, much is outlined in Chapters 4 and 7. Of some interest, however, was the LBSCR South London line, opened in association with the LCDR between 1865 and 1867. Trains run at first south east from London Bridge along the former L&G viaduct, which was again expanded in conjunction with the scheme. At South Bermondsey they then swing south and west to Peckham Rye, where the former LCDR line via Catford joins. The lines to East Brixton were owned by the Brighton but, from Brixton to Wandsworth Road, they were the Chatham's, trains passing through the densely-populated inner suburbs of Denmark Hill, Brixton and Clapham to join the approaches to Victoria. Curves from Canterbury Road Junction (West) and Cambria Road Junction (east) provide access to Blackfriars and Holborn Viaduct via Loughborough Junction. Competition from Underground, bus and private transport, together with changes in population density and employment factors, have affected the City termini to a much greater extent than the others which have been able to develop their outer suburban, off-peak and main line traffics.

Suburban rail traffic in south east London, with no direct Underground links excepting those to Elephant & Castle, New Cross, and New Cross Gate has been the

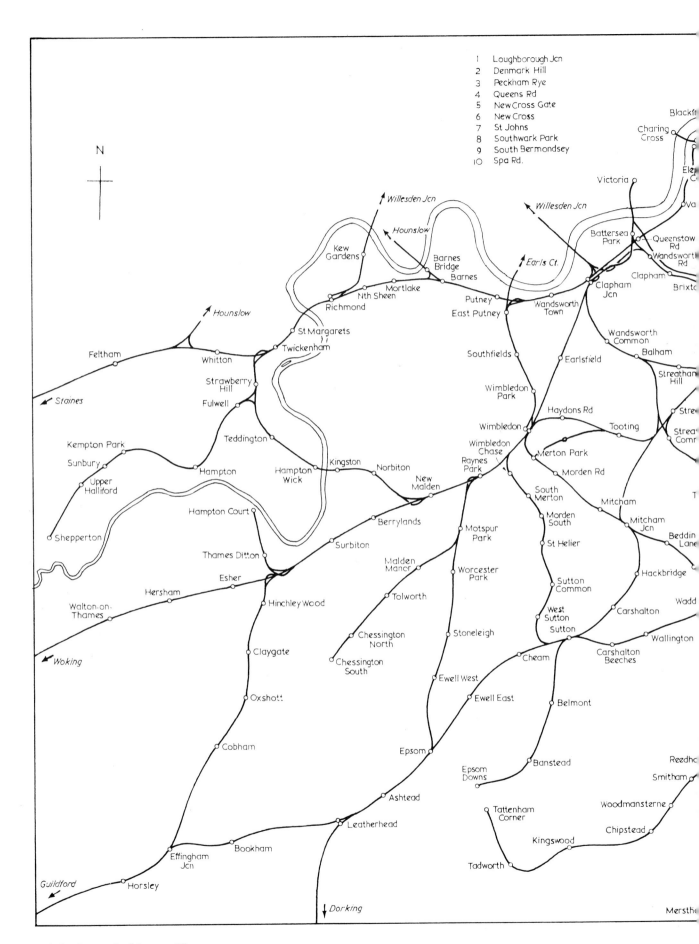

N

Willesden Jcn

Hounslow

Willesden Jcn

Blackf

Charing Cross

Ele

Victoria

Va

Battersea Park

Queenstow Rd

Wandsworth Rd

Earls Ct.

Kew Gardens

Barnes Bridge

Barnes

Mortlake

Nth Sheen

Richmond

Putney

East Putney

Wandsworth Town

Clapham Jcn

Clapham

Brixto

Hounslow

St Margarets

Twickenham

Southfields

Wandsworth Common

Balham

Streatham Hill

Feltham

Whitton

Strawberry Hill

Fulwell

Wimbledon Park

Earlsfield

Staines

Haydons Rd

Stre

Kempton Park

Teddington

Wimbledon

Tooting

Strea Comr

Sunbury

Hampton

Kingston

Norbiton

New Malden

Wimbledon Chase

Raynes Park

Merton Park

Morden Rd

South Merton

Mitcham

Mitcham Jcn

Upper Halliford

Hampton Wick

Berrylands

Motspur Park

Morden South

St Helier

Beddin Lane

Shepperton

Hampton Court

Surbiton

Malden Manor

Worcester Park

Sutton Common

Hackbridge

Thames Ditton

Tolworth

West Sutton

Carshalton

Wadd

Esher

Hersham

Hinchley Wood

Stoneleigh

Sutton

Carshalton Beeches

Wallington

Walton-on-Thames

Chessington North

Cheam

Claygate

Chessington South

Ewell West

Woking

Ewell East

Belmont

Oxshott

Banstead

Reedh

Cobham

Epsom

Smitham

Epsom Downs

Woodmansterne

Tattenham Corner

Chipstead

Ashtead

Kingswood

Leatherhead

Bookham

Tadworth

Effingham Jcn

Guildford

Horsley

↓ *Dorking*

Mersth

Suburban lines south of the River Thames.

preserve of the main line railways although the bus network is well developed. The London & Greenwich provided the initial stimulus. In 1849 the 'North Kent' line was opened via Lewisham and Blackheath, avoiding Greenwich, to gain the Thameside at Woolwich to Dartford and Gravesend, opening the way forward to Rochester. The link between Greenwich and Charlton was not built until 1878.

The 'Mid-Kent' from Lewisham to Beckenham was opened in 1857, this being extended to Addiscombe in 1864. Branches were opened from Elmers End to Hayes in 1882 and from Woodside to Selsdon in 1885. On the SER main line, Hither Green, Grove Park, Chislehurst and Orpington developed as the main suburban traffic objectives. The branch to Bromley North from Grove Park was opened in 1878.

To fill the gap between the Tonbridge line and the 'North Kent' route, the SER opened the 'Dartford Loop' in 1866 between Hither Green and Dartford, leading to the development of Eltham, Sidcup and Bexley. It was not until 1895 that the link from Blackheath to Slade Green was opened, mainly to serve the Welling and Bexleyheath areas. It is interesting how, like Strawberry Hill in south west London, the large locomotive shed at Slades Green, which was opened in 1901, was soon to be converted for electric multiple-units which replaced steam passenger workings on most of the services on the south-eastern suburban lines in 1926. The depot is adjacent to the junction with the Bexleyheath and 'North Kent' lines at Erith.

Neither the LCDR Crystal Palace (1865–1954) nor its Greenwich Park (1871/88–1917) branches were successful for suburban traffic although the 'Catford loop', opened between Nunhead and Shortlands in 1892 was more useful, particularly in serving Catford.

To the south, the LBSCR line from Peckham Rye to Sutton, running almost parallel but west of the London Bridge to East Croydon line, was opened in 1868 providing several important connections to earlier lines and opening-up a host of alternative suburban routes through junctions at Tulse Hill, Streatham and Mitcham.

An extension from West Croydon to Epsom was opened in 1847 while the lightly-used but useful link from West Croydon to Wimbledon followed in 1855. Branches were opened to Epsom Downs, Caterham and Tattenham Corner in 1865, 1856 and 1901 respectively.

Kentish Hop-pickers

Paddock Wood was for many years the centre of Kentish hop-picking, with special trains, particularly

Clapham Junction *One of the busiest junctions in the world, Clapham Junction sees a vast traffic of commuter trains pass through each day between London and its south and south western suburbs as well as on main line services. The location retains some locomotive hauled workings and this interesting picture shows two light engines Nos 74 003 and 74 004 returning from Waterloo on 18 September 1974.*
Brian Morrison

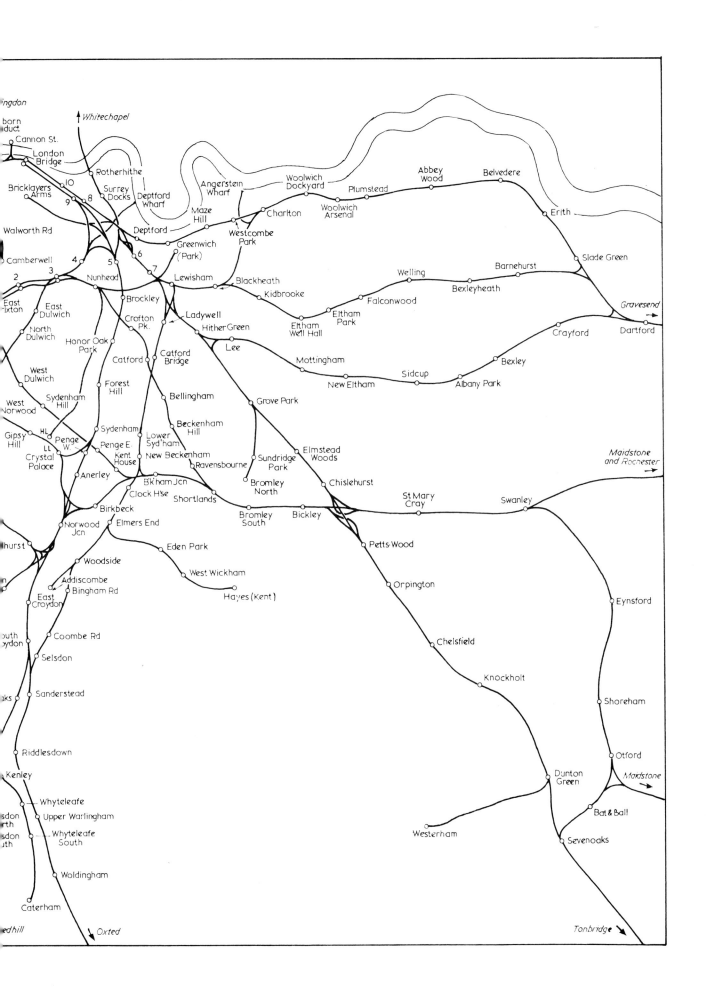

West Croydon *Terminus of the London & Croydon Railway, which opened from London Bridge in 1839, West Croydon was destined to become a through station with lines southwards to Sutton and Wimbledon. This view shows deserted platforms but a crowded locomotive yard during the 1911 railway strike.*
London Borough of Croydon

Richmond *District Railway trains reached Richmond in 1877 and were electrified in 1905. An Aldgate service waits in the platform while the LSWR Windsor and Kingston 'loop' lines, opened to Richmond in 1846, are in the foreground. These were two separate stations until rebuilt by the Southern Railway.*
London Borough of Richmond-upon-Thames

from London Bridge, forming an important part of this seasonal traffic. The need for manual labour for gathering hops and fruit in the late summer brought extra traffic to many parts of Kent, but the mechanisation of harvesting, coupled with changing sociological factors, resulted in rapid decline after World War II, leaving a traffic that was virtually dead by the mid-1950s. The trains, often formed of ageing stock, were a part of the railway scene which is almost forgotten today, with competitive road transport and changed employment patterns.

British Rail's Underground

Unique in the range of services provided by British Rail in the Capital is the Waterloo & City line commonly known as 'The Drain', presumably because of its subterranean tube construction. Although similar to the tube network of the London Underground, it has never formed part of that system, and has no physical connection to any other line. Only the Great Northern & City line from Finsbury Park to Moorgate provides a parallel for the main line companies, although this was built to main line loading gauge and was joined physically to the main line at Drayton Park.

The purpose of the line was to enable the LSWR to obtain a satisfactory link into the City. The location of Waterloo was awkward for this, and alternative arrangements via the LCDR from Longhedge via

Tonbridge *Hop pickers' specials were important seasonal workings on the Kent lines, notably from London Bridge, until the mid 1950s. Class E 4-4-0 No 1159 coasts through Tonbridge on 15 September 1934 with a hop pickers' service returning to London.* V. R. Webster

Brixton to Ludgate Hill, and by means of the connection at Waterloo Junction (Eastern) to the SER for Cannon Street or London Bridge, never proved fully successful.

The line opened in August 1898 linking Waterloo and Bank, passing beneath the Thames. In its aim the line more than justified construction, carrying large volumes of commuters across the river, and thus plays an important part in ensuring the efficient functioning of London.

Conclusion

So London and its south-eastern dormitory has grown in many respects through the influence of railways which initially provided better communications, and the necessary network which stimulated both housing and industrial development. Today, this is far less dominant, good road communications being crucial; inner-suburban rail traffic has considerably reduced as other competing transport modes, falling population and local employment, and declining housing standards have affected many inner-zone areas. Nevertheless, the outer-suburban traffic has largely taken its place, leaving the railway better placed to concentrate its efforts on what it is best suited to do, carrying a large number of people over a direct route for a journey of twenty or more miles in comfort and at speed.

6
FOR PLEASURE

'When a man is tired of London he is tired of life for there is in London all that life can afford'
(Dr Johnson)

In its broadest sense, there are few parts of London's rail network not associated with pleasure travel. Whether it be through the use of the local train service for holidays or simply a 'day out', for a trip to the theatre, shops or cinema in the West End, an art gallery, museum or place of interest, to watch a football match, or perhaps just to visit a friend, the recreational uses of London's railways are virtually limitless. This chapter seeks to identify a few of the more important aspects of London as a worthwhile place in which to live and work and, most of all, to enjoy leisure.

Holidays by the Sea

Until the coming of the railways, holidays for Londoners were almost unknown. Travel and communications by road were poor, and working conditions for the average family man were such that a holiday generally could not be afforded.

The arrival of the railway led to sometimes rapid and significant changes. Hitherto undeveloped coastal settlements such as Brighton suddenly sprang to life and in a very short while had become popular resorts. The Sussex coast from Bognor through Brighton and Eastbourne to Hastings, largely frequented by the well-to-do, was popularised this way, while Margate, Ramsgate and Herne Bay achieved similar popularity as Thanet resorts, partly in conjunction with Thames river traffic. On the north bank, Southend grew as a key holiday resort, particularly for day trippers and excursionists, as did Clacton and Walton-on-the-Naze. Today these resorts are far less frequented by the rail traveller, although day trips remain popular, the tastes of the average person now being further afield, including package tours abroad. So the traveller may well now start and end his trip by rail at Gatwick, Heathrow, Luton (indirectly) or by the Underground, from Victoria Coach Station.

Holidays in the West Country were popular with Londoners, Paddington and Waterloo on busy summer Saturdays thronging with harassed parents with heavy suitcases and happy children with buckets and spades. While still well used, the family aspect has considerably diminished as pure cost in relation to the private car, with its added convenience and flexibility, can make rail travel unattractive.

Economic and sociological changes have also reduced the demand for boat train services as air travel and general increases in sophistication of travellers has wrought the rail link outmoded. Perhaps it need not have been so, but the railway has changed to provide the services it can best and most economically undertake, often shedding traffic it no longer wished to handle.

A day at the Park

The 'Bank Holiday' was once a treasured respite for the busy office and manual worker. Crowds in their thousands used the railway to visit popular open spaces like Hampstead Heath and Epping Forest on such days. The private car, now widely available, and extra holidays have largely changed that – day trips often are much further afield and to a much broader range of activities. Yet these open spaces, and their attendant holiday fairs, remain popular and the train still carries a significant traffic, but for many the problem is not whether to take the train but where to park!

Some facilities, such as Alexandra Palace or Crystal Palace, had extensive rail connections which for brief periods were heavily used for pleasure travel. Alexandra Palace could be visited by either the ex-GN branch via Highgate (direct), to Wood Green on the GN main line or to Palace Gates by the GER. The Palace and Park, with horse racing for some years was subject to the fluctuations of factors of the Palace itself, which was somehow plagued by disaster. Paxton's celebrated Crystal Palace, removed from Hyde Park to the ridges of South London following the 1851 Exhibition, suffered a similar fate; the massive LCDR station in its

Southend Central *Southend is today chiefly a commuter centre but with the Kursaal, attractive estuary frontage and proximity to London, it was until the 1960s a popular resort for excursion traffic. A Class 4 2-6-4T draws out of Southend Central, probably for Fenchurch Street, in September 1955.* Rev. A. W. V. Mace

Gatwick Racecourse *Dappled in the late afternoon sunshine and still tranquil from its rural location, Gatwick was destined to become a busy and noisy place when London's second airport began to be developed. Opened in 1958, the present Gatwick Airport station replaced the Racecourse Station seen in this picture and also the earlier Tinsley Green of 1935 (renamed Gatwick Airport from 1 June 1936)* J. H. Aston

Boat trains *Liverpool Street, Victoria and Waterloo now chiefly deal with boat train traffic, although St Pancras (for Tilbury) and Euston and Paddington (for the Irish links) also had these activities. Waterloo was terminus for the lucrative liner trade from Southampton, in addition to present Channel Islands services from Weymouth, and here Lord Nelson class 4-6-0 No 30860 Lord Hawke rounds the curve through Clapham Junction with the Pullman 'Cunarder' on the last leg of its journey from Southampton Docks on 25 July 1956. Brian Morrison*

Gospel Oak *Hampstead Heath has been a source of relaxation for the people of North London since the nineteenth century and particularly at Bank Holidays, Hampstead Heath and Gospel Oak stations were once thronged with pleasure traffic. Since January 1981 services to Barking have terminated at Gospel Oak, diverted from Kentish Town. On 22 August 1981 the 15.25 Richmond to Broad Street approaches while the 15.55 to Barking waits in the bay. R. Davies*

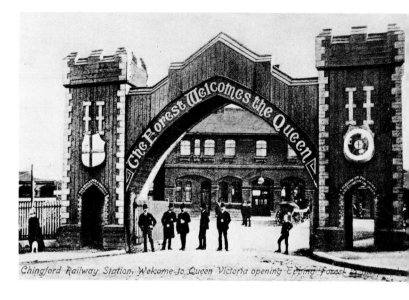

Chingford Railway Station. Welcome to Queen Victoria opening Epping Forest

Alexandra Palace *Holding a commanding position overlooking North London, Alexandra Palace has had a chequered history as the People's Palace. The Alexandra Palace branch followed its fluctuating fortunes being closed and re-opened no less than eight times between 1873 and 1898 to close completely in 1954. This view shows the station and palace ruins after the first disastrous fire of 1873.*
Greater London Council

Chingford *The Chingford branch was originally intended to reach High Beach in the heart of Epping Forest. Fortunately a large part of the Forest area was preserved for the recreation of Londoners and the extension was thrown out by Parliament. This interesting picture shows the special entrance at Chingford built when Queen Victoria came to open the Forest to the public in 1882. Vestry House Museum, London Borough of Waltham Forest.*

Crystal Palace *Like Alexandra Palace, its North London counterpart, the branch to Crystal Palace saw a burst of early popularity for recreational travel followed by years of decline especially after the destruction of the Palace in 1936. Opened in 1865 to tap excursion traffic, the branch from Nunhead was electrified but closed in 1954, with few remains today.* H. C. Casserley

shadow died a lingering death following the fire which destroyed the Palace in 1936. The Brighton station with its staple suburban traffic however remains, albeit under-utilised for the traffic it was built to carry.

The parks of Central London, together with the Zoo and related attractions, also provide recreational travel, a lot of which is LT-generated.

A Country Walk

The railway companies', BR and LT publicity departments have always sought to promote London's countryside, often successfully, through posters, handbills and sometimes very professionally produced publications. Today, the Metropolitan Railway's *Metroland* booklets of the 1920s, describing the attractions of those areas served by the Metropolitan 'main line' and its branches into the Chilterns, often related to housing developments, are valuable collectors' items and treasured possessions. The average semi-detached house was then priced around £750 in Harrow, Pinner or Eastcote, which seems unbelievable today! Similar, but usually less flamboyant productions, have advertised 'round trip' walks, promoted by the main line companies with special tickets, and giving

general details, fares and system maps for guidance. LT's *Country Walks* continue this tradition today, excellent value for a day in London's country by train.

The River Thames itself provides considerable recreational interest. The tourist may use the train to reach the West End for a river trip, or to Hampton Court or Greenwich. In the past Kew and Richmond were virtually holiday resorts, but even now the nearby stations carry significant pleasure traffic on sunny summer week-ends. Windsor, the ever popular 'out-of-town' royal residence, possesses all the ingredients of the popular centre for the day-tripper or tourist. Historical connections, good road and rail links and the river and parkland setting, all continue to generate some seasonal rail passenger traffic, although this pales into insignificance compared with the traffic carried by coaches, a good proportion of which ironically park in the former goods yard of the GW station.

Sport

Football remains possibly one of the most regular sources of special and often heavily peaked rail traffic. Home league and cup matches for the main London teams of West Ham, Tottenham Hotspur and Arsenal, with its Piccadilly line station named after the team, generate significant traffic flows. Other heavy flows are associated with, for instance, Queens Park Rangers, Crystal Palace, Chelsea, Fulham, Charlton, Orient and Millwall. Of course other teams generate travel also, but these are generally of smaller volumes or the grounds are less convenient.

Rickmansworth *'Metroland' epitomises the delights of Middlesex and the Chilterns which were opened up by the Metropolitan Railway for leisure activities for Londoners. Rickmansworth remains today attractively rural and was from 1925–1961 transfer point between electric and steam traction for Metropolitan trains. Here electric locomotive No 11 replaces an L1 2-6-4T and awaits departure south past semaphore signals.* London Transport Executive

Chesham *Another popular destination for Chiltern hikers was Chesham, served by the branch from Chalfont & Latimer. Until the completion of electrification in 1960/1 it was served mainly by a steam push-pull train here seen in the new bay with LMR Ivatt 2-6-2T No 41272 and the coaches now preserved on the Bluebell Railway. During the interim period after the conductor rails were energised but before full electric services were introduced, the London–Chesham peak hour trains were worked right through by Metropolitan electric locomotives. No 2 is running round its train on a Saturday mid-day working from Liverpool Street.* G. M. Kichenside

Windsor & Eton Riverside *As a result of its attractive riverside location and royal connections, Windsor became a popular objective for day trippers. While the GW Windsor & Eton station undoubtedly holds the commanding position for the Castle, Riverside is the LSWR terminus well situated for Thameside ramblers.* R. Davies

Football and other events at Wembley create such heavy traffic flows that they often necessitate special travel and often crowd control arrangements at the nearby stations. Although Wembley Stadium station has gone, Wembley Park, Complex and Central stations still carry large passenger volumes for such events, and incorporate special facilities. Similar generators of traffic include rugby at Twickenham, the Boat Race, the Henley Regattas, and cricket at Lords and The Oval. White City and Crystal Palace regularly stage well-supported athletic events, while in tennis 'Wimbledon Fortnight' is ever popular. Dog and stock car racing at Hackney, Walthamstow and Harringay stadiums also attract railborne patronage.

Special services for horse racing meetings have been a prestige traffic that the railways have sought to serve and maintain. Epsom, with its two branch links, and Kempton Park, with special platforms on the Shepperton branch, are good examples. Royal specials to Epsom on Derby Day exemplify this arrangement.

Exhibition Traffic

No survey of recreational travel would be complete without reference to the contribution of Earl's Court and Olympia to London's pleasure market. Although the Birmingham Exhibition centre (rail served from London) has stolen some of the regular favourites such as the Motor Show, Motorfair remains very popular as do the Ideal Home Exhibition and many other traditional large shows. The centre virtually keeps Kensington (Olympia) open as a station, the special, mainly LT, exhibition services being predominant usage, although these run only when there is an exhibition warranting a service. Wembley has in recent years also tried to generate exhibition facilities with the good rail services it can offer.

Wembley Stadium *For the Empire Exhibition, the LNER opened Wembley Stadium station in 1923 on a single track loop west of Neasden which was used for football traffic until 1968. The picture shows Class N7 0-6-2T No 997E (BR 69619) drawing into Wembley Stadium on 4 July 1925 with an Exhibition train from Marylebone, with the 'Never-stop' Railway on the right. H. C. Casserley*

Other

Preserved railways can themselves be classed in this category, the Bluebell line in Sussex, the GW Railway Centre at Didcot, the Quainton Railway Society north of Aylesbury and the Stour Valley Railway in Essex being the main examples in the London and South East area.

BR 'Merrymaker' excursions, 'Awayday' tickets and main line steam on other parts of the BR system do much to encourage use of the rail network from London, and hopefully provide an enjoyable day out for Londoners and others.

Epsom Race Specials *The railways have always been a popular mode of transport for race meetings and have often vied for this prestige traffic. Epsom still sees considerable activity for meetings and in this picture a royal special for Epsom passes Belmont in the charge of LBSCR 4-4-2T No 78. London Borough of Sutton*

7
SOUTHERN ELECTRIC

Those in search of the *Art Deco* style with its echoes of the 1930s would do well to study Richmond station and its booking hall. While it has been modernised, basically it remains as reconstructed by the Southern Railway in 1937 to emphasise the modern transport service that 'Southern Electric' provided. The company at first concentrated on its London suburban service but by 1938, had extended its electrified network to 622 route miles from the 83 miles it inherited from its constituents in 1923.

On its incorporation the Southern found that its three main constituents, the London Brighton & South Coast Railway (LBSCR), the London & South Western Railway (LSWR) and the South Eastern & Chatham Railway (SECR), had answered the demands of their suburban traffic differently, although the problems were largely the same. The London County Council, which had been created in 1889, began to purchase the independent street tramway companies from 1891, determined to improve and electrify them. Its electric trams were inaugurated in 1903 and conversion then proceeded fairly rapidly on the South London system. At the same time, the London United Tramways Company electrified its system in the south-western suburbs from 1901. Major bus competition began from around 1905, the year that the District Railway was electrified completely, and the tube was opened to Hammersmith in 1906. Earlier, 1902 saw the incorporation of the 'Underground' group, which would integrate the tube, tram and bus companies as a predecessor of London Transport. In short, there was considerable development on the transport scene, and the Southern's constituents had to do something to meet the increased competition which affected their suburban traffic.

The LBSCR

The LBSCR had been the first to introduce electric trains over its South London Line between Victoria and London Bridge via Denmark Hill, on 1 December 1909. In 1903 the company had obtained Parliamentary powers to electrify the whole system and on the recommendation of its consulting engineer, Philip Dawson, adopted a system of alternating current fed to the trains from overhead wires. This system made power supply easier than a direct current system; the track was kept free of conductor rails and the system was suitable for extension to the South Coast. Work started in 1906 but the first trial train did not run until 17 January 1909. Virtually everything was experimental so progress was slow, although since the line had almost every physical feature of a railway, much was learned.

Eight three-car trains were built, seating 74 first- and 144 third-class passengers; an innovation was the absence of second-class, not abolished elsewhere on the LBSCR suburban lines until June 1911. A carriage repair shop and shed were erected at Peckham Rye, while five platforms were electrified at Victoria and six at London Bridge. Until June 1912 services before 07.30 on weekdays were steam, after this electrics ran about every 15 minutes and took 24 minutes for the journey of nine intermediate stops, 12 minutes faster than the steam service. Little change was made to fares but electrification told its own story. The eight million passengers on the line in 1902 had more than halved by 1909; the first year of electric services saw 7½ million carried.

So successful was the South London Line that the next step was to electrify the lines to Crystal Palace. Work went forward rapidly and the service from Victoria via Streatham Hill opened on 12 May 1911, the day that King George V opened the Festival of Empire at the Palace. Electrification was carried through to Norwood Junction and Selhurst to reach workshops and sidings but the section from Peckham Rye to West Norwood could not open until the London Electric Supply Corporation had installed extra generating capacity. Officially fixed for 1 June 1912, electric trains began to run on 3 March as a miners' strike had made locomotive coal scarce. Thirty three-car sets with 48 first- and 170 third-class seats were built. Service frequencies of between three and five trains an hour had its effect in a 70% increase in passengers.

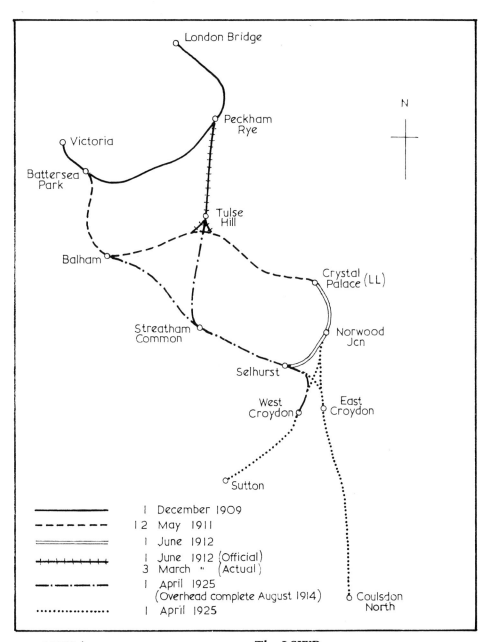

————————	1	December 1909
– – – – – –	12	May 1911
════════	1	June 1912
┼┼┼┼┼┼┼┼	1	June 1912 (Official)
	3	March " (Actual)
—·—·—·—	1	April 1925
		(Overhead complete August 1914)
··············	1	April 1925

Electrification progress on LBSCR lines.

In 1913 the company decided to electrify almost all of its suburban services. A good deal of the work had been done by August 1914, with overhead equipment erected from Balham Junction to Selhurst and West Croydon and Tulse Hill to Streatham Common and Streatham South Junction. Alas, the system of electrification was German. After war broke out essential material could not be obtained and work was abandoned for the duration. After the war the schemes were reviewed, electrification to Brighton and Eastbourne being approved in principle by the Board. Work did not recommence until 1922 when it resumed on the Coulsdon and Sutton lines, but was not complete by 1 January 1923 when the Southern took over.

The LSWR

While the electric trains of the District and LNWR ran over LSWR tracks, it was not until 1913 that the LSWR announced its electrification plans, perhaps spurred into action by the Central London Railway's authorised extension to Richmond. More significant was the appointment of Mr H. A. Walker as General Manager on 1 January 1912, when the reduction of suburban traffic was one of the first problems to face him. He knew of the LNWR suburban electrification, as he had previously worked for that company, and would have borne the LNWR experience in mind when developing the LSWR schemes. The intention was to cover the lines from Waterloo to Wimbledon via East Putney, the Kingston and Hounslow loops, the Shepperton and Hampton Court branches, and the routes to Guildford via Woking, Cobham and Epsom. In the six years to 1913 receipts of over £100,000 had been lost on these lines, and electrification was the only way to regain the traffic.

Following a visit to America by its Electrical Engineer, and on the advice of its consultant, the LSWR decided to adopt a 600-volt direct current third-rail system. Although work was delayed by the outbreak of World War I, it did not cease. Consequently, on 25 October 1915 the first electric trains commenced between Waterloo and Wimbledon via East Putney on a regular 20-minute interval service. Electric services on the Kingston Loop and Shepperton lines were announced for 5 December 1915, but problems with alleged interference with Post Office telephones delayed this until 30 January 1916. The Hounslow loop service began on 12 March, the Hampton Court branch on 18 June and electrification reached Claygate on 20 November.

To work these services, 84 three-coach trains were provided, converted from existing steam-hauled coaches. Again, only first- and third-class was provided, the first time on the LSWR that second-class was excluded, and about a quarter of the 172 to 190 seats in each train were first-class. Sheds and repair shops were built at Durnsford Road, Wimbledon, south of the power station which supplied the system, and later the steam locomotive shed at Strawberry Hill was converted to a depot for electric trains.

Timetables were not necessary, as trains ran at fixed minutes past each hour and were between two and four an hour. There was no variation to the timetable at peak hours but the three-car trains were strengthened to six. Journey times were a third less than those of the previous steam service. Results were as expected, the decline from 25 million passengers carried on these lines in 1913 to 23.3 million in 1915 was reversed. By 1916 it was 29.4 million and by 1920 52.6 million. 1920 saw the introduction of 24 two-coach third-class trailers to work between two of the motor sets, but there development stopped. Indeed, it had already gone slightly into reverse; the Claygate service was withdrawn in July 1919 in order to release rolling stock to cope with the additional traffic. And so it was in this form that the LSWR electric system passed to the Southern Railway.

The SECR

On the SECR Parliamentary powers for electric working were obtained in 1903, but little happened until 1913. With a continuing loss of traffic to other forms of transport, and perhaps inspired by the neighbouring LBSCR's adventures with electric traction, the subject was raised at the shareholders' half-yearly meeting. The Chairman stated that electrification of the system would be complicated and therefore expensive, while he did not think it advisable to go to the shareholders for money. The outbreak of war put paid to any further plans, although as it caused the closure of a number of suburban stations and services it made the eventual task simpler.

After the war, the SECR intended to use £6.5m of state aid to electrify the suburban area in three stages. Increases in speed of 30-40% and 30-60% in frequency were expected from a 1500V direct current system which would employ separate conductor and return rails. Three-car multiple-units were to be employed with seating in first- and third-class for 256. Through passenger and goods trains would be worked over the electrified section by electric locomotives. In 1922 the SECR sought permission to build its own power station, a task in which it was unsuccessful. On absorption by the Southern Railway, no work had been started.

Southern Development

So the infant Southern Railway, on its incorporation in 1923, found that its three principal constituents had developed three different systems of electrification. Clearly the first step was to standardise on one system. After due consideration, a departmental committee recommended the adoption of the LSWR direct-current 600-volt third-rail system, for ease of installation and the low cost of construction and maintenance. The Directors accepted this on 1 February 1923, very early in the life of the SR, but as the former LBSCR extension to Sutton and Coulsdon was so far advanced, they decided that it should be completed. Whereas the SECR had attempted and the LSWR actually did generate its own power, the Southern Railway had to accept that in future it would have to purchase electricity from electric supply concerns, for whom railway demand was a useful base load.

Meanwhile, the Southern had to do something to restore its image on the suburban services. Changes in working hours had concentrated the daily peaks into shorter periods, especially on the former SECR Charing Cross and Cannon Street services, making operation with resources run down in World War I more difficult. To do something quickly, the Southern took up the plans of its constituents. SECR plans were ready, the change of system to the new standard was relatively minor so on 5 July 1923 the Board sanctioned work on the scheme. Next the uncompleted sections of the LSWR scheme were sanctioned with the line from Leatherhead to Dorking North taking the place of Hampton Court Junction to Guildford via Woking.

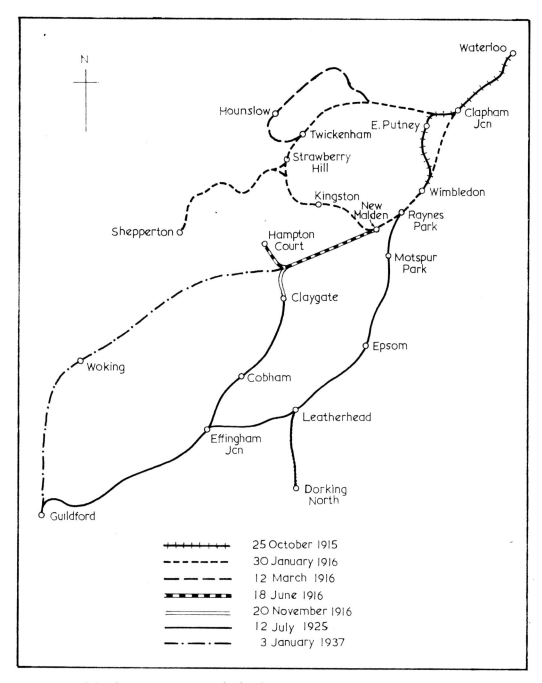

++++++++	25 October 1915
- - - - -	30 January 1916
— — —	12 March 1916
■■■■■■	18 June 1916
═══════	20 November 1916
————	12 July 1925
—·—·—	3 January 1937

Electrification progress on LSWR lines.

Here incorporation of the former LBSCR Leatherhead to Dorking line knitted together two constituents of the SR. Finally, on 6 December 1923, agreement was given to the completion of the former LBSCR scheme. Thus work could be started whilst the future pattern of electrification was decided.

The first stage of the modernisation of the former SECR routes involved electrification from Victoria and Holborn Viaduct to Orpington via Herne Hill and Catford, together with the Crystal Palace branch. In addition, the lines from Brixton to Loughborough Junction and Cambria Road Junction were electrified,

although no regular service of electric trains used them. Substantial rationalisation took place with some rebuilding at Brixton, Herne Hill, Loughborough Junction, Nunhead and Shortlands. The platforms at Ludgate Hill were too short for eight-coach trains so its services were restricted to peak-hour steam services from the inception of electrification. Training runs began from Nunhead to Crystal Palace on 1 April 1925 and trial running from St Paul's to Shortlands on 8 June. Public services began on 12 July, the same day as

103

Chelsfield *Electric services to Chelsfield were provided as part of the Southern's extension of electrification from Orpington to Sevenoaks in January 1935. In this view the changes electrification has brought are apparent, the 3-car electric unit 1518, built for the 1925 scheme, conductor rail, lineside cabling and a substation, but semaphore signals still remain.* Rev. A. W. V. Mace

they began on the Dorking North and Guildford lines on the former LSWR.

The second stage on the ex-SECR lines covered the routes from Charing Cross and Cannon Street to Orpington, Bromley North, Hayes and Addiscombe, together with the spur to Beckenham Junction. As the electric services were intended to run direct to each terminal, instead of to Charing Cross via Cannon Street which had been the practice until then, the introduction of these services depended upon the rationalisation of the track layout as far as London Bridge. Charing Cross was tackled first. When it was complete and temporary electrification arrangements made at Cannon Street, these services were announced to commence on 1 December 1925, but problems with power supply delayed this until 28 February 1926. Staff training took place on the Elmers End to Hayes line where branch services had been worked electrically from 21 September 1925. Cannon Street was reconstructed from 5 June to

28 June 1926 when, to assist the work, it was completely closed. After a period of temporary services for staff to familiarise themselves with the new layout, full services commenced on 19 July.

The third stage involved the routes to Dartford via Greenwich, Blackheath, Bexleyheath and Sidcup. Again, it was the rationalisation at Charing Cross and Cannon Street which determined the date of introduction of these services. While a few electric trains had run between Charing Cross and Dartford during the General Strike and more during the closure of Cannon Street, the full service had to wait until 19 July 1926.

As further parts of the rationalisation work a number of inner suburban stations, closed in World War I, were removed from 1923 and colour-light signalling was introduced in 1926 from Holborn Viaduct to Elephant & Castle and from Charing Cross and Cannon Street to Borough Market Junction. Stock was provided by a mixture of new sets and reconstruction. 29 three-car sets were built with seats for 56 first- and 180 third-class passengers whilst 105 sets of similar specification were converted from former SECR steam stock and 70 two-car trailer sets of 180 seats from LBSCR stock. Stabling for these trains was provided in sheds at Orpington and Addiscombe while the former engine

104

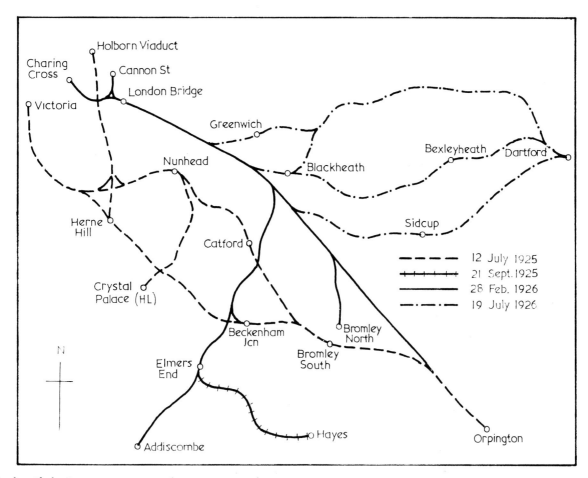

Electrification progress on SECR lines.

shed at Slade Green was converted to serve as an electric depot and a new building erected as a repair shop. Apart from the station rebuilding already mentioned, Bromley North station was rebuilt and brought into use in December 1925.

Completion of the former LBSCR overhead system had started in 1922 and was continued by the Southern, but the opening of the extensions from Balham and Tulse Hill to Coulsdon and Sutton had to be postponed until 1 April 1925 because of problems with the electricity supply. The rolling stock comprised 21 motor vans, 60 driving trailers and 20 trailer coaches. Essentially locomotives, the motor vans were marshalled into five-car sets with seats for 64 first- and 240 third-class passengers, which ran singly in off-peak and in pairs at peaks. The new service ran mainly at twenty-minute intervals eased to half-hourly at less busy times. Incidental works were mainly limited to the conversion of Beeches Halt to Carshalton Beeches station and track alterations at Sutton.

On the erstwhile LSWR lines, the formal opening took place on 9 July 1925, an occasion used by the Southern to obtain some valuable publicity. A special train ran from Waterloo to Dorking North and, after a short stop, returned to Leatherhead and then ran to Guildford. Here, at a civic lunch, the Southern's Chairman announced that 67 single-track miles had been electrified and 104 coaches provided for the project without exceeding the estimated cost of £833,000. Public services commenced on 12 July 1925, when the new Motspur Park station opened, and followed the principle of regular interval trains.

With the completion of these plans of its constituents the Southern turned to its own schemes. Having decided that the standard system was to be dc third-rail, the inevitable happened when it was announced in August 1926 that the former Brighton overhead system would be converted to the standard as part of plans to extend electrification on the former Brighton suburban system. Conversion took place in three stages. Services from London Bridge to Victoria and Coulsdon North on 17 June 1928, from Victoria to Crystal Palace on 3 March 1929 and finally between Victoria and Coulsdon North and Sutton on 22 September 1929.

Work went forward throughout the remainder of the 1920s so that the inauguration of electric services on 6 July 1930 to Windsor, Gravesend and from Wimbledon to West Croydon saw the virtual completion of the

Coulsdon North *When the LBSCR overhead electric system was completed in April 1925, it extended to Coulsdon North and to Sutton. However, conversion to direct current working meant the last train on the overhead system left Victoria for Coulsdon North only just over four years later on Sunday 22 September 1929. In October 1981, No 4738, a 4-SUB set of 1949, stands in the terminal platform whilst a 4-CIG of 1964 passes on its way towards East Croydon. R. Davies*

electrification of the suburban area. The 1930s were therefore spent in extending the system to cover the main line services and providing additional facilities in the suburban area, required by growth in traffic and the expansion of London's housing.

The extension of main line electrification had started with the Brighton line. To relieve unemployment, the 1929 Budget had abolished the duty on first- and second class fares provided that the capitalised value of the duty was spent by the railway companies on improvement

Addiscombe *The second stage of electrification of the SECR lines involved the branch to Addiscombe, on which electric services commenced on 28 February 1926. This view shows 1417, one of the sets whose bodywork was converted from former SECR coaches, at Addiscombe on that day. On completion of reconstruction at Charing Cross and Cannon Street, Addiscombe was to have a train an hour to each terminus.* London Borough of Croydon

Lewisham *As part of a plan to direct cross-London freight trains away from London Bridge, the former SECR Greenwich Park branch was truncated and by means of a new spur diverted to join the North Kent lines at Lewisham in 1929. The connection was electrified in 1935 for peak hour services from Dartford to St. Pauls (Blackfriars), again to relieve the London Bridge area. No 1749 leaves the spur and runs into Lewisham in 1936. Rev. A. W. V. Mace*

schemes. The Southern's share was just over £2 million, which was to be spent on extending electrification from Purley to Reigate, Brighton and West Worthing, using the existing system, which would enable suburban stock to be used for excursion traffic. Starting in 1931 the project involved the customary re-signalling, rationalisation of tracks and rebuilding of stations. Public services began on 1 January 1933 super-imposing main line trains on the suburban system. Results were immediate. Nearly 80% more tickets were collected at Brighton over Easter compared with 1932, and this success was to be repeated with the conversion of services to Eastbourne, Hastings and Portsmouth.

Before turning to two case studies of suburban lines built by the Southern in the 1930s, it would be useful to review the principles which lay behind the Southern Electric system. Perhaps the most important was that every aspect of operation was reviewed to see whether it met the contemporary requirements and, if it did not, what changes were necessary. Electrification therefore meant much more than just adding a third rail and con-verting from steam haulage.

The first stage would be to rationalise track layouts, stations and operating practices. The 1926 announce-ment of electrification of the LBSCR lines therefore meant that the track layout between London Bridge and Bricklayers Arms Junction was completely rearranged to provide two up and two down lines controlled by one signalbox, instead of the previous awkward layout, a legacy of LBSCR and SECR independence. One consequence of this new layout was the need to rebuild South Bermondsey, which otherwise would have been left with a platform for one direction only, and the resited station was opened on 17 June 1928. A change in operating practice was evident in the same scheme when Tadworth and Caterham trains were diverted to terminate at London Bridge in peak hours. Until then they had run to Charing Cross and Cannon Street throughout the day but had to cross from former LBSCR lines to former SECR lines just outside London Bridge. In the intensive peak working of the electric service this would have been likely to cause delays. Rationalisation of stations took place on electrification to Epsom, where the LSWR had a separate station from the LBSCR, although the latter's trains ran through the LSWR station. Rebuilding produced one station to serve both groups of services. On the Windsor line new stations were provided at North Sheen and Whitton, both opened with electric services on 6 July 1930. Existing facilities were altered or supplemented to complement the new service specification.

The second stage was the timetables and publicity for the line. Herbert Walker, the Southern General Manager, was convinced of the need for regular headways and frequent services, maintaining that the public should have no need to consult timetables. He had carried on this plan on the LSWR electrification and it became Southern Railway policy. Thus in 1938 a passenger from West Croydon to Wimbledon knew that on weekdays the trains left at 11, 31 and 51 minutes past each hour in the peaks and at 14 and 44 minutes past in the off-peaks. Even if the times were not known, the maximum wait would be thirty minutes. As far as possible this was repeated on each line electrified. Organised publicity started on the Southern with the appointment of John Elliot as public relations officer in January 1925. The LBSCR had adopted the trade mark of 'Elevated Electric' no doubt because its first electrified line was on viaduct and embankment. The Southern adopted the 'Southern Electric' tag to market its services and it was prominently displayed in green-and-white enamelled signs on station frontages. The speed and frequency of the services were the major selling points so, for example, passers-by at Crystal Palace (High Level) station were faced with a sign 'Southern Electric. Frequent Trains to City and Victoria. Weekly Seasons. Cheap Tickets Daily.' Sometimes a flash symbol was used over the words 'Southern Electric' written in the distinctive 'sunshine' lettering.

The third aspect was the use of electric multiple-units in fixed formation sets. The use of multiple-units cut down the number of movements necessary at the terminals and therefore the time spent in them. A locomotive-hauled train having arrived at the terminus required another locomotive to attach at the country end to work the train away. This would enable the original locomotive to clear the platform and move to a siding, ready to back on to the next train to arrive. By contrast a multiple-unit would arrive, requiring only the driver to walk to the other end and drive the train away. Four moves had been replaced by two. With this reduction in movements for each train, more trains could be dealt with at any terminal, enabling the train service to be increased.

The fixed formation enabled trains to be strengthened at peak times but trains could also be split or joined en route. Thus units from Caterham and Tattenham Corner were joined at Purley to form one train to Charing Cross or London Bridge, whilst in the other direction the process was reversed. The LSWR practice of route indication was continued, as a stencil plate in front of an opal glass panel was shown on the leading end. Letters were used to indicate routes which was put to good use by Hovis bread in carriage advertisements. Five trains were shown, each with different headcodes, H for Hampton Court, $\bar{\text{O}}$ for Hounslow, V for Kingston, I for Claygate and S for Shepperton; together they spelt 'H$\bar{\text{O}}$VIS'. ('The Route to Health – Go b(u)y it', the panels proclaimed).

Lastly, depot facilities had to be provided for the new stock. Peckham Rye and Selhurst had been provided for the LBSCR scheme and Wimbledon for the LSWR. These three depots had been specially constructed for electric stock but subsequently existing steam facilities were adapted for this purpose. Strawberry Hill locomotive depot, in the triangle formed by the Shepperton branch and the Kingston Loop, had been opened in the 1890s and enlarged in 1908. Some of the depot was used for electric stock from 1916 but, when steam locomotives were transferred to Feltham in 1922/3, it became exclusively used by electric multiple-units. Slade Green depot on the South Eastern section was a further example of the conversion process; Orpington and Addiscombe were especially built for the same scheme. So as electrification progressed, this mixture of new building and adaption of existing facilities went on to provide stabling and maintenance.

Southern Case Studies I – The Wimbledon & Sutton Branch

The first example of a line to be built and opened by the Southern Railway was the 5¼-mile branch from Wimbledon to Sutton. Ideas for such a railway had been floated from as early as 1883, but it was not until 1910 that powers were obtained for the line. Initially an

Brighton Belle *On the electrification to Brighton in 1933, three five-car sets were provided for the* Southern Belle, *later the* Brighton Belle, *service from Victoria, the first all-electric Pullman trains in the world. Making three journeys each way on weekdays, increased to four in 1963, the service was suspended from 1942 to 1946 and finally withdrawn in 1972. Here 3053 in chocolate and cream livery waits at Victoria.*
C. R. L. Coles

independent company, it came under the control of the District Railway in 1912. Preliminary works were started in 1913 which would have enabled the District to extend its Wimbledon service to Sutton, but World War I stopped further progress. After the war plans changed. The Underground Group, parent of the District, intended to extend the City & South London tube from Clapham Common to Morden, to build the Wimbledon to Sutton line and to construct a depot at Morden for both tube and District stock. The prospect of tube trains reaching Sutton was too much for the Southern. After Parliamentary clashes in 1923, compromise was reached. The tube was to be extended to Morden but there was to be no junction with the Wimbledon & Sutton which the Southern would take-over and build.

While the Southern adopted the line by an Act in 1924, preliminary work was delayed until 1927 and Sir Robert McAlpine & Sons, the main contractor, did not begin work until July 1928. Work was pressed forward to allow the line to be opened from Wimbledon to South Merton on 7 July 1929. Electric trains began to run on to Sutton from 1 January 1930; the public service did not commence until Sunday, 5 January and was provided by a Holborn Viaduct to West Croydon service with trains running every twenty minutes in the peaks and every half-hour at other times.

The six stations on the line were built to a common pattern. All had island platforms, capable of taking eight-car trains, with a closed canopy covering part of the platform and the waiting rooms and lavatories, beyond which was a room for staff. Access to the platforms was gained by flights of steps going down at South Merton, St Helier and Sutton Common, up at Wimbledon Chase and Morden South, while at West Sutton steps led up to cross one of the tracks and then down to the platform. Concrete buildings at street level were provided at Wimbledon Chase, St Helier and West Sutton, faced with tiles at Wimbledon, and all followed the same pattern. A wide entrance flanked by shops and protected by a small canopy, led into a circulating hall. Passengers bought their tickets at a passimeter booking office on the opposite side of the

Clapham Junction *Old and new stock is apparent in this 1980 view of the south end of Clapham Junction. EMU No 4637, a 4SUB, on a Kingston Loop train, is at the boundary of the former LSWR lines. All four tracks to the right of it were the LBSCR lines, where No 7805, a 4VEP, and No 7317, a 4CIG, pass from and to Brighton.*
Brian Morrison

Peckham Rye *Evidence of the Brighton overhead system is apparent in this view of No B184 on a Brighton–London Bridge train at Peckham Rye on 15 May 1927. This was on the original section of Elevated Electric, converted in 1928. After the system was abandoned, the gantries were put to use elsewhere, although in places the bases can still be detected.* H. C. Casserley

hall from the entrance and then walked ahead to reach their trains by going up or down the flight of steps. Passengers leaving the station had their tickets collected on the other side of the booking office. The entrance hall was tiled and lighted by a centre roof skylight. Foundations for such street-level buildings were provided at the other stations, (indeed, the booking office section was built at Sutton Common) against the time they would be required, but temporary facilities were provided at platform level. All stations except South Merton had a station forecourt.

The stations acted as local centres, and at all except South Merton and Morden South there were adjacent shops. Housing development took place all along the line in the 1930s, a mixture of LCC development and private estates of mainly small terraced houses.

Hampton Court *Hampton Court was also provided with LSWR electric services in 1916, initially served from Waterloo by three trains an hour for the greater part of each weekday, aided by the flyover, to enable branch trains to leave the main line, opened in 1915. Rationalisation saw the closure of the goods yard in 1965 and the installation of colour light signalling in 1970. Now passenger facilities are effectively confined to the island platform at which 508 020 arrives.* R. Davies

Kingston *Kingston was served by LSWR electric services from 1916 but was reconstructed to its present form by the Southern Railway from 1934. The three low level terminal bays were abolished leaving two through platforms and a bay. The recent type of EMU, 508 026, stands at the down platform bound for Shepperton whilst 5105, a 4-EPB of 1951, stands in the bay with a train for Waterloo via Richmond.* R. Davies

Slade Green *Stock for the Eastern Section Suburban electrification of 1925–26 was provided with maintenance and stabling facilities at Orpington, Addiscombe and Slade Green. No 5334, a 4-EPB of 1960, passes Slade Green with a train from Dartford to London Bridge. To the left is the former steam locomotive shed converted on electrification for EMU stabling and behind it is the repair shop of the same vintage.*
Brian Morrison

Slades Green *A 1925 view of Slades Green (today Slade Green) shows it in its days as a steam depot with locomotive No A169 to the left and A308 on the right. The shed dated from the formation of the SECR, with its determination to develop suburban services, which also extended to the establishment of carriage sidings close to the depot. The development bore fruit which ultimately necessitated electrification.*
H. C. Casserley

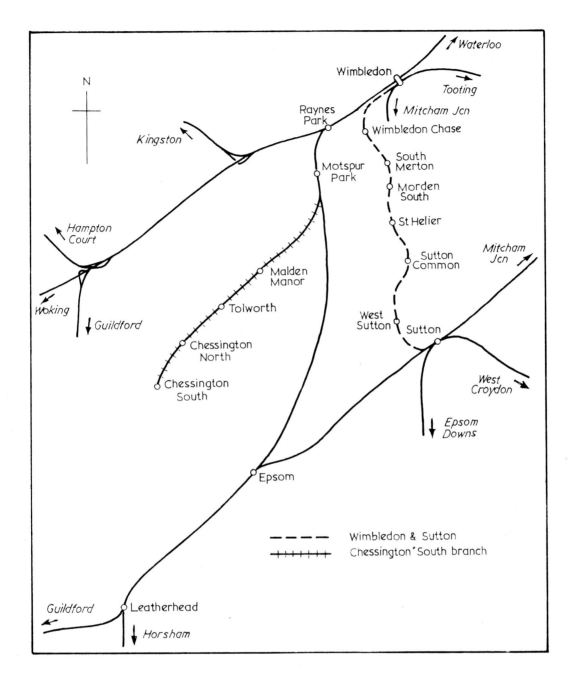

Case studies: Wimbledon & Sutton and Chessington lines.

Wimbledon Chase, St Helier and Morden South were on main roads but all the others were on minor roads. At St Helier, where its estate was intended to have 10,000 houses, the LCC paid for a station, but parklands were near to South Merton, Morden South and Sutton Common. Freight services were limited to serving an Express Dairy and a goods yard at St Helier, and the only signalbox on the line was at St Helier. Signalling, originally solely upper-quadrant semaphores with posts made of old rail, is now a mixture of semaphore and colour-light. Sharp curves were exemplified at West Sutton where rail greasers are installed on the Sutton branch line for the 30mph restriction. In this

area two concrete retaining walls were necessary to minimise the land which had to be acquired where the line joins the LBSCR main line at a gradient of 1 in 44.

Southern Case Studies II – The Chessington Branch

The second example of 'Southern Electric' in practice is the line from Motspur Park to Chessington South. This was part of a greater design for a line to Leatherhead which would serve the area between the Claygate and

113

St. Helier *St. Helier is typical of the style of the stations on the Wimbledon & Sutton line. From its opening by the Southern in 1930 it provided transport facilities for the LCC estate, begun in 1929, represented by the parade of shops at the top. Indeed the LCC conveyed 12 acres, part of the land needed for the station, free to the SR.*
Lens of Sutton

Epsom lines of the former LSWR. Anticipated housing development was the principal reason for its promotion, and the Act for its construction was obtained in 1930. Problems over land acquisition delayed the start of construction as the activities of land speculators drove up prices and broke the land into small portions anticipating profits from its value for housebuilding. However, by November 1933 the SR Board had agreed that all the land required for the branch should be purchased. With the advance of London, house building began at its northern end in 1932 and 1933. Accordingly the line was divided into two sections and contracts were let for the section to Chessington South in 1935. Sir Robert McAlpine & Sons began work at Motspur Park in 1936 and the section to Tolworth opened to passengers on 29 May 1938. Almost a year later the remaining two miles to Chessington South were opened on 28 May 1939. In both these areas the section of line was available for staff training for a fortnight beforehand. Beyond Chessington South the track stopped after some 20 chains but the embankment continued towards

Leatherhead. World War II prevented the completion of the project and the subsequent designation of the land beyond Chessington South as Green Belt precluded further housing development. Although powers to construct the Chessington South to Leatherhead section were kept alive until 1961, completion of the project now seems unlikely.

Motspur Park, the junction station for the branch, was opened in July 1925 in anticipation of suburban development and was similar in style to those on the Sutton line. An island platform, capable of holding eight-car trains, was provided with all facilities to which access was gained by footbridge from both sides of the line. About half a mile beyond the station towards Epsom the line diverged on the 3¾-mile run to Chessington. All the four stations on the line were built to a common pattern which was varied to suit the site. The street-level buildings were provided in the corner of the station forecourt. The central entrance was flanked by a shop on one side and a parcels and luggage office on the other and led into a booking hall lit by roof lights. To one side was the booking office, and to the other a ladies' toilet, a bookstall and a store with a telephone in the corner. Ahead was the ticket barrier, beyond which was the entrance to the gentlemen's toilet, alongside the booking office. Except for Chessington South, where only one platform was in use, the passage then bifurcated to lead to steps up to each platform.

The steps led up to platforms 540ft long capable of holding eight-car trains, sheltered in part by platform awnings integral with the building, and provided with fluorescent lights. Each platform was provided with a waiting and staff rooms, in some cases with a booking office window to make for one-man operation, and from the ground level parcels and luggage office, one was served by a lift shaft which in the event never contained a lift. Chessington South, which can be seen from the North station, differed as only the down platform was brought into use and, although the up platform was built together with its awning, its line was used only as a siding, a similar arrangement to that when Tolworth was the temporary terminus of the line. Once through the ticket barrier, here steps led down to the platform which conformed to the standard pattern. Provision was made for a footbridge but its entrance beyond the barrier was boarded-off. Station materials were largely re-inforced concrete, also the predominant building material in bridgeworks and viaducts, although the street-level facilities at both Chessington stations were built in brick. The concrete has not weathered well in places, but when painted can look attractive. The interior of the booking hall and the passageways were tiled with framed spaces for posters. At all stations but Chessington North a gated exit from the platform gave access to a ramp to street level.

Housing development moved out along the line and each station became the focal point for its local area, except for Tolworth where the centre was fixed just north of the road intersection on the Kingston By-Pass.

Malden Manor and Chessington North had a parade of shops nearby but the former's was from the 1930s and the latter's the 1950s. Certainly the area around the two Chessington stations owes more to the 1950s than the 1930s, while Chessington South was on the edge of the Green Belt.

A goods yard and signalbox were provided at Tolworth and Chessington South, but both facilities have now changed. The former are now coal concentration depots and the latter have been removed.

Envoi

The line to Chessington South was almost the last to be electrified by the Southern Railway; that distinction fell to the lines to Maidstone and Gillingham in Kent in July 1939. A month later the country was at war. The years after it were a time of austerity and the task of electrification was not resumed until 1956. By that time the Southern Railway no longer existed, but from 1952 a bust of Sir Herbert Walker had looked out on the concourse of Waterloo to review the 'Southern Electric' he had created.

Chessington South *Chessington South looks very new with an EMU terminating in what was planned as the down platform. However, because of the intended extension of services, it was signalled as a terminal platform and the up platform as a siding but the latter has never been brought into use and is now greatly overgrown. The goods yard lay ahead of the unit under a road bridge, whilst Chessington North is visible in the distance behind it.* Lens of Sutton

8
LONDON TRANSPORT'S RAILWAYS

'Underground to Anywhere!'
(An Underground Electric Railway Poster – May 1908)

No survey of London's railways would be complete without reference to the special contribution made by London Transport's rail network. Predominantly developed in North London because of the way in which the tube and Underground grew around the centre, the Underground complements the intensive SR electric services south of the Thames. The lines fall conveniently into two groups, sub-surface and tube, both of which contrast markedly with their main line counterparts. A particularly interesting aspect was the expansion of the system to absorb sections of several former 'main line' branches.

The Underground is an everyday part of the London scene and is easily taken for granted. Few travellers are aware of its history as they catch their daily trains to town or use its services for recreational purposes. Few also take time to notice the architectural contribution made to London as they pass quickly through in the daily round of rush hours, ticket queues and changing trains. Fewer still consider how reliable their daily journey is, finding time only to grumble when things go wrong.

With services now only of electric multiple-unit stock, much of the former character of some of its lines has been lost, and it is the purpose of this chapter to outline briefly the history of the development of the LT rail system and to try to bring alive its atmosphere and history as part of London's railways.

Sub-surface

The Metropolitan and District:
Underground portions of these sections of the present LT network were built on the 'cut-and-cover' principle, a method of first cutting and lining the trench in which the trains were to run, before covering, often with a road, and owe their origins to two one-time competitors, the Metropolitan and District Railways. In their construction, loading gauge and operating styles they were closely related to main line companies, and even today maintain a separate identity from the deep 'tube' lines and BR services.

The Metropolitan opened the first Underground line from Paddington to Farringdon Street in 1863 which was initially worked by the GWR. In conjunction with the District Railway's lines between South Kensington and Aldgate, and by extensions of the Metropolitan from Paddington and Farringdon Street, the 'Inner' Circle (today's Circle Line) was completed by 1884, providing valuable links between the bulk of London's main line termini, the City and parts of the West End.

Several of the stations on the Circle are of interest for their remaining historical and architectural features. Paddington (Circle), Baker Street, Farringdon, Liverpool Street, Aldgate and Mansion House are of special note. The section from Kings Cross to Moorgate, commonly known as the City Widened lines, has additional interest because of links to the former Great Northern (withdrawn since 1976) and Midland Lines, whose trains began operating over the Metropolitan in 1863 and 1868 respectively. At first GN trains ran on the Metropolitan tracks, but in 1866 the first section of the 'Widened' lines was opened between Farringdon and Moorgate, used initially by GW trains only. Additional tracks were opened from Kings Cross to Farringdon in 1868, GN trains being extended to Moorgate in 1869. Now BR electric trains from the Bedford line use these separate tracks, paralleling the LT lines, and cross from the east to the west side at Farringdon to terminate at their own platforms in the rebuilt Moorgate (Met/Circle) station. Just to the south of Farringdon Station the tunnel mouth of the closed link from the Widened lines to the LCDR at Snow Hill can still be seen. This route, opened in 1866, was little used by passenger services after 1916 but remained an important cross-London freight route until 1969.

Westward extensions took the District to West Brompton in 1869, Putney Bridge in 1880, and by use of LSWR to Wimbledon in 1889. In 1872 a connection from Earl's Court to Addison Road, now Kensington (Olympia), was opened enabling both the 'Middle' and

'Outer' Circle services to be introduced. 1874 saw a further extension to Hammersmith, running powers being granted to operate over the LSWR from Studland Road Junction to Richmond in 1877, with a branch from Turnham Green to Ealing Broadway following two years later.

The Hounslow branch was opened from Acton Town to Hounslow Town in 1883, a single-track extension to Hounslow Barracks (later Hounslow West) being finished a year later and subsequently doubled. As part of the Heathrow Extension of the Piccadilly Line, this branch was further extended to Hatton Cross, finally reaching Heathrow Central in 1977. By the mid-1980s the line will be extended as a single-track loop to serve a new station to be built as part of Terminal 4. A branch was opened also from Ealing to South Harrow in 1903, District trains being extended in 1910 to Rayners Lane where they joined the Metropolitan's Uxbridge branch, opened in 1904 from the 'main line' at Harrow. In the early 1930s District trains were replaced by those from the Piccadilly Line, extended from Hammersmith.

Of these western outposts of the District, Earl's Court stands out as a busy focal point situated in the

The Metropolitan 'Widened' Lines *The northern part of the Circle line is of interest not only for being the first section of Underground opened in 1863, but also for its BR services which use the 'Widened' lines to Moorgate. Formerly served also by the LNER and cross-London links to the London Chatham & Dover Railway, it is now only used by Midland trains. Farringdon is seen here on 23 August 1947 with, in the background, LNER Class N1 No 9484 awaiting freight banking duties.* H. C. Casserley

complex scissors track formation between High Street Kensington, Gloucester Road, West Kensington and West Brompton. The four-track section from Hammersmith to Acton Town, used by District and 'fast' Piccadilly line services, recalls the erstwhile LSWR route from Richmond to the West London line over which passenger services where withdrawn in 1916. Intermediate stations to Turnham Green are of 'main line' style. Lillie Bridge depot provides a fascinating complex at West Kensington, and further depots can be seen at Ealing Common and Northfields, together with the main rolling stock overhaul works at Acton. The modern design of the Heathrow Extension, suitable only for tube stock, is in marked contrast to the remaining architecture of the Hounslow branch built for District rolling stock.

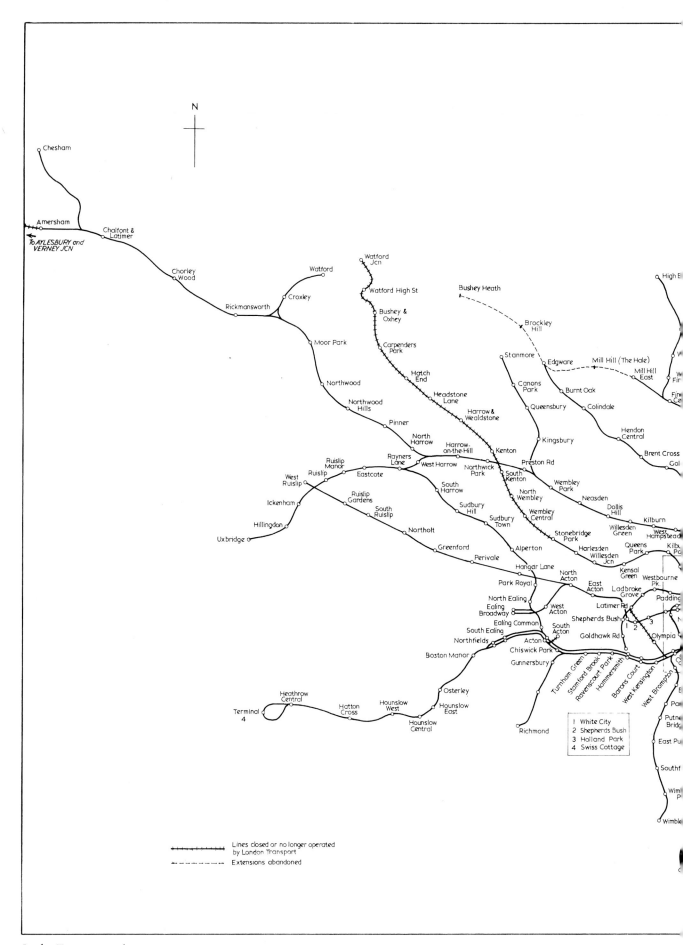

London Transport network.

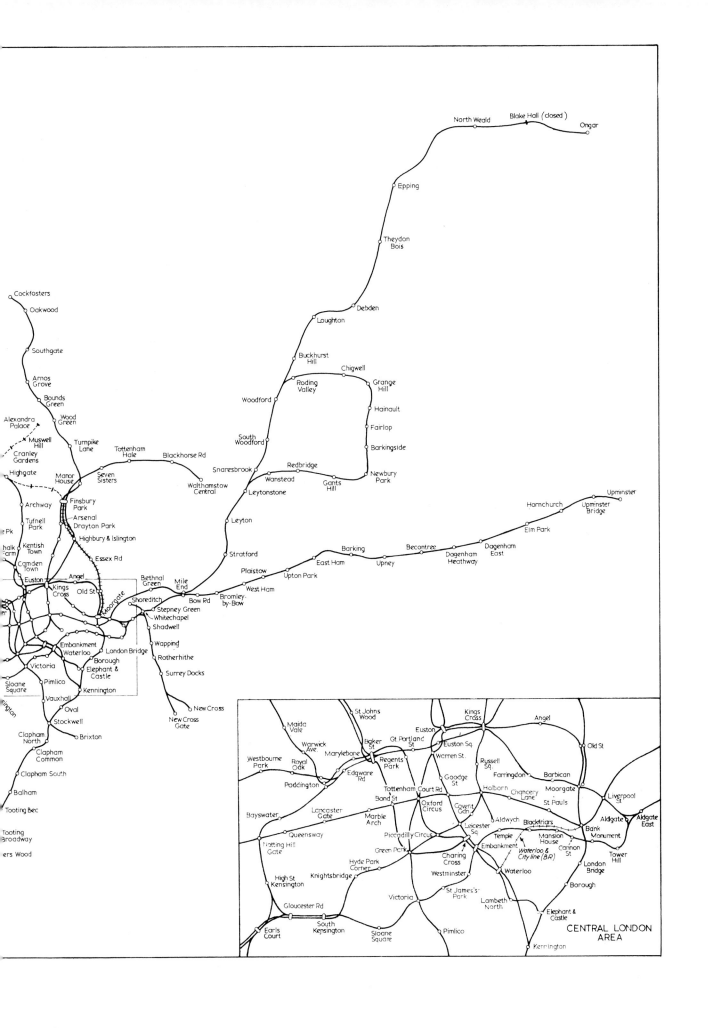

Cockfosters
Oakwood
Southgate
Arnos Grove
Bounds Green
Alexandra Palace
Wood Green
Muswell Hill
Turnpike Lane
Cranley Gardens
Highgate
Manor House
Seven Sisters
Tottenham Hale
Blackhorse Rd
Walthamstow Central
Archway
Tufnell Park
Finsbury Park
Arsenal
Drayton Park
Highbury & Islington
Essex Rd
Leyton
Snaresbrook
Wanstead
Leytonstone
Redbridge
Gants Hill
Newbury Park
Barkingside
Fairlop
Hainault
Grange Hill
Chigwell
Roding Valley
Woodford
South Woodford
Buckhurst Hill
Loughton
Debden
Theydon Bois
Epping
North Weald
Blake Hall (closed)
Ongar

Chalk Farm
Kentish Town
Camden Town
Euston
Kings Cross
Angel
Old St
Moorgate
Bethnal Green
Mile End
Bow Rd
Bromley-by-Bow
Plaistow
West Ham
Upton Park
East Ham
Stratford
Barking
Upney
Becontree
Dagenham Heathway
Dagenham East
Elm Park
Hornchurch
Upminster Bridge
Upminster

Shoreditch
Stepney Green
Whitechapel
Shadwell
Wapping
Rotherhithe
Surrey Docks
New Cross
New Cross Gate

Embankment
Waterloo
London Bridge
Borough
Elephant & Castle
Kennington
Victoria
Pimlico
Sloane Square
Vauxhall
Oval
Stockwell
Clapham North
Clapham Common
Clapham South
Balham
Tooting Bec
Tooting Broadway
Brixton
ers Wood

CENTRAL LONDON AREA

Maida Vale
St Johns Wood
Kings Cross
Angel
Warwick Ave.
Baker St
Gt Portland St
Euston
Euston Sq
Old St
Marylebone
Warren St.
Westbourne Park
Royal Oak
Regents Park
Russell Sq.
Farringdon
Barbican
Moorgate
Edgware Rd
Paddington
Goodge St
Liverpool St
Bond St
Tottenham Court Rd
Holborn
Chancery Lane
St Pauls
Bayswater
Lancaster Gate
Oxford Circus
Covent Gdn
Aldgate
Aldgate East
Marble Arch
Leicester Sq
Aldwych
Blackfriars
Bank
Monument
Queensway
Piccadilly Circus
Temple
Mansion House
Notting Hill Gate
Green Park
Embankment
Cannon St
Tower Hill
Hyde Park Corner
Charing Cross
Waterloo & City line (BR)
London Bridge
High St Kensington
Knightsbridge
Westminster
Waterloo
Borough
Gloucester Rd
Victoria
St James's Park
Earls Court
South Kensington
Sloane Square
Pimlico
Lambeth North
Elephant & Castle
Kennington

A service was introduced in 1905 between South Acton and Hounslow Barracks over the Acton 'Loop line' completed in 1899, although this was cut back in 1913 to a shuttle between Acton Town and South Acton. In the 1920s services again ran through from South Acton to South Harrow and Uxbridge as well as to Hounslow. In 1932, however, the final pattern of a shuttle service from a new bay platform (No 5) at Acton Town to South Acton was introduced, which remained until withdrawn in 1959. Today there are few traces of this interesting service.

West of Paddington the Hammersmith branch, promoted by the Hammersmith & City Railway, was opened from Westbourne Park to Hammersmith in 1864, being absorbed into Metropolitan services in 1865. Two years later it was taken over by the GW and Metropolitan jointly and is now part of the present Hammersmith & City section of the Metropolitan line, operating over the northern portion of the Circle in the form of a Hammersmith to Whitechapel and Barking service. From Edgware Road, trains diverge from the Circle, calling at platforms in the Bishop's Road suburban section of Paddington main line station. At Royal Oak the approaches to Paddington can be observed before the train dives under the main lines to swing away south-westwards from Westbourne Park. The line crosses the West London line at Shepherds Bush and the Central line's White City depot can be briefly glimpsed. The flavour of cosmopolitan West London is also apparent as the line takes its elevated route across cramped suburban areas to terminate at the substantial Hammersmith (Met) station.

The stub of the alignment of a connection between the H&C and the WLR (1864–1940) can still be seen at Latimer Road. This was used by 'Middle Circle' trains, although by 1910 services had been reduced to a shuttle from Edgware Road to Addison Road, which ceased after the link line sustained severe bomb damage in World War II and was not considered worthy of re-instatement.

In addition to District trains, the Metropolitan provided a service to Richmond from 1877 by means of the H&C and the LSWR, reached by the Kensington & Richmond via Grove Road Junction, Hammersmith. These services ceased in 1906 and are reputed to have been the last regular steam-hauled passenger services through Baker Street. LSWR trains to Kensington via Shepherds Bush were withdrawn in 1916 and there are few remains north of Hammersmith of this former link, although the local road pattern in the Shepherds Bush area reflects the previous alignment.

Extensions on the eastern side of London took the Metropolitan and District services to Whitechapel in 1884 as part of a through route to New Cross and New Cross Gate over the East London line. The ELR originated from a pedestrian tunnel built by Marc Brunel beneath the Thames, and incorporated into the line from Shoreditch to New Cross and New Cross Gate, opened between 1869 and 1876. The ELR enabled through services from south of the Thames to operate into Liverpool Street. Although used by cross-London services in the late nineteenth century, the route was less utilised than it might have been, and has mainly operated as a self-contained part of the Metropolitan line since 1941. BR cross-London connections by this route were finally withdrawn in 1966. Remaining services over the line call at somewhat Dickensian stations where development rests on the rejuvenation of the Docklands area and the now faded possibility of a new tube line to South East London.

In 1902 the District was extended from Whitechapel to Bow, where connection was made with the LTSR lines. District electric services reached Barking in 1908 and Upminster in 1932, providing the service to intermediate suburban stations and relieving the LTSR trains, which west of Upminster now call only at Barking and Stepney.

At its western end, the District ran a short-lived service to Windsor between 1883 and 1885 while, more successfully, trains operated between Ealing Broadway and Southend from 1910 until 1939, using special LTSR stock.

The first section of the District electrified was in 1903 between South Harrow and Acton, following earlier experiments. In 1905 District electric services were introduced from South Acton to Hounslow, between Ealing and Whitechapel, over the Wimbledon and Richmond branches and, by the Metropolitan, on the Inner Circle. In the following year a remnant of the Middle Circle between Aldgate and Kensington was electrified although this was cut back to Edgware Road in 1910. H&C trains were similarly converted in 1906 and Metropolitan steam trains to Richmond withdrawn. The East London line was electrified in 1913.

District meets the LTSR *Campbell Road Junction, Bow was where the District joined the LTSR, the extension being opened by the Whitechapel & Bow Railway in 1902. Quadrupling to Barking was completed in 1908, the year in which District electric trains reached Barking. A Wimbledon branch train approaches Bromley-by-Bow on 30 August 1958 having just crossed the River Lea and the Fenchurch Street – Southend LTSR tracks are on its right.* H. C. Casserley

Baker Street *Baker Street station, and its associated Chiltern Court complex above, looks very new in this picture. Note the cab road and covered entrance to the station.* London Transport Executive

Metropolitan Pullman Facilities *The Metropolitan was unique amongst the Underground railway companies in that, from 1910 until 1939, it operated two Pullman Cars,* Mayflower *and* Galatea, *on services between Verney Junction, Chesham and the City. The comfort of these cars is shown by this interior view, a far cry from the standard A60 stock of today. London Transport Executive*

Northwood *As part of the Metropolitan line improvements in the early 1960s the former bottleneck between Harrow North Junction and Watford South Junction, near Moor Park, was quadrupled. At Northwood new platforms were built on the new slow lines while the existing tracks became the fast lines. Part of the old station can be seen on the extreme left. An A60 train bound for Baker Street draws to a halt. G. M. Kichenside*

On the north side of the Circle, Baker Street is the hub of Metropolitan services, and also serves as terminal for Metropolitan 'main line' trains from *Metroland* and the Chilterns. The present Baker Street complex dates from the early twentieth century although work at the station was not completed until 1929. Its ramped former cab road on the frontage to Marylebone Road provides access to the concourse by steps from the road.

Trains first began operating from Baker Street to Swiss Cottage in 1868 being extended to Willesden Green in 1879. The Metropolitan, then under the control of Sir Edward Watkin, reached Harrow in 1880, Pinner in 1885, Rickmansworth in 1887 and Chesham in 1889. Branching from Chalfont Road (now Chalfont & Latimer), it reached Aylesbury in 1892 and, having taken over a local company, the Aylesbury & Buckingham, in the previous year, commenced through services to Verney Junction by 1897.

The London extension of the GCR line joined the Metropolitan just north of Quainton Road, opened to passenger traffic in March 1899, although used for goods traffic some months earlier. Together with the Brill branch (1871–1935), which also came into Metropolitan operations, services over these lines to Harrow were transferred to the Metropolitan & Great Central Joint Committee in 1906. Metropolitan branches were added to Uxbridge in 1904, Watford in 1925 and Stanmore in 1932.

Today, the present Metropolitan line A60 and A62 stock operating from Baker Street and the City to Amersham, Chesham, Watford and Uxbridge fails to create the romance of the former electric locomotive-hauled 'main line' services to Aylesbury and beyond, which from 1910 until 1939 encompassed Pullman cars. Electric trains reached Harrow and Uxbridge in 1905, but the locomotives of main line services were changed at Wembley Park until 1908 when facilities were provided at Harrow. Electric operation was extended to Rickmansworth in 1925 and this was the transfer point for steam traction until 1961, when Amersham and Chesham became the northern termini of electric services and Aylesbury was exclusively served by BR diesel multiple-units.

The complex transport corridor at Finchley Road, through which the Metropolitan, GC, Jubilee, Midland and North London lines pass, provides the first point of interest after Baker Street, although remains of the three former intermediate stations can still be seen between Finchley Road and Baker Street. Exchange sidings with the Midland goods yard at Finchley Road provided an outlet for goods to the main line. At Neasden, the extensive LT depot is on the east side, while Wembley Park has additional facilities to service major sporting events at Wembley Stadium. Junctions

are made at Harrow with BR tracks to Marylebone and the Uxbridge branch. North of Harrow to the junction with the Watford branch, tracks were quadrupled between 1959 and 1962. Pinner and Northwood stations reflect traditional Metropolitan architecture, which is largely unspoilt at Rickmansworth and at all stations to Aylesbury.

Steam on LT

Apart from the Metropolitan Line, where they lasted until 1966, BR steam locomotives ran over LT lines until the early 1960s when diesels replaced passenger and freight workings on the Widened lines and steam-hauled freight via Bishop's Road ceased with the closure of Smithfield Market depot in 1962. Freight workings, latterly diesel-hauled, were withdrawn over the Edgware and Barnet lines by 1964. LT steam remained in service for engineers' trains until 1971, working from Neasden and Lillie Bridge. The locomotives were former GWR 0-6-0 pannier tanks, the last remaining Metropolitan and District locomotives having been withdrawn in 1963.

The Tubes

The Northern:

This line has two areas of interest, sections across Central London built to relieve congestion in overcrowded streets, and sections into the suburbs, the extension to East Finchley absorbing existing GN branches which were developed for commuter use.

The first tube as part of the present system was opened in 1890 by the City & South London Railway from King William Street, near Monument, to Stockwell. Northward extensions, which included abandonment of part of the line to King William Street, took services to Moorgate in 1900, Angel in 1901 and Euston in 1907. Southwards, the line reached Clapham Common in 1900.

Linked with the CSLR was the Charing Cross Euston & Hampstead Railway, forerunner of the London Electric Railway. This company opened its branches from Golders Green and Archway to Strand via Camden Town in 1907. An extension was made to Embankment in 1914; connection with the CSLR was effected between Camden Town and Euston in 1924, and between Embankment and Kennington in 1926 concurrently with southward extension to Morden. 1924 saw completion of the Edgware line while, as part of the 1935/40 New Works Programme of the LPTB, extension from Archway to the former GNR group of branches at East Finchley was completed in 1939.

Owing to World War II the electrification scheme for these branches was only partially completed, the

North Harrow *Serving the then newly developing* Metroland, *North Harrow Station entrance shows its dual service to Baker Street (Met) or Marylebone (GCR). Single-deck London General Omnibus route 230, forerunner of today's H1, waits outside.* London Transport Executive

Wembley Park *The Metropolitan 'Main Line' north of Finchley Road remains today an impressive transport corridor carrying Metropolitan, Jubilee and BR services to destinations in Middlesex and 'Metroland'. Wembley Park is an important suburban station and this view looks south with the Wembley Stadium Platform on the left and the former Metropolitan Railway power station in the background. A GC line suburban service overtakes two northbound Metropolitan line trains in the distance.* London Transport Executive

The rebuilt Euston station with a Class 86/2 Bo-Bo electric locomotive waiting to leave with an express for the north, formed of Mk 2 air-conditioned stock. John Glover

Southall with a Class 50 locomotive heading an up express for Paddington while an Inter-City 125 HST disappears at speed on the down main line. A local DMU on the down relief line in the background makes a call on all stations to Slough service. John Glover

Contrasts in London stations, with, left, the new era of Inter-City 125 High Speed Trains at Paddington and, below, the last years of the LNER Pacifics at King's Cross in the late 1950s. A Peppercorn Class A1 leaves with a northbound express, while Gresley A3 No 60067 stands in the shed yard. Diesels have begun to infiltrate, with one of the short-lived EE Baby Deltic Type 2 locomotives on empty stock duty. BRB and T. B. Owen/Colour-rail

Right upper: Guildford is an important junction on the Waterloo–Portsmouth line where it meets the routes from Reading, Aldershot, Surbiton via Cobham, and Redhill. Moreover on the Portsmouth line itself express services are often scheduled to overtake stopping trains. In 1957 a Waterloo express, formed of 4COR units, in the foreground at platforms 6/7 will go ahead of the stopping service composed of 2BIL units on the far side at Platform 3. B. J. Swain/Colour-rail

Right lower: For over 35 years Bulleid's spartan 4SUB units, distinguished by their curved bodysides and rounded windows, have worked on Southern suburban services. Here two 4SUB units, Nos 4742 and 4651, pass at Leatherhead on London–Dorking/Effingham Junction workings. John Glover

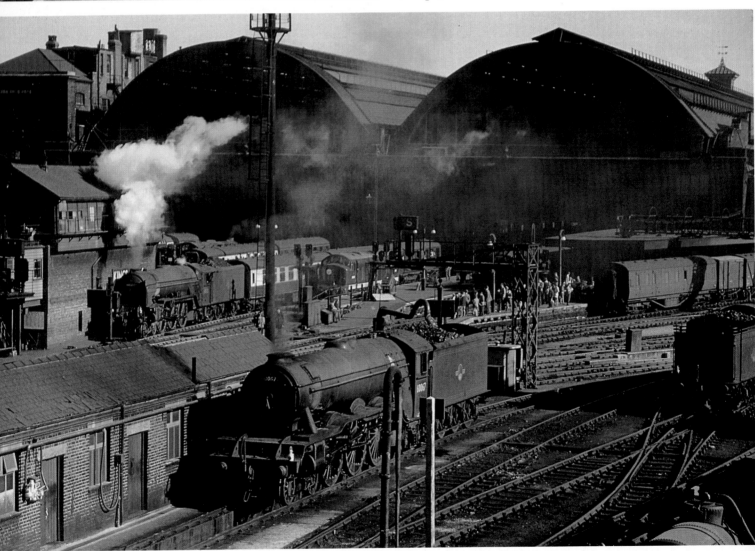

For its Broad Street–Richmond/Euston–Watford electrification in 1916/22 the LNWR introduced saloon electric trains with Oerlikon electrical equipment and quite spacious interiors, though with single end sliding doors heavily laden trains were slow to unload. One of these trains is seen at Kenton in the late 1950s, a year or so before withdrawal. G. M. Kichenside

Moorgate in the 1950s with Metropolitan compartment type T stock in brown livery on a peak working to Watford, a former District F stock train behind waiting to leave for Uxbridge, while nearest the camera is LMS Fowler 2-6-2T No 40024 running into the locomotive headshunt to wait for its next working to St Albans. The latter service survives in modern form as part of the Midland suburban electrification on the Widened Lines. J. G. Dewing/Colour-rail

tube reaching High Barnet and Mill Hill East in 1940 and 1941 respectively. The integration of the Alexandra Palace branch, the tube service extension from Mill Hill East to Edgware and Bushey Heath and use of the Great Northern & City line to Moorgate were all abandoned following post-war stringencies, perhaps mercifully in view of the complexity of the system had it been completed throughout as planned.

The Northern line as it became provides a variety of interest to the observant passenger. Its Central area stations are a mixture ranging from island platforms (eg Angel), lift served (eg Goodge Street) and modernised (eg Charing Cross). Interchanges are made with other lines at many of the stations. Hampstead, on the Edgware branch, is the deepest station on the system, while the open-air stations from Golders Green to Edgware are of similar period but varied styles. Golders Green and Edgware are important bus/rail interchanges. Highgate, on the Barnet branch, is of interest as a result of the unsuccessful extension scheme which would have incorporated the original GN High Level station into the Northern line network. East Finchley is an excellent product of its age, having been rebuilt as part of the New Works scheme, while Finchley Central and stations beyond continue to reflect their nineteenth century origins. Morden, again an important bus/rail interchange, is a worthy terminus in an early Holden style at the southern end of the line.

Linked with the Northern until absorbed into the GN electric service in 1976 was the Great Northern &

Steam Service Locomotives *To replace the stud of ageing Metropolitan tanks retained mainly for Engineers' trains, thirteen ex-GWR 0-6-0 pannier tanks were purchased by LT from BR. The first arrived in 1956 and the remaining three were withdrawn in 1971, these being the last steam locomotives in regular use on public lines in the London area. This picture shows L98 (BR No 7739) hurrying westbound past West Kensington, with the Piccadilly line emerging from the tunnel.* Chris Cheetham

City, opened from Moorgate to Finsbury Park in 1904. This line, scene of the tragic accident at Moorgate in 1975, is now chiefly of interest as part of the electric services to the GN main line. It gave the ex-GN route a City terminus in 1976 – its original objective in 1892 – and between these dates it was never certain what the role of the line was.

The extensive system has resulted in the provision of stabling at several depots, Morden and Golders Green being of chief interest. Wellington Sidings, Highgate, are also of note because of the former link with the BR system. This was used until 1970 for the regular transfer of LT Northern City stock for maintenance and major overhaul purposes from Drayton Park to Highgate Sidings and Acton Works. Structural weakness of bridges between Park Junction and Finsbury Park resulted in re-routing of these workings until their withdrawal in 1975, after transfer to BR of this part of the Northern Line. Highgate is a tranquil spot, worthwhile visiting and exploring for the remains of the Edgware and Barnet line, with the associated branch to Alexandra Palace closed in 1954. Other stabling sidings are at Barnet and Edgware. The Aldenham bus overhaul

works was built as part of the abandoned Bushey Heath Extension and also intended as a stabling depot.

The Central:
'The Twopenny Tube', by which the present Central line was known for many years because of its one-time flat fare, was opened from Shepherds Bush to Bank in 1900, being extended to Wood Lane and Liverpool Street in 1908 and 1912 respectively. The line was further extended to Ealing Broadway in 1920, and as part of the 1935/40 New Works Programme the branch to West Ruislip, paralleling the GWR Birmingham 'Direct' line from North Acton, was finally completed in 1948. On the east, extension took the Central to Stratford in 1946 and a year later to Woodford and Newbury Park. By 1948 electrification of the 'Hainault Loop' and to Loughton was completed. Electric trains reached Epping in the following year but the Epping-Ongar service remained steam-operated until 1957.

In Central London, Oxford Circus is the chief interchange, further enhanced since 1969 by Victoria line services. Although layout and design conforms to a similar pattern at all stations, the complexity of interchanges between lines adds considerable interest. On the extensions, Hanger Lane in the west stands out as classic of its time, the late 1940s, matched by Newbury Park in the east. A number of stations on the Eastern Extension reflect their GER origins, while for rural antiquity and tranquility the Ongar branch and parts of the Hainault loop starkly contrast with most other sections of LT's rail operations.

The Bakerloo and Jubilee Lines:
The Bakerloo originated as a scheme to improve communications across the West End, later being extended to relieve Metropolitan services in the northern suburbs and tapping the localities served by the LNWR.

The central section from Baker Street to Elephant & Castle was opened in 1906, followed by extensions to Edgware Road in 1907, Paddington in 1913 and

East Finchley *Opened in 1867 by the Edgware Highgate & London Railway, a large part of this ex-GN branch was incorporated into the Northern Line of London Transport, LT trains commencing on 3 July 1939. The central tracks at East Finchley were the original lines to and from Finsbury Park and are still used by tube stock stabling at Wellington Sidings, Highgate.* B. R. Hardy

The Great Northern & City *Opened in 1904, the line linked Finsbury Park with Moorgate and was used from 1939 until 1975 by Northern Line tube trains into which system the branch was nearly absorbed. The other platform of the Moorgate terminus was the scene of LT's worst accident when, on 28 February 1975, a terminating train crashed with the loss of 43 lives. Moorgate is now terminus for BR trains from the ex-GN suburban lines.* R. J. Greenaway

Queen's Park in 1915, finally being projected over the LNWR 'New Line' to Watford in 1917. Services were operated on this section jointly with BR until 1965 when through services were withdrawn, except for the four peak-hour trains to and from Watford. These in turn were withdrawn in 1982, leaving only the Stonebridge Depot workings beyond Queen's Park.

As part of the New Works Programme, the Bakerloo was extended in 1939 from Baker Street to Finchley Road at which point Metropolitan tracks were re-arranged to enable Bakerloo trains to provide services to the intermediate stations from Finchley Road to Wembley Park. The Metropolitan branch to Stanmore was further absorbed into the tube extension.

Regent's Park is of interest on the central section, being little altered since it was opened. Queen's Park is a substantial structure at ground level, tube trains using the centre and BR trains the outer faces of two island platforms. Car stabling sheds are provided at both ends.

Extensive alterations to Bakerloo services were made in 1979 with the opening of the first stage of the Jubilee Line, which absorbed the Stanmore branch and provided a new cross-London link between Baker Street and Charing Cross via Bond Street and Green Park. Further extensions to Fenchurch Street and south-east London were proposed, but because of financial constraints and traffic reasons may possibly never proceed. As part of the change a new depot for Bakerloo line stock was opened at Stonebridge Park, while Jubilee line trains stable mainly at Neasden and Stanmore sidings. At the south end of the Bakerloo, trains continue to stable at London Road depot, a difficult location to staff and for maintenance of the facilities, but remaining for essential operational needs.

The Piccadilly:
Amalgamation of two smaller companies, the Brompton & Piccadilly Circus and the Great Northern & Strand Railways led to the main part of today's Piccadilly line being opened from Finsbury Park to Hammersmith in 1906. The peak-hours-only Aldwych branch, opened a year later, was a truncated portion of the Great Northern & Strand, a quirk of history for which various extension schemes have never successfully been pursued.

In the west, Piccadilly trains were extended from Hammersmith over the District lines to South Harrow in 1932 and Hounslow and Uxbridge in 1933, providing the present pattern of services. Concurrently, the Cockfosters extension was built in the north-east, the line opening throughout on 31 July 1933.

In Central London, stations have similar characteristics to those of other lines, although those on the extensions provide the most interest (eg Arnos Grove).

The interest of the line has been further enhanced by the introduction in late 1975 of 1973 tube stock, operating to Heathrow Central since 1977. The main depot at the eastern end is situated between Cockfosters and Oakwood, still today on the edge of London's built-up area. Northfields depot provides the principal facility at the western end, with South Harrow sidings adding additional stabling on the Uxbridge branch.

The Victoria:

The zenith of modern tube engineering in London came with the construction of the Victoria line, a cross-link which enhanced travel by Underground largely by its speed and diversity of interchange. Although Stage 1 of the Jubilee line is later, as presently built it is much less ambitious. The Victoria line was opened in sections first from Walthamstow to Highbury, thence onwards to Warren Street in 1968 and to Victoria in March 1969. The Brixton Extension was opened in 1971, Pimlico opening in the following year.

Being the first line on the Underground to be run throughout by automatic train operation (the Woodford-Hainault service and limited trials on the District being of less significance) it created a good deal of interest and has generated a large amount of traffic by its attractive design, speed, reliability and convenience. It is the only line on the tube network to have its public service entirely underground, only the extensive depot at Northumberland Park, not open to the public, being on the surface.

A last glance

The whole atmosphere of the tube lines is of course different from the sub-surface facilities, tube stations requiring escalators or lifts rather than stairs to the platforms, although there are many common features where the tube has thrust on the surface into suburbs.

The Underground did so much in the 1920s and 1930s to generate the growth of suburban housing development which would have continued further had

North Weald *The GER Loughton branch was extended to Ongar on 24 April 1865 having reached Loughton nine years previously. While Central line tube services reached Epping in 1949, the Epping-Ongar service remained steam operated until 1957. Class F5 2-4-2T No 67202 is seen at North Weald in tranquil surroundings in 1957 just prior to electrification.* Alan J. Willmott

not imposition of the Green Belt after World War II curtailed expansion. Fifty years on, these services still perform an essential function in the efficient working of London as part of the Capital's overall rail network. However, it is of interest that the two newest tubes, the Victoria and Jubilee lines, have been intended as much to improve service in the Central area as they were to better serve parts of the suburbs.

Today, London Transport remains a major undertaking employing a workforce of some 60,000, half of whom can be directly related to bus operations. Although the period to World War II under Frank Pick and Lord Ashfield were the Golden Years for London's public transport development, the challenges of today are, like those of its main line brother, British Rail, no less demanding or exciting.

The creation of the London Passenger Transport Board in 1933 was the climax of years of gradual coming together by both the railway and bus undertakings in London, which gave the opportunity for overall development and integration under a single unifying operator. This certainly provided the ingredients to take advantage of the favourable social and financial climate for public transport of the depressed years through the 1920s and 1930s. Not surprisingly, therefore, the rapid advances brought about by the 1935/40 New Works Programme and the inter-relation of design and construction which had

Co-ordination *One of the most successful schemes for transport co-ordination was seen on the LNWR 'New Line' between Euston and Watford from 1916 when Bakerloo tube trains were extended on the same tracks from Queens Park to Watford. New jointly-owned stock was built but was not ready for the start of services and Central London Railway trains were borrowed, as seen here between Harrow and Kenton.* Locomotive Publishing Company

Oakwood *Enfield West (now Oakwood) on the Piccadilly line extension to Cockfosters, was opened on 13 March 1933 although services did not reach Cockfosters until July that year. This view of East Pole Farm just prior to the commencement of engineering work shows the former rural setting, the farm being approximately by the present entrance to Cockfosters depot.* London Borough of Enfield

occurred in the 1920s, just before the creation of London Transport, are attributed to the far-sighted leadership of key men such as Lord Ashfield and Frank Pick. They were able to tap the latent talent of other individuals, notably Charles Holden who was responsible for so much of the advanced architectural contribution of London Transport at that time. Even today, while their newness has mellowed to relative maturity, the exciting image created by Holden's Piccadilly line stations, his Head Office masterpiece, 55 Broadway, and other important work, still depict the advances of that era.

Today's problems are somewhat different. Those of Pick and Lord Ashfield were of a rapidly-expanding London, ripe for capital investment in transport. Car ownership was still low, yet the growing population was demanding more and better public transport services to provide improved mobility. Now the difficulties are of maintaining an ageing infrastructure, a static or declining population, and a labour-intensive industry in times of high labour costs and inflation against a background of higher ownership of private cars. Whereas in the 1930s the loss-making services could be adequately cross-subsidised, the profitable base has become sadly inadequate resulting in the inevitable need for subsidy. Therefore, with most of the necessary infrastructure built, the job of managing London Transport railways has become one of struggling to maintain and raise standards rather than expansion.

In its efforts to achieve this aim, the two main events affecting London's public transport since the war have been the transfer of policy-making and financing from Central Government to the Greater London Council under the Transport (London) Act, 1969, and in 1980 decentralisation resulting from a major internal re-organisation. Both factors aim to create the conditions whereby smaller organisations can better meet local needs, be more accountable and tap the talents of managers. However, this process needs to be planned and co-ordinated and perhaps a modern day successor to Lord Ashfield, 'Creator of London Transport', may yet lead the Underground into a new 'Golden Age'.

Stonebridge Park *In 1965 Bakerloo Line Watford trains were withdrawn except at peak hours but in 1982 the Watford service was withdrawn completely. As part of the Bakerloo/Jubilee Line arrangements, a new depot was opened at Stonebridge and the picture shows the depot link diverging to the right, now the northernmost point worked by Bakerloo trains on this route. B. R. Hardy*

9
FREIGHT

By contrast to the glamour of passenger services, freight traffic was much more humdrum and workaday, often being handled out of sight of the public. The only real exceptions were the marshalling yards that passengers passed on their way to or from the main London termini. Here wagons of all types could be seen in transit to and from the Capital, and this chapter aims to indicate what those wagons contained, where they were destined, and how they would be handled on their journey. Parcels traffic will be excluded as will be the specialist forms to and from the docks.

The Economic Background

The general economic scene has had a number of effects on railway freight, but some of the more important can be discussed. The first is the dominance of coal as a source of energy in the Victorian period. Steam was the major source of power for factories, and this of course demanded considerable amounts of coal. Electricity and

oil did not become important until the 1920s and although gas was used, it had to be produced from coal. With such reliance upon coal, carryings to London were bound to be heavy. Second, the railways were the only effective method of long-distance transport until after World War I, when road vehicles with their greater convenience began to become important in the carriage of freight. This meant that the virtual monopoly of railways in the Victorian era was gradually lost and rail freight carryings decreased as the competition increased. Third, so long as road transport was restricted to a horse and cart the area that could be served by one railway depot was limited. Inevitably

Wendover *The Metropolitan Railway, with its aspiration to main line status, operated freight services from several goods stations but after its absorption into the LPTB these services were transferred to the LNER. By 1939 the LNER had also purchased its locomotives such as No 6156, formerly Metropolitan 0-6-4T 'G' class No 96 Charles Jones, seen near Wendover. H. C. Casserley*

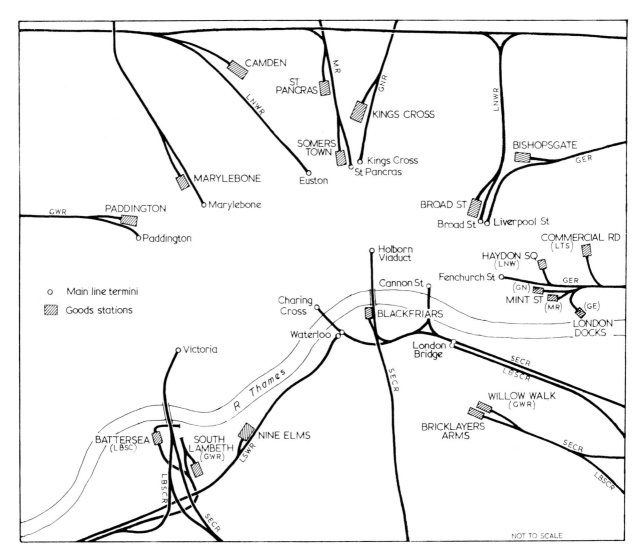

Goods depots in Central London.

therefore there had to be a large number of small depots each serving a small area, so virtually every station dealt with freight. Fourth, the absence of refrigeration meant that food had to be dealt with in a different way to today. For example, cattle were brought to market in London live so that the time between their being killed and eaten was minimised; alive, the meat would be less prone to disease. Last, changes in the markets for goods hauled by rail has had an effect; the decreased demand for coal has already been mentioned, another example is potatoes. Increased affluence has reduced the importance of potatoes in the family diet and they are now more often sold ready-prepared. As the need for potato markets and warehouses has declined so have the rail facilities to serve them.

Types of Traffic

Traditionally rail freight traffic has been categorised into three groups – coal, mineral and general merchandise. Coal traffic is self-explanatory; mineral traffic which as well as true minerals such as iron and steel, included a number of other products. General merchandise was the remaining commodity – principally manufactured products. With no mines and considerable consumption, the flow of coal class traffic would be up to London from the coal mining areas, with a return flow of empty wagons. The same pattern would broadly be true of mineral traffic, but in the case of general merchandise the flow would be more evenly balanced, as finished goods would be brought up to London for sale and the products of London's industries would be despatched to other parts of the country.

Each company had distinctive traffic depending upon the part of Britain it served. Coal was the concern of the

Great Northern, Midland, London & North Western, Great Central and Great Western Railways, whereas the three southern companies had little. To supply South London with its coal therefore, 'foreign' companies like the Midland and London & North Western opened coal depots at places such as Wandsworth Road and Peckham Rye respectively. Indeed the Midland had a coal depot on the District at High Street Kensington, reached from Willesden Yard through Acton, Hammersmith and Earl's Court. Similar services would produce a complex pattern of freight train routes travelling over the tracks of a number of companies. The Great Eastern, serving the agricultural area of East Anglia, was concerned in the business of feeding London, even going as far as operating its own fruit and vegetable market at Stratford. Potatoes were a staple traffic of the Midland Railway and the Great Northern, with a special market at Somers Town goods depot on the former. But perhaps the Midland's best-known traffic was beer in barrels from Burton-on-Trent. It was stored at ground level in arches under St Pancras station, to which wagons gained access by a hoist on the country end of the platforms.

Methods of Handling

Railways are especially suited to handling bulk flows over distances of some 150 miles or more. The speediest and most economic method of dealing with it is a complete train running directly from origin to destination.

Midland Coal Trains *One of the principal traffics on the Midland Railway route to London was coal from Nottinghamshire and Derbyshire. Marshalled into trains at Toton yard, it was brought south from 1927 to 1958 by Beyer-Garratt 2-6-6-2Ts such as No 47995. Even as late as 1960 there were 22 coal trains up to London each day with slightly fewer return workings of empties.*
Real Photographs Co Ltd

This 'trainload' operation as it is termed is the principal method of operation today, and can be seen in use for instance to deal with the oil traffic from North Thameside. The principle has been embodied into Freightliner operation, Willesden being a good example of a London freight centre, occupying the site of the former locomotive depot on the down side of the main line.

However, as has already been mentioned, the horse and cart was the only competition in Victorian days, so in order to deal with freight traffic the railways developed a complete network of depots linked by a system which used the wagon as the unit of movement. Under this system of operation the goods to be transported would be brought into the station by the sender or by the railway company, but in either case by horse and cart. Once at the station it would be loaded onto a wagon which awaited the arrival of the daily pick-up freight. This set out from a main marshalling yard to serve a number of stations by shunting the goods yard at each, detaching from its train wagons consigned to the station and attaching wagons consigned from the station to elsewhere. Having done this job at a number of stations, it would return to the marshalling yard and

137

Uxbridge High Street *Uxbridge High Street was the terminus of the GWR branch from Denham from which passenger services were withdrawn in 1939. Freight services lasted for another 25 years but No 5564 is seen in January 1964 a month before services ceased. By this time the single line terminated in two sidings where the two 16-ton mineral wagons have been unloaded and their coal put in the stacking ground on the left.* T. Wright

Temple Mills *Temple Mills Yard dating from around 1880 was reconstructed and modernised between 1954 and 1959 to become the main yard for the Great Eastern lines. In this picture the hump is at the top right, the 48 tracks of the main yard lie between it and the road bridge, beyond which lies the group of eight departure sidings. The Control Tower, on the centre line of the yard, supervised shunting operations.* Aerofilms Limited

leave in the reception sidings the wagons it had collected. Here there would be other wagons collected by similar pick-up freights or brought in by trunk trains from other marshalling yards. Wagons of both types would be sorted into either trunk trains for other marshalling yards or for pick-up freights in the area. Thus a wagon from one station would go on one pick-up freight to a main marshalling yard, on one or more trunk freights between yards and finally arrive at the station to which it was consigned by another pick-up freight. From this final station it could be collected by the public or delivered by railway cartage.

It can be readily seen that this system by its very nature was slow and produced variable transit times. In 1963, for example, the average turn-round time between loading for one trip and the next was just under 12 working days, the average loaded transit time was between one-and-a-half and two days, and the average journey length 67 miles. Whilst there were wide differences between individual instances hidden by these averages, they did indicate an uncompetitive service compared to same day transit by road. This system had two further implications on the rail wagon fleet. The slow journeys necessitated an enormous wagon fleet, nearly 863,000 in January 1963 compared to 138,000 in January 1980, many of which would be poorly utilised. As any wagon might need to be sent anywhere and couple to any other, this need for the new to match the old held back technical progress. Faced with this situation, it was no surprise that the Beeching Report concluded that this wagon-load system should be progressively displaced.

Freight Working

To illustrate freight working it would be best to look at London railways in the 1950s before the development of the changes envisaged in the Beeching Report had changed it considerably.

The first thing to note is the pattern of marshalling yards. Each pre-grouping company had a yard some five to ten miles out from its terminus. Starting in the east the Great Eastern had Temple Mills, the Great Northern Finsbury Park and Ferme Park, the Midland Brent, the Great Central Neasden, the London & North Western Willesden, the Great Western Acton, the London & South Western Feltham, the London Brighton & South Coast Norwood and the South Eastern Herne Hill and Hither Green. Ripple Lane on the former LTSR system dates from 1937, when the former yard at Ilford became too small to deal with the volume of traffic. Ripple Lane was rebuilt and re-opened in 1958. All these yards received wagons from its parent system and distributed them to its goods

depots and to other London yards, as well as dealing with a similar flow in reverse.

The second fact to observe is that the main goods depots were closer to London than the marshalling yards, and ringed its centre. North of the Thames, these depots were generally adjacent to the main passenger terminals such as Kings Cross, Marylebone and Paddington. An exception was Camden Depot where Camden Bank intervened between the goods depot and the passenger terminus at Euston. South of the Thames the main goods depots were some distance from the passenger terminals to avoid using expensive land and the need for viaduct construction. All of the South London depots, apart from South Lambeth, were originally passenger terminals which were later taken over for goods work. Battersea, Nine Elms and Blackfriars adopted this goods role when the main lines they served were extended to passenger terminals nearer the centre of London. Bricklayers Arms was a passenger terminal which was established because of inter-company quarrels, whose resolution put paid to its passenger role.

The South Lambeth depot, some 12½ acres in extent, was a GWR enclave in South London which was reached from Acton via the West London Line and running powers over the SECR low-level lines from Longhedge Junction. Entry to the depot was controlled by South Lambeth Goods signalbox but because of the awkward layout, incoming trains had to run onto five-chain headshunts and then set back into the depot. Built on the side of the Southwark and Vauxhall Waterworks, the depot was opened for milk traffic in 1910, to goods in 1911, and was completed on 1 January 1913. Dealing principally with merchandise rather than coal, the depot incorporated a large warehouse and was equipped with a 35-ton crane. Private sidings for the CEGB Battersea Power Station and for the Metropolitan Water Board were connected to the depot tracks. The depot remained under Western Region management until its transfer to the Southern Region on 5 February 1968 and saw 12 years' further use before closure on 1 November 1980.

With this complete pattern of marshalling yards and goods stations, a network of freight routes was necessary in order to cater for the flows between each. Consequently a number of lines were predominant for cross-London freight traffic. North of the Thames there were two main routes – the Tottenham & Hampstead and the North London. The Tottenham & Hampstead and the associated Tottenham & Forest Gate ran from Woodgrange Park on the LTSR through Tottenham, where there was a link to the GER, to junctions with the Midland at Kentish Town and with the North London Line at Gospel Oak. 1940 saw the restoration

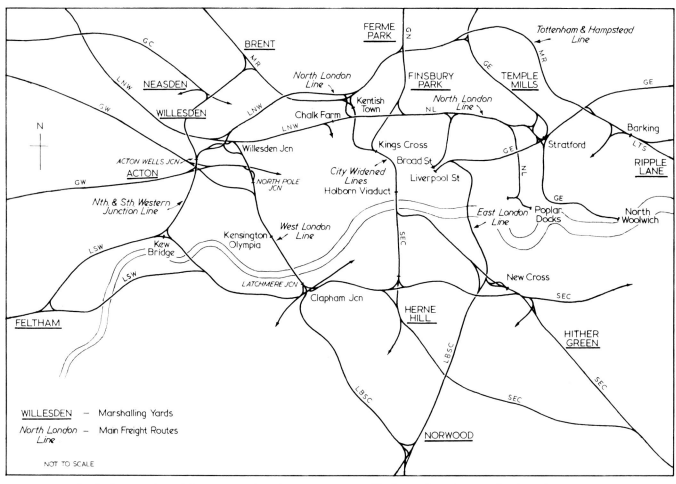

Cross-London freight routes, their radial connections and marshalling yards.

of the connection to the former GNR at Harringay Park. The North London line extended from Poplar to Camden Town where it joined the LNWR, and its extension, the Hampstead Junction, branched-off at Camden to run to Willesden Junction via Gospel Oak. The first section had connections to the GER at Victoria Park and the GNR at Canonbury.

Of the four north-south routes, only two today carry goods traffic, one is closed and lifted, and one exclusively dedicated to passenger traffic. Of the lines still in use, the first is the North & South Western Junction from Willesden to Kew. The focal point on this line is Acton Wells Junction, where five routes converge. From the north comes the Midland line of 1868 from Brent, the N&SWJ itself from Willesden, and the Hampstead Junction of 1860 from Willesden High Level. To the south the N&SWJ runs to Kew, whilst a spur runs down to the former GWR yard at Acton. Junctions at Kew enable trains to run onward either via Brentford or Barnes.

The second line in use is the West London, from a junction with the former LNWR at Willesden to meet

at Clapham Junction with the three pre-grouping southern companies. North Pole is the principal intermediate junction where the line is joined by a spur from the Great Western. This is by far the most important cross-London link today, carrying scheduled passenger trains as well as freight trains.

The City Widened lines no longer have any freight services and are the exclusive preserve of the St Pancras suburban services. However, freight trains from the Midland and Great Northern systems joined the Metropolitan Railway at its Kings Cross station for the run to Farringdon, where they diverged onto the SECR link to Holborn Viaduct. Opened in 1866, this line rose at 1 in 39 from Farringdon and was the reason for the provision of a banking locomotive. Locomotives using this route were fitted with condensing apparatus in an endeavour to reduce the amount of smoke produced; a pipe returned the exhaust steam to the water tanks where it condensed back to water.

The last link was the East London Line from a junction with the Great Eastern at Shoreditch to the LBSCR and SECR at New Cross. The difficulty with this route was that traffic had to be worked via Liverpool Street, as the junction at Shoreditch faced that station. Some relief was afforded by a hydraulic hoist for wagons at Spitalfields, joining the East London to the GE Spitalfields Goods Depot. In 1904 the Great Eastern opened a goods depot in the LBSCR yard at New Cross, again an awkward layout as it required a double-reversal to reach the East London line. Nowadays the line only sees passenger traffic as a self-contained part of the Metropolitan Line.

The main route across South London runs from Clapham Junction and the West London Line through Brixton and Peckham Rye to reach the erstwhile SECR at Lewisham. When the City Widened lines route was in operation for freight a considerable amount of traffic came on to this route from Loughborough Junction, exemplified in the flows from Ferme Park. A particularly interesting traffic on this route was coal for the joint Midland and LNWR depot at Peckham Rye. The Midland coal was collected from Battersea, reached by either the North & South Western Junction or the City Widened Lines, and the LNWR coal came via the West London Line.

Ferme Park Transfer Freights 1946

Some idea of the complexity of freight movements in the London area can be obtained from a flow diagram which has been compiled from the LNER Working Timetable for May to October 1946. It shows the number of trains to and from Ferme Park Yard which ran daily from Monday to Friday. It is important to remember that other transfer freights left or arrived from Clarence Yard and East Goods Yard at Finsbury Park. As these two have not been included for clarity, the total number of transfers to and from the London

area GN yards was higher than shown.

Three groups of services can be distinguished. The first group was trains to the Great Western at Acton and some of the services to the Southern at Feltham. These immediately left the Great Northern main line to reach the Tottenham & Hampstead at Harringay Park Junction. Joining the North London Line at Gospel Oak, they ran along it to Acton Wells where trains for Acton diverged, leaving the others to reach Feltham via Old Kew Junction. The second group comprised trains for the North London Line to reach goods depots on the North London and Great Eastern. These trains would diverge at Finsbury Park to reach the North London at Canonbury.

By far the predominant flow was the third group, trips to the Southern via Kings Cross, the Widened Lines and Holborn Viaduct Low Level. Once across the river, trains travelling through London Bridge diverged at Blackfriars Junction to reach it via Metropolitan Junction. The majority continued to Loughborough Junction, where trains separated into three groups to Hither Green, Herne Hill and, the predominant group, to Battersea and Feltham.

The two routes to Hither Green are apparent, although the majority of trains ran via Loughborough Junction. This arrangement was caused by the interference that slow-moving freight trains would have on

Southall *Although seen here on a van train at Southall in 1958 0-6-0PT No 9710 was one of the eleven Collett pannier tanks built with condensing equipment in 1933 to enable them to run over the Metropolitan from Paddington to the GWR freight depot at Smithfield. Opened in 1869 this was reached by a connection off the City 'Widened' lines, which were gained on transfer trips from Acton Yard, at Farringdon.* A. R. Brown

Nine Elms *This aerial view of Nine Elms shows the goods station behind Tite's original terminal buildings whilst the two crossings of Nine Elms Lane can be seen. That on the left led to the original goods yard and wharf of 1838 whilst that on the right led to Belmont Wharf. After the opening of Waterloo in 1848 Nine Elms served goods until its work was transferred to the adjacent former GWR South Lambeth Depot in 1968.* Fairey Aviation Ltd

Walworth *Walworth Coal Depot, although on the LCDR 'City Line' between Herne Hill and Farringdon, was opened by the Midland Railway in 1871 to further its mineral traffic. Reached by running powers, it was reconstructed in 1958–59 with reception and departure sidings, seen under the signalbox, 50 unloading bays on either side of a traverser, on the right, and three turntables. Intended for 70,000 tons a year, the reconstructed depot was closed in 1973.*
The Museum of London

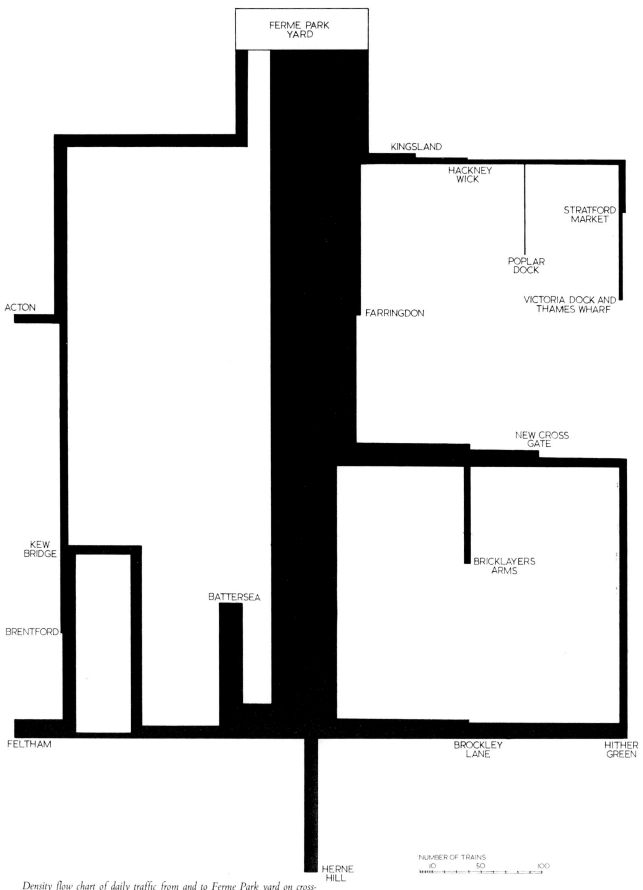

FERME PARK
YARD

KINGSLAND

HACKNEY
WICK

STRATFORD
MARKET

POPLAR
DOCK

ACTON

FARRINGDON

VICTORIA DOCK AND
THAMES WHARF

NEW CROSS
GATE

KEW
BRIDGE

BRICKLAYERS
ARMS

BATTERSEA

BRENTFORD

FELTHAM

BROCKLEY
LANE

HITHER
GREEN

NUMBER OF TRAINS
10   50   100

HERNE
HILL

Density flow chart of daily traffic from and to Ferme Park yard on cross-London freight services, summer service 1946.

Neasden *Neasden Yard was the main Great Central yard in the London area. It was strategically located where the route to the North via Rickmansworth could join the Midland cross-London line from Cricklewood to Acton Wells by a spur. These two GC lines of 1899 were supplemented in 1905 by the route via Northolt, putting the yard at the confluence of three routes. A transfer freight via Kew East Junction arrives behind 4-6-0 No 30457 Sir Bedivere in 1952.*
Brian Morrison

Ferme Park *Ferme Park marshalling yard was opened by the Great Northern Railway in 1888 as its principal yard in the London area. In the foreground is the up yard, separated from the down yard by the main line. Transfer workings between the two halves of the yard crossed the main line by a flyover, whose approach can be seen to the middle left of this 1956 picture. British Rail*

the regular-interval electric services through London Bridge; going by the alternative route avoided this.

Alternative routes to Feltham via Acton and Brentford, via Holborn and Richmond, and via Holborn and Brentford were apparent, being the result of similar plans to avoid interference with other services. Indeed, the timetable records times when freight trains were not to run on certain lines. So, for example, no freights were allowed on the Up line of the City Widened Lines between 06.30 and 09.30, as between these hours the lines were dedicated to the LNER and LMSR suburban services to Moorgate. On the Widened Lines an LNER banking engine was provided at Farringdon at all times, apart from 00.45 to 17.55 on Sundays, for services destined for South London which required this facility.

A further peculiarity of working notable on the diagram was that trains for Bricklayers Arms from Ferme Park would have had to reverse to reach their destination. To avoid the need for the locomotive to run around the train, the Southern allowed such trains to be propelled into Bricklayers Arms. Similarly to avoid this running-round they could propel out on the return journey. However, it was laid down this could not be done during foggy weather, and at such times the trains were diverted to Hither Green. During normal times traffic for stations on the lines to Addiscombe and Hayes had to be worked on the Bricklayers Arms trains. This avoided an awkward movement on the Southern, as a train from Hither Green to Addiscombe or Hayes would need to run up

Feltham *Feltham Marshalling Yard came into use in 1920, although some ancilliary facilities were finished later. It replaced inadequate yards at Nine Elms, Woking and Willesden and was designed as a hump-yard to enlist the assistance of gravity in shunting. With 14 reception sidings 33 sorting roads and a secondary yard of 8 flat sidings, its location enabled trips to be run easily to the lines north of the Thames.*
C. R. L. Coles

the main line and reverse in order to reach its destination.

A final injunction to operating staff was 'The times of arrival and departure of freight trains at stations and sidings are based on the normal requirements, but wherever practicable and desirable the trains must be got away earlier by arrangement with control'.

Feltham Yard

In order to obtain a clearer idea of the operation of a London marshalling yard, Feltham Yard on the Southern Railway will now be studied. The yard was sited south of the Waterloo to Windsor line, approximately 14 miles from the London terminal. Brought into use in 1920, it was one of the first hump yards in the country. Flat shunting, the previous practice, meant that a locomotive had to place the wagons for one train in one siding, then place the wagons for a second train in another siding and continue the process until it had sorted its train. It was a slow process as it involved much locomotive movement in the marshalling sidings. If the wagons were pushed over a hump, they could roll down by gravity into the collecting sidings, and the number of locomotives in the marshalling sidings reduced. This greatly increased the throughput of a yard and was the reason for its selection at Feltham.

The yard was effectively two side by side. The Up Yard dealt with traffic destined to depart towards London and the Down Yard away from it. Both were similar in design and in operation. A train on arrival would run into the reception sidings and the locomotive would detach from the train. Shunters would then uncouple the train into sections or 'cuts', corresponding to the marshalling siding into which the wagons should be placed. A locomotive would then push the train from the rear up the gradient to the hump summit at a slow walking pace. As the wagons passed over the hump, they would run down into the marshalling sidings in the sections into which they had been divided. Each of the sidings was reserved for particular destinations and the wagons would be guided by successive pairs of points after the hump into the correct particular track. When sufficient wagons for a particular destination were collected on a track they would be coupled, a locomotive and brake van attached and form a timetabled train for their destination. As well as these tracks to make-up trains, there was a cripple siding and a brake van track. The former held wagons unfit for travel because of some defect until the problem could be rectified, the latter held all the incoming brake vans until they were used on outgoing trains.

In addition to the yard there were a number of other facilities apart from the obvious offices and mess rooms for staff. The first was a wagon repair shop sited between the down hump and the up marshalling sidings; with a considerable throughput of wagons in the yard it made sense to have repair facilities for them there. The second was a shed, capable of housing 36 locomotives. Again, with locomotives working to and from the yard, facilities to stable and maintain them were necessary, including coaling and watering. Among the locomotives based there were the Urie G16 4-8-0 tanks introduced in 1921, specially designed for hump shunting at Feltham, and the Urie H16 4-6-2 tanks introduced in the same year for trip services to Brent and Willesden. The third facility was cattle pens so that livestock in transit could be fed and watered if necessary; the last a transfer goods shed to enable goods to be transferred between wagons if required.

Access to the main lines was controlled by Feltham Junction signalbox at the London end and by Feltham East at the Windsor end. The distance between these two signalboxes was 1,712 yd. From its opening, Feltham Yard became the principal London yard on the former LSWR system and its transfer trips to the yards north of the Thames continued until the mid-1960s. In 1953 there were some 30 trains each way from the yard to others such as Neasden, Ferme Park and Temple Mills, bringing a wide variety of motive power. The run-down in wagonload freight brought closure of the yard and depot. Today only wasteland remains as a silent reminder of this once-busy yard.

The Present Freight Scene

The virtual demise of traditional wagonload traffic by the early 1980s has led to the closure of all the former freight terminals around inner London, while the marshalling yards that still exist are mere shadows of their erstwhile importance. These sites are valuable for commercial redevelopment. Somers Town, for example, has become the location for the British Library; proposals for the Neasden sidings site will create a major freight and commercial complex.

There are now few small goods yard facilities left, while depots handling specialised traffics like livestock and milk have long vanished.

Although these changes have stripped much of interest and fascination from the London railway scene, modern freight operation still makes a significant contribution to London's rail services. As an example, Stratford has been developed as a major international freight and Freightliner depot, with associated warehouse and forwarding facilities, to cater for export and import needs.

The remaining wagonload traffic in many cases incorporates modern braking methods, which dispense with the traditional brake van. New Speedlink terminal-to-terminal services are being developed to supplement Freightliners, and to bridge the gap between container and complete trainload needs.

The commercial basis for present-day BR freight operation has resulted in a competitive approach to road transport, with few frills. Yet these services, which connect a limited number of London termini, and which are concentrated on a few main line routes to key provincial centres, form an essential and stable base on which to project the benefits of rail freight in meeting changing commercial and environmental needs in London.

10
TO THE DOCKS AND THE RIVER

Introduction

London has been a port since at least Roman times, while river transport must have been used before that. The development of railways in the nineteenth century consequently found a well-established system to which they reacted and supplemented. Based upon the Thames, it is convenient to distinguish six areas, the Upper Thames extending as far downstream as Teddington, the Upper Tidal Thames thence to London Bridge, Docklands to Woolwich, Lower Thameside to Thameshaven, beyond which is the Sea Reach and Estuary. It is with Docklands and Lower Thameside that this chapter will be principally concerned. Inevitably the Port of London Authority, founded in 1909 to control the river and docks from Teddington to the sea, figures largely in the story.

From the inception of the port until the opening of the West India Dock in 1802, ships loaded and unloaded at quays along the banks of the river. While the number of ships using these quays remained small, it was a perfectly satisfactory system. With the growth of trade by 1796, 1,400 ships had to compete for facilities designed for 613; the consequent congestion led to the development of additional capacity in wet docks which would be unaffected by the Thames tidal range of more than fifteen feet. The success of the West India Dock meant that by 1830 four more docks had opened; London Dock in 1805, East India Dock in 1806, a precursor of the Surrey Commercial Docks improved an existing dock in 1810, and St Katharine Dock opened in 1828–9. Built before the Railway Age, railway facilities in this group were poor; only the East and West India Docks were to be directly rail-served.

However, the development of rail facilities was greatly influenced by the 'free water clause' introduced in the West India Dock Act. Fearing that their livelihood would disappear with the introduction of the wet docks, the operators of river craft were successful in obtaining the concession that all barges arriving or leaving the wet docks could do so free of charge to load or unload from ships in the docks. By unloading into a barge which could then take the goods to a riverside

wharf owned by the railway company, the dock company's charges could be avoided. To capitalise on this, the railways set up their own wharves whilst also serving the docks directly. The principal wharves were Brentford (GWR), Chelsea (WLER), Battersea (LBSCR), Nine Elms (LSWR), Blackfriars (LCDR), Deptford (LBSCR) and Angerstein Wharf (SER). Their story will be told later.

Dock Railways

Rail facilities to the London and St Katharine's dock system were therefore restricted to a branch from London Docks Junction on the line into Fenchurch Street, authorised in 1860. It reached the East Smithfield depot and the wool warehouse, but the awkward and congested layout of the dock area precluded rail tracks on the dockside. Rail facilities for the Surrey Commercial Docks were provided by a spur from the Deptford Wharf Line from New Cross, opened in 1851, but fell into disuse for dock traffic, until revived by a new connection in 1930–1. These two dock systems were unique in another respect. In the remaining docks the rail facilities came to be operated by the dock companies and subsequently the Port of London Authority. Here they remained in the hands of the railway companies and subsequently BR. East Smithfield depot closed on 1 September 1966; the Deptford Wharf line closed on 1 January 1964, although dock traffic ceased earlier.

The East and West India Docks, although initially built and operated by separate companies, combined in 1838 to meet competition from the London and St Katharine docks and can be treated as one. The initial rail service was provided by the London & Blackwall, whose story is told elsewhere, but an alternative was provided by the East & West India Docks & Birmingham Junction Railway (E&WID&BJR), authorised in 1846. The aim of the company was concisely indicated by its name and its intention was to give rail facilities equal to the Victoria Dock further downstream. It ran from Camden Town on the London

147

& North Western Railway to the Docks and opened in sections, being finally complete in 1852. South of a junction at Bow with the London & Blackwall Extension Railway, only goods services were provided but passenger trains were first run to Poplar in 1866, being extended over the London & Blackwall to London Railways, but rail facilities had to await the opening in 1868 of the Millwall Docks, south of the West India Docks on the Isle of Dogs, catering for the expansion of dock trade. Rail facilities were provided from the outset in the Millwall Docks and had to be extended back through the West India Docks to join

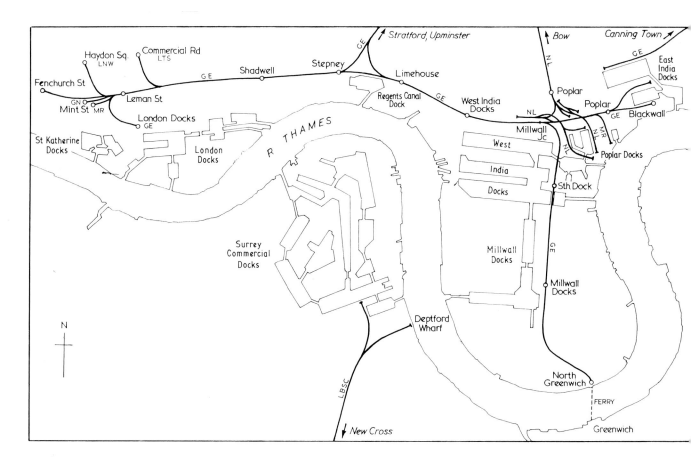

Blackwall from 1870. Twenty years later they reverted to their original terminus.

The railway acquired its own dock at Poplar from 1850 by leasing from the dock company the site of what had been two reservoirs to maintain the level of water in the dock. Originally intended for coal, it became an ordinary waterside depot. Indeed, as well as the North London (as the E&WID&BJR had become in 1853), the London & North Western, the Great Northern and Great Western had depots at Poplar Dock. Because the London & Blackwall ran east to west immediately to the north of Poplar Dock, NLR trains had to cross above it. Consequently, the line from Camden Town bifurcated; the line to the east side of the Dock crossed the London & Blackwall directly, but the line to other parts of the Dock involved a reversal before the climb.

The West India Docks proper were served by connections to both the London & Blackwall and the North

the existing railways. As the tracks had to conform to the existing restricted dock layout, sharp curves were inevitable, limiting the design of the locomotives to work them. From 1872 until 1926 a passenger service to North Greenwich made use of these dock lines, although it was operated by the Great Eastern Railway which had leased the London & Blackwall in 1865.

The East India Docks had two places of rail access. One was from the London & Blackwall to serve the Export Dock, while the Import Dock was connected to the GER branch to North Woolwich. The acquisition of the Export Dock for an electricity generating station in 1947 meant the end of the connection to the London & Blackwall. Interestingly enough the Great Northern had a goods depot off the connection to the Export Dock, whilst the Midland had a branch from the London & Blackwall to its own Poplar Dock. Nineteen chains in length, it was an enclave reached by running

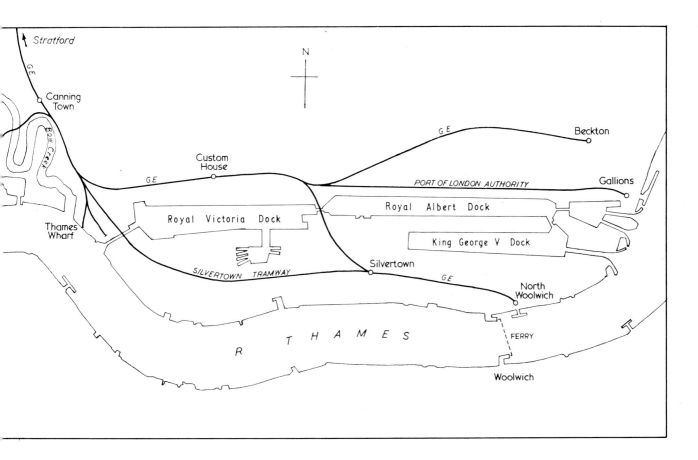

powers over the Great Eastern from Tottenham West Junction.

Thus in all the cases above except the Millwall Docks, the railway had to fit an infrastructure that was already in existence. In contrast in the remaining groups, the Royal and Tilbury Docks, railways were provided from the outset and in the case of the latter

acted as a spur to development.

The inception of the Royal Group of the Royal Victoria Dock, the Royal Albert Dock and the King George V Dock dates from the opening in 1855 of the Victoria Dock, the first dock in the port with main line railway connections. It was amalgamated in 1864 with the London & St Katharine Dock in a merger designed

Railway connections to the London and Tilbury Docks.

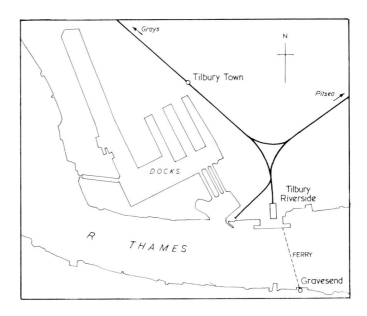

Poplar *Poplar was one of the original stations on the London & Blackwall but this view, taken after its closure to passengers in 1926, shows the connection to the GER East India Docks and GNR Blackwall Goods Depots going off to the left at the platform end. Both of these depots remained open until 1967, served by trains using the north to east spur at Limehouse.* London Borough of Tower Hamlets

Millwall Extension Railway *The Millwall Extension Railway was opened from Millwall Junction to North Greenwich in 1872 and on its first section passed through Millwall Dock, utilising three separate swing bridges to cross parts of the basin. Because of the light construction of the bridges and danger of fire in ships' sails, horses were at first used for haulage instead of locomotives.* London Borough of Tower Hamlets

to meet the competition from the East and West India Docks, which had combined in 1838, and to cater for the increasing size of ships. The Royal Albert Dock opened in 1880 (when the Victoria Dock acquired the prefix 'Royal') and the King George V Dock in 1921. The whole group provided about half the deep-sea berths in the five dock systems of London and dealt with ships from 10,000 to 30,000 tons.

Before the docks were built the area was flood-plain of nothing more than agricultural value. Across this

under-developed area, the Eastern Counties & Thames Junction was authorised in 1844 to build a 2½ mile line from Stratford to Thames Wharf on Barking Creek. Realising that an extension of 2½ miles would enable Woolwich to be served by a ferry, a further Act for another company to do that was obtained in the following year. The line opened from Stratford to Canning Town on 29 April 1846 and through to North Woolwich on 14 June 1847. By 1847 the Eastern Counties Railway had taken-over both companies.

The line to Woolwich had run broadly parallel to the river bank but the construction of the Victoria Dock necessitated a diversion, since the lock entrance was at the west end of the dock and crossed the railway. Rail operations would have been severely restricted by a swing bridge to let vessels into and out of the dock, so the tracks were diverted to run to the north of the dock, regaining the original route at Silvertown. The portion abandoned as a through route remained as the 'Silvertown Tramway' to serve the works which sprang up along the river bank. The opening of the Royal Albert Dock posed the same problem as it joined the Victoria Dock at the latter's east end where the Woolwich line had been relocated. This time the solution was to put the railway in a 600yd tunnel beneath the docks, with approaches on a gradient of 1 in 50, the tracks being 23ft below low water. The existing length of railway was retained and together with a road crossed the dock on a swing bridge of 90ft span. Originally signal boxes were provided at each end of the bridge, for goods trains of over 25 wagons that were precluded from using the tunnel.

Both sides of all three docks were served by tracks belonging to the dock company, which in 1909 was merged into the Port of London Authority (PLA). The hub of the rail system in this group was the Royal Victoria Exchange Sidings, located between the Woolwich branch and the north side of the Victoria Dock. Access from the main line was at A Box junction behind the site of Tidal Basin station. B and C Boxes for regulating movements between sections of the Exchange sidings were removed in 1917 but D Box at the extreme east of the sidings was retained.

The sidings comprised three groups, outwards of 10 tracks accommodating 369 wagons, reception of 11 tracks for 464 wagons and shunting and marshalling of 10 tracks for 367 wagons. Within the dock system five different types of traffic could be distinguished. Inwards freight traffic comprised about 22 daily trains in 1952, which were brought into the Reception Sidings by BR. A PLA locomotive took the train forward to the inwards marshalling sidings where trains were made up for the various ships and sheds. Outward freight largely reversed this process, but the perishable nature of much

West India Docks *Although taken in the 1950s this picture of unloading wool from South Africa in West India Docks is from a vanished world. The wool came over the ship's side in bales and was largely dealt with by hand; the only mechanical aids were a crane and barrows. Note the short-wheelbase of the PLA saddle tank to enable it to traverse more easily the sharp curves of the railway system in this group of docks.* The Museum of London

Silvertown *This 1960 view of Silvertown shows two of its three stages of railway development. Class L1 2-6-4T No 67716, with its train of quint-arts for North Woolwich, is climbing from the tunnel under the water connection between the Royal Victoria and Royal Albert Docks. The two tracks to the left cross the same connection by a swing bridge whilst the Silvertown Tramway, the original line, lies out of the picture to the left.* T. Wright

Docks Railways *A train of banana vans stands at the Exchange Sidings for the Royal Group of docks in LNER days. Typical of the perishable traffic dealt with through this Group, vans would be placed on the berths by 08.00, loaded and moved to the exchange sidings by three services at 12.00, 14.30 and 16.30 ready for same day despatch.* Fox Photos

Ocean port *Tilbury Riverside station was laid out to accommodate boat train passengers arriving and departing by ocean liners but the station was also used by local trains between Southend and Fenchurch Street which had to reverse there. Stanier three-cylinder 2-6-4T No 42505 leaves Riverside for Fenchurch Street on 28 June 1958.* G. M. Kichenside

Horse shunting *At many riverside wharves and sidings horses were used for shunting.*

of the traffic, meat and fruit, called for a speedy service and specialised wagons.

Brief periods of hectic activity were commonplace. At 17.00 between six and ten trains converged onto the Outwards Sidings from all parts of the dock, to be reformed into eight outward trains for BR, the first due to leave at 17.50. Private siding traffic, notably for coal, grain and flour, involved haulage over the dock line and shunting at each siding. Internal traffic consisted mainly of frozen meat from ship to store and non-perishable goods from ship to warehouse. To deal with this traffic, the PLA maintained its own wagons, some 548 in all, of which 310 were open trucks.

The final source of traffic was passenger traffic of two types. The first comprised special trains for embarkation or disembarkation at the docks. In the Royal Group the

PLA issued tickets for these trains, either on the ship on the day of arrival or at temporary booking offices. About two-thirds of a ship's passengers used the special train, and for a ship carrying 900 passengers three specials would be needed. In contrast to freight practice, it would be hauled along PLA lines by a BR locomotive with facing points clipped and under the control of a flagman, with road crossings guarded by flagmen or dock police.

The second was passenger traffic of a specialist nature carried on the Gallions branch. When the Royal Albert Dock was authorised, the dock company was empowered to build a 1¾-mile branch from the Woolwich branch to Gallions. Built and worked as a double track running along the north wall of the dock, it had stations at Connaught Road, Central, Manor

Way and Gallions. Under the Act the company had power to convey only passenger and parcels traffic and had to provide cheap trains for workmen's use. The section to Central was opened on 3 August 1880 with approximately half-hourly service from 08.30 to 18.00, but by November it was open throughout. Initially operated by the dock company with second-hand equipment, including three former LNWR 2-4-0 tank engines, the Great Eastern operated it from 1 July 1896. By October 1900 there were 54 weekday trains to Gallions, of which 17 were from Liverpool Street or Fenchurch Street. A similar pattern operated in the reverse direction. Improvements in tram and bus services caused the closure of the shuttle from Custom House to Gallions on 6 June 1932, but through trains continued. The LNER as successors to the GER provided the trains, but the PLA staffed the stations, crossings and signalboxes. In the end the line was a casualty of war. Damaged by bombs on 7 September 1940, it was repaired for wagon storage, until it was formally abandoned in 1950.

The final dock group, at Tilbury, was the East & West India Dock Company's answer to the competition of the Royal Albert Dock. The location, 26 miles downstream of London Bridge, was selected to avoid most of the shallows then found in many reaches of the Thames. To overcome the distance from London it was designed for rail transit, using the London Tilbury & Southend Railway, which had arrived in 1854. No warehouses were built. Instead facilities were provided in London at the Commercial Road Depot, served by a 27-chain branch from the approach to Fenchurch Street.

Opened in 1886, Tilbury was for some time a costly failure which was only developed after the formation of the PLA in 1909. Connection to the main railway system was at two places. The principal point, North End Junction, between Grays and Tilbury Town, had exchange sidings comprising an outward section for 220 wagons, reception for 120 wagons and six tracks of marshalling sidings for 220 wagons. A subsidiary entrance at South Junction by Tilbury Riverside had in later years only a ground frame, and was only open between 18.00 and 06.00 when North End Junction box was closed.

Alongside Riverside station, the PLA and the LMSR, successor to the LTSR, constructed a floating landing stage, opened by Ramsay MacDonald in 1930. This enabled liners to berth at all states of the tide and rail services to be provided for passengers from Riverside. Passenger trains also used the dock railway system, but the only regular service was via South Junction to the PLA terminus, Tilbury Marine, in connection with the ferry service to Dunkirk. Inaugurated on 13 May 1927, it only lasted until 1 May 1932, a victim of passengers' preference for a short sea crossing. Operated by collaboration between the LMSR and the Nord Railway of France, it was an overnight service in both directions using at first three and later four steamers, which had belonged to the constituents of the LMS and which were renamed for the new service. Marine station was a simple platform where the LMS hired a booking office from the PLA and issued tickets to continental and inland destinations itself. By use of this service a passenger could leave St Pancras at 22.30 and be in Paris

Tilbury Docks *The Port of London Authority railways are epitomised by this 1950 view at Tilbury Docks of Hudswell, Clarke 0-6-0T No 45 of 1915. The 10ft wheelbase of the locomotive enabled it to use sharp curves in the Dock area so that, at Tilbury, rail access was possible to the front and rear of every berth in the system.* Chris Cheetham

LTSR Docks Services *Few warehouses were originally provided at Tilbury Docks as the East & West India Dock company agreed with the LTSR to lease a depot at Commercial Road, Whitechapel. Special trains were provided from Tilbury to the depot from its opening in 1886 and this view shows the 12.50 Tilbury to Commercial Road at Grays in 1908 headed by No 75 Canvey Island, built that year.*
LCGB Ken Nunn Collection

St Pancras *Ivatt 2-6-0 No 43019 heads a Swedish Lloyd Boat Train to Tilbury at St. Pancras in October 1961. Scandinavian and Australian boat trains were inaugurated from 1894, on the opening of the Tottenham & Forest Gate Railway, lasting until 1963 and the electrification of the LTSR. The Midland inaugurating this service felt it would help passengers from the Midlands, destined for Tilbury sailings, to avoid crossing London with luggage. M. Mensing*

Nord at 10.20, although if he were travelling third-class this would be delayed to 11.45.

Ferry Services

Ferry services operated by railway companies can best be considered by starting at London Bridge and moving downstream. The first, between North Greenwich on the Isle of Dogs to Greenwich, dated back to 1550, but the rights for foot-passengers were leased in 1871 to the Thames Steamboat Company which in turn conveyed them to the London & Blackwall Railway in 1874. In turn they passed to the Great Eastern Railway, which to encourage use of the Millwall Extension Railway issued through tickets from Fenchurch Street and Greenwich. At the turn of the century some 1.3 million passengers used the ferry annually, but the opening of an LCC free pedestrian subway in 1902 saw the withdrawal of the service on payment of £8,000 compensation.

The ferry between North Woolwich and Woolwich dates from the opening of the railway to North Woolwich in 1847 when two steam ferries were operated. Built at a Barking shipyard, they were later joined by a third vessel plying between the two railway piers. The opening of the South Eastern Railway line to Woolwich on the south bank in 1849 dealt a severe blow to through traffic to London, but the industrial and dock development of the north bank brought a twice daily flow of workmen to replace it. The railway ferry managed to continue after the LCC ferry, a short distance upstream, was introduced on 23 March 1889,

somewhat surprisingly as the former charged a penny to cross and the latter was free. Perhaps it continued on through bookings to GER stations but it finally bowed to the inevitable and was withdrawn on 1 October 1908.

Further downstream, the London Tilbury & Southend Railway had obtained powers in its original Act of 1852 to enable it to serve Gravesend and the pleasure gardens at Rosherville from Tilbury on the north bank of the Thames, but only passengers proceeding to or from its trains were to be carried. On expiry of these powers in 1868 they were allowed to lapse but were renewed in 1875. In 1880 two rival ferries on the route were absorbed to obtain a monopoly, a situation which remains today.

Railway Wharves

Railway wharves formed a small part of the 639 wharves on the tidal Thames that existed in 1951 and which made use of the barge fleet to serve ships. Most of the wharves were within two miles upstream or downstream of London Bridge, looking back to the quays from which the Port first developed, but the railway wharves had to be located wherever the particular company could make a line to the River.

Tilbury Ferry Edith *represents today's sole remaining railway ferry from Tilbury to Gravesend and is one of three ships built for the service in 1961. Of some 220 tons and capable of carrying 475 passengers, she is seen in 1977 in front of the PLA landing stage and customs hall with Tilbury Riverside station to the right.* E. Wilmshurst

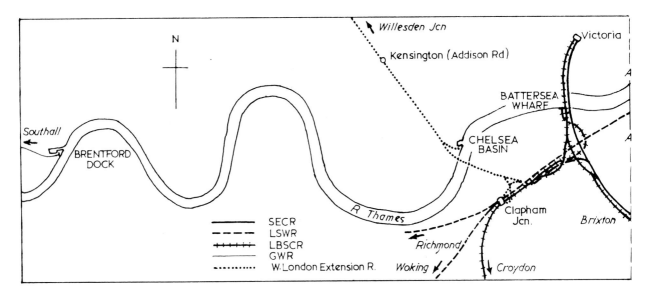

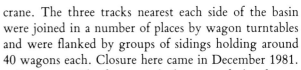

The Great Western Railway approach at Brentford was made through the medium of the Great Western & Brentford Railway. Opened to goods on the broad gauge on 18 July 1859, standard gauge was added in October 1861. By 1956 Brentford Dock forwarded some 137,000 tons of merchandise and coal and received 63,000 tons. Although most was carried by barge, Dutch coasters did reach the Dock. The dock closed on 31 December 1964, and has since been developed as a marina, encircled by new houses. Part of the branch remains to serve Brentford Town Yard with its GLC refuse transfer depot.

The Chelsea Basin of the West London Extension Railway was one of the remaining parts of the Kensington Canal, which had been filled-in to form the route of the railway north of the river, the climb to the river bridge leaving the basin to be served by a branch from the main line. The canal was subsequently widened to form a basin in the centre of the depot. Broadly square in shape, the basin had a goods shed, on the opposite side to the entrance, served by a one-ton crane. The three tracks nearest each side of the basin were joined in a number of places by wagon turntables and were flanked by groups of sidings holding around 40 wagons each. Closure here came in December 1981.

Battersea Wharf occupied the site of the former Pimlico terminus of the West End of London & Crystal Palace Railway Company. Opened in 1858 on the south side of the river, it was replaced by Victoria on the north side two years later. Nevertheless, the London, Brighton & South Coast Railway used it as a goods depot with road and river access. In 1904 the depot equipped with 10 tons of crane power handled goods and livestock but the Great Northern, Midland and London & South Western Railways also used the depot, making use of running powers to do so. Together with Deptford Wharf it formed the river outlet of the LBSCR, until it closed on 4 May 1970.

Much the same origin was found on the LSWR Wharf at Nine Elms; the former London & Southampton Railway terminus was handed-over to goods traffic after the extension to Waterloo had been opened in 1848. The Nine Elms site had been selected because it offered proximity to a berth for the river vessels that were to link the line to the City. A single line crossed Nine Elms Lane into a ¾-acre yard, which from 1936 was dominated by a granary by the river bank where lighters were loaded by crane. Traffic was withdrawn by 1968.

The final example of a passenger terminus becoming a goods wharf was Blackfriars on the London, Chatham & Dover's City Extension. Opened on the south side of

Southall *A freight train from the Brentford Dock branch joins the Great Western main line at Southall in May 1960 hauled by 0-6-0PT No 4673. The branch climbed past the depot, and goods traffic terminated in sidings on the south side of the line beyond the station. At this time the seven weekday trips were allowed 18 minutes for the four mile branch. A. R. Brown*

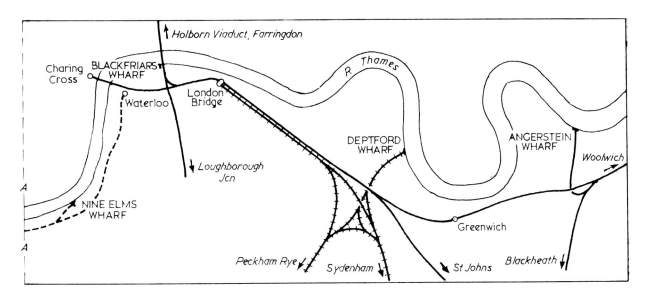

Railway connections to riverside wharves.

the Thames on 1 June 1864 its passenger role came to an end in 1885, when both the rail and street levels were devoted to freight working. Cramped in site, wagons had to be lowered by hydraulic hoist to the wharf. No doubt the cramped conditions, which involved wagons being sorted for the depot at Herne Hill, did not encourage the development of river traffic at the only place the LCDR could deal with it. The depot closed in 1964.

Brentford Dock *Brentford Dock was opened in 1859 and this view, around the end of World War I, shows cranes dealing with the lighters to and from the Pool of London moored in the dock basin. This was reached from the Thames through lock gates and had a covered area at its western end. Behind the second crane is the grain warehouse.*
British Rail

Chelsea Basin *Chelsea Basin depot was situated on the West London Extension Railway whose tracks rise from the right to cross the Thames on the way to Clapham Junction. The tracks between the two signals split into a group on each side of the basin whose site is marked by the crane jib.* R. Davies

The Deptford Wharf has already been mentioned for its access to Surrey Commercial Docks, but it was opened from New Cross Gate on 2 July 1849 to provide a goods service to the Thames. It passed over the Grand Surrey Canal by a moveable bridge, under the Greenwich viaduct, climbed to cross a road and the canal again, and finally dropped to ground level. Lines spread out to serve the wharf area so that the final road crossing before the basin was reached had seven widely-spaced tracks. Locomotives stopped short of the crossing, over which the wagons were hauled by rope and capstan. Coal, timber and stone were the principal traffic until closure in 1964.

The final wharf is Angerstein, named after the man who built this one-mile branch from the South Eastern Railway's North Kent line at Charlton. Opened in

Deptford and Angerstein Wharves *Exclusively used for goods traffic, the Deptford Wharf and Angerstein Wharf branches were not greatly photographed except by the passengers of an occasional enthusiast special. Deptford Wharf was the LBSCR's outlet and is seen in March 1958. The special stands on the New Cross side of Grove Street Crossing, the limit of locomotive working.* H. C. Casserley

Angerstein Wharf in 1956 is seen in its workday role with Class C2X No 32551 on a short freight. The track on the right served the LCC Tramways Central Repair Depot on which an LCC steam locomotive could be seen shunting. Three years later the branch was electrified on the overhead wire system but, as it was subsequently removed, services on the branch are now diesel hauled. Alan A. Jackson

1852, the line and wharf were leased by the SER which had ideas of a ferry to Blackwall. Instead, its use was restricted to freight and it was electrified on the overhead system for Class 71 freight locomotives in 1960. Although the wharf is no longer used, the line remains to serve private sidings.

Pleasure Traffic

The final connection between railways and the river is pleasure traffic, of which two types may be discerned. The first can be found above Richmond where little industrial use was made of the Thames. Here lay the Thameside resorts of Henley, Marlow, Cookham and Maidenhead served by the Great Western main line or its branches, while Staines marked the border, being served by the GWR and the LSWR. The latter also served the downstream towns of Hampton Court, Kingston and Richmond. The pleasure traffic to these places was typified by the *Three Men in a Boat* who took the LSWR to Kingston to start their trip up river and caught the GWR from Pangbourne on their return.

Thorpe Bay *The LTS line to Southend was heavily used for business and pleasure with commuters travelling to London from Southend and its neighbouring dormitory suburbs in the morning and back in the evening, with day trippers travelling in the reverse direction. Even in the 1950s trains of 11 to 13 coach non-corridor sets ran at about five minute intervals in peak hours. Here LMS Fairburn 2-6-4T No 42679 heads for Shoeburyness with the 12.05 from Fenchurch Street on 27 July 1957. G. M. Kichenside*

The second type of pleasure traffic is trains to London's seaside resort of Southend, which owes its rise to the London, Tilbury & Southend Railway. On the opening of the direct line via Laindon in 1888, the distance to London was shortened by 7¾ miles and the service greatly increased. Southend's population grew eightfold in the next 30 years, aided by the opening of the Great Eastern branch from Shenfield in 1889. Although the two lines competed, particularly from 1892, the LT&S had the faster route, and still remains the principal route to Southend. In addition, the connection to the District Railway near Bromley-by-Bow station enabled a through service from Ealing Broadway to Southend to be introduced in 1910. Hauled by electric locomotives to Barking, the trains were taken on by LTSR tank engines. By 1912 the service had been increased to four trains on weekdays and six on Sundays but this service was withdrawn in 1939, never to return. Since World War II Southend has lost much of its pleasure role to office and shopping functions.

11
DEPOTS AND WORKS

Table 2 at the end of the chapter shows how much London was a mecca for the steam locomotive connoisseur. In the area covered directly by this book, there were some 39 motive power depots, excluding sub-depots, taken into British Railways on 1 January 1948. In addition there was a number of recognised locomotive servicing points provided to reduce wasteful movements to engine sheds between short layovers. Examples of these were Ranelagh Bridge at Royal Oak, serving Paddington, and Kings Cross locomotive yard, although many of the other termini still have or had similar facilities. Finally, locomotive, carriage and wagon repair shops completed the variety.

Throughout the nineteenth and early part of the twentieth centuries, changes to locomotive sheds were generally to provide for modernisation or expansion, perhaps on a new site. Rationalisation of locomotive servicing depots began in the 1920s and 1930s with the Southern Railway electrification programmes, and a number of depots which had provided locomotives for the extensive suburban network were closed or modified for other uses.

Former engine sheds at Strawberry Hill and Slade

Kings Cross (Engine Sidings) *Prototype* Deltic, *now preserved in the Science Museum London, and forerunner of the successful Class 55 locomotives on the East Coast main line, eases gently over the points in Kings Cross locomotive stabling sidings, on 9 February 1960.* J. Oatway

Green, for instance, were converted for electric multiple-units, while the SER shed at Purley still stands, clearly displaying '1890' and 'SER' over the entrance, having been closed in 1927; Orpington is a further example of conversion embodying the original building. The approach to Victoria is of interest for the remains of the former roundhouse of the LBSCR Battersea Park depot. Examples of buildings of historic interest because of their former railway origins include the Roundhouse Theatre at Chalk Farm, once the London & Birmingham Railway engine sheds, and the Eastern Counties Railway 'engine house' at Gidea Park, used for many years for industrial purposes.

Although many depots, such as Kentish Town, Willesden, Kings Cross and Stratford, were extensively rebuilt in the 1930s to achieve better efficiency, rapid modernisation of motive power following the 1955 Railway Modernisation Plan of BR led to further substantial change in locomotive facilities. Diesel and electric locomotives are much more flexible for stabling,

requiring less cleaning and servicing than steam locomotives (and no turntables, either) while the bulk of suburban services were progressively replaced by diesel or electric multiple-units. As a consequence most of the steam depots were closed by the first half of the 1960s, although some were partly or wholly converted for diesel operation before later closure. A few remain for this purpose, for instance Old Oak Common and Hither Green, or have been converted to other uses, such as Kentish Town. In most cases, little evidence now remains of these former facilities which provided employment and often a lifetime's work for several thousand railwaymen.

Apart from the conversions for diesel or electric operations, which included Stewarts Lane, Camden, Hornsey and Devons Road, provision for which began on a very small scale in the 1930s with the introduction of diesel shunters at marshalling yards, some purpose-built diesel and electric maintenance depots were constructed. Examples were at Willesden, Cricklewood, Stratford, Finsbury Park, Ripple Lane and Hitchin. In addition, sheds for stabling and maintenance purposes are provided at various points to service electric and diesel multiple-units for suburban and High-Speed Trains.

In the days of steam operation, moving trains at the termini and along the line for passenger or freight

Camden *Camden epitomised the 'top link' shed, its primary purpose being servicing locomotives for main line work and station duties. On 6 July 1958, Patriot Class 4-6-0 No 45546* Fleetwood *has just been turned ready to back down to be coaled, while in the shed others await their next duties.* Brian Morrison

Rickmansworth (Engine Sidings) *On 7 April 1947, Met 4-4-4 tank locomotives Nos 9807 and 9808 stand ready to return northwards from Rickmansworth after the change from electric traction. A Met 'T' stock EMU stands in the sidings controlled by a lower quadrant signal.* H. C. Casserley

Shoeburyness *For much of its independent life the LTS line was worked by 4-4-2Ts but during the 1930s Stanier, the LMS cme, designed a three-cylinder version of his suburban 2-6-4T which operated almost entirely on the Tilbury and Southend lines, later supplemented until the end of steam by LMS Fairburn and BR 2-6-4Ts. Shoeburyness shed had the job of looking after most of them.* G. M. Kichenside

working were fascinating to watch, and much of the attraction was in the way that the steam locomotive gave the appearance of being 'alive'. However, the locomotive depot held a special appeal, for this was where the mystique of the working steam locomotive could be observed and discovered. This is less so with diesels or electrics, where so much more standardisation and a sense of sterility has replaced the traditional smell of smoke and hot oil.

The purpose of this chapter is to re-create something of the atmosphere of the working steam locomotive shed in London, examining the types of locomotives and trains operated, the variety of depots found and the typical routine of the running shed, together with the

supporting activities of locomotive workshops and the ancillary facilities of carriage and wagon repair shops. A comparison will be made also between the diesel and electric maintenance depots and the steam running sheds which they replaced.

Types of Engine Shed

Although it is not possible to categorise exactly the diverse range of London sheds, four types of steam motive power depot can be identified and these are given in the table. These are categorised for this purpose as main line, suburban and local, freight, and branch, miscellaneous and minor work.

Main line:

These depots were above all concerned with the provision of express passenger locomotives to service main line trains. Of course, other types of duty were dealt with by the depots, mainly for suburban and empty coaching movements, parcels and station pilot duties, but the importance of these sheds was such that all types of working were usually catered for. Stratford, for example, had a great variety of different types of work, with a large allocation of tank locomotives to handle the extensive Liverpool Street suburban services, as well as freight locomotives to cope with Docklands traffic and the demands of Temple Mills and other freight yards in East London, in addition to 'top link' passenger locomotives for main line express work. This

Stewarts Lane *The pride of Stewarts Lane, amongst its range of main line duties, was the* Golden Arrow. *West Country Class pacific No 34091* Weymouth *stands immaculate outside the shed ready to leave for Victoria and so begin its journey on 2 August 1958.* J. Oatway

Cricklewood Diesel Depot *Located on the east side of the Midland main line opposite the site of the former steam shed, which occupied space on the other side of the main lines, this view is of the main diesel maintenance shed on 29 October 1978. Nos 47202 and 47443 share accommodation with a 'Peak'.* Brian Morrison

Guildford *Guildford was an important 'mixed traffic' shed with a range of local passenger and freight work. The depot took the form of a semi-circular roundhouse, probably to make the best use of limited space. The shed-pilot for many years, 0-4-0ST No 30458* Ironside, *built in 1890 for the Southampton Dock Company, is seen by the entrance on 20 April 1952.* P. H. Wells

went for the other depots also, but perhaps the cross-section was greatest at Stratford, which had no major freight specialising depot, as was the case in most of the other 'main line' sheds, but several small sub-sheds providing mainly out-station facilities for the extensive suburban passenger services into Liverpool Street.

Suburban and local work:

This was the largest group of depots, which were generally smaller sheds at key points to service the outer ends of suburban workings or operate local, cross-country or branch passenger and freight services.

Freight:

These, being complementary to and sometimes more important than their neighbouring 'main line' sheds, were involved principally with the provision of suitable locomotives for freight services and shunting duties and were located often close to major marshalling yards. These were not, however, the 'Cinderella' sheds that their work might suggest, since powerful locomotives and express types often were involved in this work as well as providing support motive power for passenger services, but perhaps they lacked the glamour of the 'top link' work of the main line running sheds. From the enthusiast's point of view it was often these depots which had the more interesting varieties of locomotive 'on shed', since freight trains brought a diversity of movement and diagramming not found so frequently on passenger and termini-related work. Cricklewood and Willesden, for instance, had superior repair facilities etc. to Kentish Town and Camden.

Branch, miscellaneous and minor work:
These were small sheds or servicing points generally dealing with no more than a handful of locomotives on branch or suburban workings, and were sub-sheds of larger depots. Sometimes they did not even have a shed building, providing only basic maintenance facilities and staff signing-on points.

Depot Layouts

The two variations of shed accommodation, the roundhouse based on lines radiating from one or more turntables and the straight shed with several parallel lines running the length of the shed, were both found in London but it was the latter which predominated. Of the straight shed type, these were either through or single-ended.

The reasons for choosing any of these layouts has

probably never been recorded in detail, but has a lot to do with the location of the depot and the site that was available, the types of locomotive housed and the operating practices of the originating company. The GWR and the Midland, for instance, tended to favour the roundhouse, Old Oak Common being the prime example with four inter-connected turntables under one roof. Cricklewood and Kentish Town were Midland roundhouses in London, while until its demolition in 1931 Kings Cross had a roundhouse of Midland origin established at 'top shed' from the period to 1868 before Midland services transferred to St Pancras. Guildford was a good example of a roundhouse being built to fit into a very restricted site. Willesden had both a roundhouse, added by the LMSR in 1927, and a straight shed.

In broad terms, the roundhouse offered the advantage of flexibility of locomotive movement against the straight-shed type, where shunting would be required to move locomotives in or out of the shed. Here the through shed gave more flexibility than the single-ended building. The roundhouse could be economical in the use of space in a limited area, although this was not the case overall, since much space was used between the tracks of the fan, although this could again be advantageous where space was needed for maintenance and equipment. The roundhouse was also safer to work in and generally less draughty than the through shed. The disadvantages of the roundhouse were where the turntable was outgrown by the size of locomotives, a breakdown, or need for maintenance of the turntable which resulted in the 'trapping' of locomotives or temporary non-use of the shed. While the straight shed had been generally more popular with the British railway companies, European and American practice favoured the roundhouse, and the last major sheds constructed by BR incorporated roundhouses.

Diesel and electric maintenance depots which have replaced the defunct steam sheds are very different in both concept and atmosphere. The purpose of the diesel depot is principally to service the complex maintenance of the locomotives. They are not running garages in the same sense as the steam shed of necessity had to be with its daily routine of firing, ash cleaning, boiler-washing, coaling and watering as well as for other types of maintenance. Thus the diesel or electric locomotive is not tied to a depot except for the needs of planned regular maintenance, and as refuelling and inspection points. Stabling can be where operational requirements best dictate, and today this is the case; train crews also can pick up their locomotives at the most convenient and operationally economic points rather than being tied to fixed depots.

As the steam locomotive was phased-out the smoke, ash, soot and coaldust of the steam shed died out also.

Cricklewood *The roundhouse was not common in London but two main Midland depots, Kentish Town and Cricklewood, were of this pattern. Three 0-6-0T Class 3F, two fitted with condensing apparatus for working on the 'Widened' lines, and a Class 4F 0-6-0 stand in war-damaged Cricklewood on 2 June 1945.* H. C. Casserley

Old Oak Common *The roundhouse was exemplified by Old Oak Common which serviced main line operations from Paddington. An unidentified Castle and sister engine No 4077 Chepstow Castle sandwich Nos 6968 Woodcock Hall, 4919 Donnington Hall and 6984 Owsden Hall in the shed on 23 July 1958.* J. Oatway

Although there was a lot of charm and atmosphere generated by this, the smoke and noise of the locomotive shed was a constant nuisance in residential areas such as at Camden or Nine Elms. The change from steam to diesel brought considerable working environment improvements and economies. A good deal of the traditional heavy, dirty, hot and sometimes dangerous work of the steam shed was replaced by much cleaner and pleasant working conditions and one in which the 'control' of the engine was by press of a button rather than through a long process of raising steam. It is true that many of the footplatemen regretted the passing of the old skills and perhaps the redundancy which came in the wake of change, but they recognised the new opportunities as well and benefitted from the considerable investment in the new and improved facilities.

Types of Locomotives and Trains Operated

There was naturally a direct relationship between the type of steam locomotive shed and the locomotives allocated or serviced by that depot. Sheds involved principally with main line passenger work had a stud of Pacifics or equivalent classes of locomotive to haul the major expresses. Thus in BR days, Kings Cross had an allocation of Classes A1, A2, A3, A4, and A10 Pacifics

(including world steam speed record-holder *Mallard*), Stratford some Britannias. Camden had Coronation and Princess Royal classes. Kings were at Old Oak Common, while Nine Elms, Stewarts Lane and Bricklayers Arms shared Merchant Navy, West Country, Battle of Britain, and Britannia class locomotives. These were supported by a range of express and mixed-traffic locomotives, often named, such as BR Standard and Stanier Class 5, Jubilee, Royal Scot and Patriot, B1, B17, K1, K3 and V2, County, Castle, Hall and Grange, Lord Nelson, King Arthur and Schools classes, the 4-6-0 wheel arrangement predominating.

The importance and range of work at these depots was indicated by their support locomotives for all other types of work. Class 28XX and 47XX 2-8-0s, 43XX 2-6-0s, 2251 class 0-6-0 and 61XX 2-6-2Ts, in addition to a host of 0-6-0 pannier tanks, were regularly seen at Old Oak Common. Camden was mainly a passenger shed, supported by Jinty 0-6-0T and 2-6-4T engines, while Kings Cross had Classes L1 2-6-4T and N2

Hornsey *Until the run-down of wagon-load freight during the 1960s, London was ringed by busy marshalling yards, usually with a motive power depot nearby, from which a good deal of transfer traffic was generated. Often this was inter-regional and Hornsey's stud of Class J50 0-6-0Ts, some of which are seen here on 4 March 1961, worked through to other parts of London. Hornsey depot today is part of the principal electric unit stabling depot for Kings Cross/Moorgate suburban services.* J. Oatway

New Cross Gate *The shed site at New Cross dated back to 1839 and the opening of the London & Croydon Railway. It was an extremely busy LBSCR depot, being its main London shed for many years, but electrification and the transfer of work to other depots resulted in its final abandonment by BR. Class I3 4-4-2T No 32091 uses the turntable on 23 June 1951.* Brian Morrison

0-6-2T locomotives for suburban and empty coaching work. Stratford had a large range of support classes. Classes J15, J17, J19 and J20 0-6-0 and J67, J68 and J69 0-6-0T engines were mainly concerned with freight shunting and miscellaneous duties, while Classes L1 2-6-4T and N7 0-6-2Ts provided all-round support, but mainly on suburban duties. Some Ivatt Class 4 2-6-0 and Jinty 0-6-0Ts were also allocated to the depot in addition to WD 2-8-0 freight engines. Kentish Town continued the Midland tradition of smaller locomotive types for many years. A group of Fowler Class 3 2-6-2Ts and Class 3F 0-6-0Ts were allocated to work over the Widened Lines and were fitted with condensing apparatus – some Class N2s at Kings Cross and a batch of 57XX pannier tanks at Old Oak Common were similarly fitted. Midland 4-4-0s, 2-6-2Ts and 2-6-4Ts and Class 8F 2-8-0s were also at Kentish Town. The Southern depots had a range of types from H and M7 0-4-4T classes, 0-6-0 Classes C, C2X, Q1 and 700, 0-6-0T and 0-6-2T Classes E1, E2, E4 and E6, 4-4-0 Classes V, D1, L and L1, through to Classes U and N 2-6-0s and H15 4-6-0s. Before the Kent Coast electrification and dieselisation resulted in their transfer back to the London Midland Region, a number of Ivatt 2-6-2Ts and LMS 2-6-4Ts were allocated to Central and Eastern section SR sheds, although these were partly exchanged for BR standard locomotives for mainten-

ance reasons. Similarly several former GWR pannier tanks and Fairburn 2-6-4T locomotives were allocated to Nine Elms as ageing Southern tanks were withdrawn.

Although these were the main classes allocated to these depots, locomotives from other sheds of different classes required servicing, and BR Standard types of most classes could also be seen. With the introduction of diesel power these were often stabled alongside steam locomotives, particularly where maintenance facilities were provided.

The number and great variety of locomotives to be seen in the London area was a feature until cessation of steam. Inter-regional workings of both passenger and freight regularly brought locomotives from other regions and, apart from classes traditionally allocated almost solely to depots in Scotland, North East England, the former Central Division of the LMSR (ie ex Lancashire & Yorkshire) and Wales, there were few classes not found in London from time to time.

The depots concerned more with freight work

provided a different but complementary range of services to those of the 'main line' sheds and were situated near major yards on the edge of London's inner suburbs. Willesden, Cricklewood, Hornsey, Feltham and Southall were good examples, with substantial allocations and a wide variety of work, involving some cross-London freight transfer traffic using the Jinty, J50 or Q1 right through to 8Fs and WDs.

One of the main changes to occur in locomotive operation with the transfer from steam motive power was to move towards standardisation of classes. As the transition period was so short this was not as planned as it might otherwise have been and several less successful diesel types were introduced which had a relatively short life. As this has occurred, together with electrification, the run-down of 'trip' freight working and the introduction of multiple-unit operations including

HSTs, the variety of locomotive types and their respective trains in the London area gradually diminished.

The initial introduction of diesels, however, was an interesting period of change and experiment in motive power and, while the locomotives changed, there was at first little noticeable alteration to operating practices.

The Western Region was different, as always, trying several types of diesel-hydraulic in the Warship and Western Classes, as well as the useful Hymeks – several have been preserved. English Electric Type 4 locomotives became the regular motive power on the West Coast route which had hitherto only seen the LMS prototypes Nos 10000/1, built at Derby Works in 1947, on regular use on main line services. Southern-inspired Nos 10201-3 of Ashford similarly worked on the SR. Several prototypes were tried, including *Deltic*, which was the forerunner of the successful 3,300hp Class 55 locomotives which took over the main 'top link' duties on the East Coast route, Brush *Falcon*, a development of the Bush Type 4, and the gas turbine locomotives Nos 18000 and 18100 used mainly on the WR. While some classes, such as the Peak (Classes 44, 45 and 46), Type 4 (Classes 40 and 47) mixed-traffic

Kentish Town *Fowler 2-6-4T No 42342 awaits its next duty by the water crane at Kentish Town on 15 April 1961 overshadowed by the massive coaling tower. Locomotive coaling and watering facilities were an integral part of the steam railway scene swept away in the 1960s by dieselisation and electrification. J. Oatway*

locomotives (Classes 25, 26, 27, 31 and 33) and the ubiquitous shunters (notably Class 08) have seen upwards of twenty years' service, others such as the D57XX, D59XX, D82XX and D84XX series went comparatively early, because of changing traffic, or indifferent performance in service.

Routine of the Shed:

Although methods of operating a shed varied with the size and layout, types of locomotive and the duties worked, most depots in steam days had similar facilities and required the same kind of routine. Often locomotives on quick turnrounds on passenger duties were serviced and turned at the terminus yards at Euston, St Pancras, Marylebone, Paddington, and Liverpool Street, but where servicing at the depot was needed the engine would arrive 'on shed' requiring to be turned (although not always in the case of tank engines) coaled, fire dropped and smokebox cleaned at the ashpit and sandboxes refilled. The locomotives would be moved to be examined in another part of the shed where any running repairs could be made quickly. The fire would then be re-made, water replenished and lubrication undertaken ready for the next duty.

At regular intervals or as necessity dictated, locomotives required fuller attention and would be stabled in the shed for boiler washouts and more detailed periodic boiler and other checks or repairs. Following such activities, on returning to work the fire had to be re-lit and steam raised, a process taking several hours. Cleaning was another aspect of shed work subject to local pride, especially at the main line running sheds, but this suffered in the 1950s and 1960s, as manpower became more difficult to recruit and steam was being run down. With dieselisation all of this was swept away and replaced by a much more controlled environment with maintenance carried out, using much more complex equipment, to more defined schedules and based on the transfer of components.

Heavy Repairs and Works

Repair facilities at the main depots were provided and at the principal running sheds, such as Old Oak Common, Kings Cross, Bricklayers Arms and Willesden, these were quite extensive with lathes, wheeldrops, overhead cranes etc. They were therefore able to perform the full range of shed repair work. Bricklayers Arms, indeed, had been fitted out by the Southern Railway in the 1930s almost as an outstation of the main SR locomotive works and provided repair facilities for the whole of the SR's activities in the London area. Similarly, Kentish Town had the most extensive outstation

shop on the Midland and the locomotive superintendent ranked second only to the chief mechanical engineer at Derby. Cricklewood also had such a facility, and these outstations were effectively erecting shops in miniature and replicas of the individual shops at Derby Works.

Only Stratford and Bow remained as full locomotive workshops in London, the SECR establishing its main works at Ashford, LBSCR at Brighton, LSWR at Eastleigh, GWR at Swindon, LNWR and MR at Crewe and Derby respectively, GCR at Gorton and the GNR at Doncaster.

Bow provided a complete range of workshop facilities for the North London Railway, the works being fully established by 1863. They eventually covered some 31 acres on both sides of the NLR main line, mainly in a triangle formed by the LTSR to the south and NLR spurs from Bow Junction to Gas Factory Junction, which the NLR used to gain access to Fenchurch Street, and by the eastwards link from Bow Station towards Barking. The overhaul of steam locomotives continued until the 1950s. Carriage and wagon repairs had ceased by the mid-1960s. The original NLR running shed by Bow Junction was rebuilt in 1882 to become the locomotive erecting shop section of the works, the locomotives being transferred to new engine sheds at Devons Road to the south. Most of the site was demolished by 1970, and little remains now of the works and locomotive sheds.

While Bow was interesting in that it was a substantial facility to service a relatively small railway, Stratford was the one remaining main works not moved out of London, and was at the hub of the GER. Today there are few remains of the locomotive and carriage works which closed in 1963, employing at that time over 1000 in the locomotive workshops, nearly 800 in the carriage shops and some 500 at the wagon works at Temple Mills. Most of the 'Old Works' buildings to the east of the Cambridge lines were demolished in the early 1970s, except the Office block (a listed building) which is still in use, while the 'New Works', on the other side of the tracks, were not demolished until 1979. Wagon repairs continue at Temple Mills, although this may cease with the run-down of the wagon fleet.

Workshop facilities were established at Stratford in 1841 by the Northern & Eastern Railway, comprising engine, carriage and wagon sheds and workshops. These were rebuilt and enlarged by the Eastern Counties which had absorbed the N&E and, having run out of space at Romford by 1847, transferred its facilities to Stratford.

The first locomotives built at Stratford in 1851 were 2-2-2 well tanks designed by Gooch, although until the early 1880s the majority of all new locomotives were

Bow Works *The North London Railway was self-contained to the extent of having its own workshops which were very extensive for a railway of its size. The works remained in use for heavy repairs for smaller classes well into BR days, and the interior of the locomotive shop is seen on 16 April 1955. The locomotives are Nos 47487, 41921, 43762 and 43729.* Brian Morrison

supplied by contractors. Improvements made to the Works under Massey Bromley (1878–1882) and T. W. Worsdell (1882–5) enabled all new construction to be met by Stratford from 1884 onwards, except 20 locomotives built by Beardmore in 1920. The peak of construction was in 1891/2, with 83 new locomotives being built in both years, while in December 1891 Stratford took the world record for locomotive construction, building in 9¾ hours an 0-6-0 goods engine and tender, which was then immediately steamed – a record that was never broken.

Carriages and wagons were built at Stratford from early ECR days, but these were usually special or 'pattern' vehicles which were loaned to successful tenderers for bulk construction. As with locomotives, Stratford built most if not all of the new construction from the mid-1880s. Wagon repairs were being undertaken at Temple Mills, about a mile north of Stratford on the Cambridge line, by the 1880s, and in 1896 the whole of the wagon works was transferred there, its place at Stratford being taken-over by the carriage works.

At the Grouping the combined works and shed site totalled 108½ acres, consisting of 24½ acres for locomotive construction and repair, 40 acres for carriage and road van building and repair, and 44 acres for the engine sheds. The Temple Mills wagon works comprised a further 24 acres. These figures probably included vacant land at High Meads, on the north-west perimeter of the works, purchased by the GER with the intention of transferring the carriage works to this site, and used subsequently by the LNER for sidings.

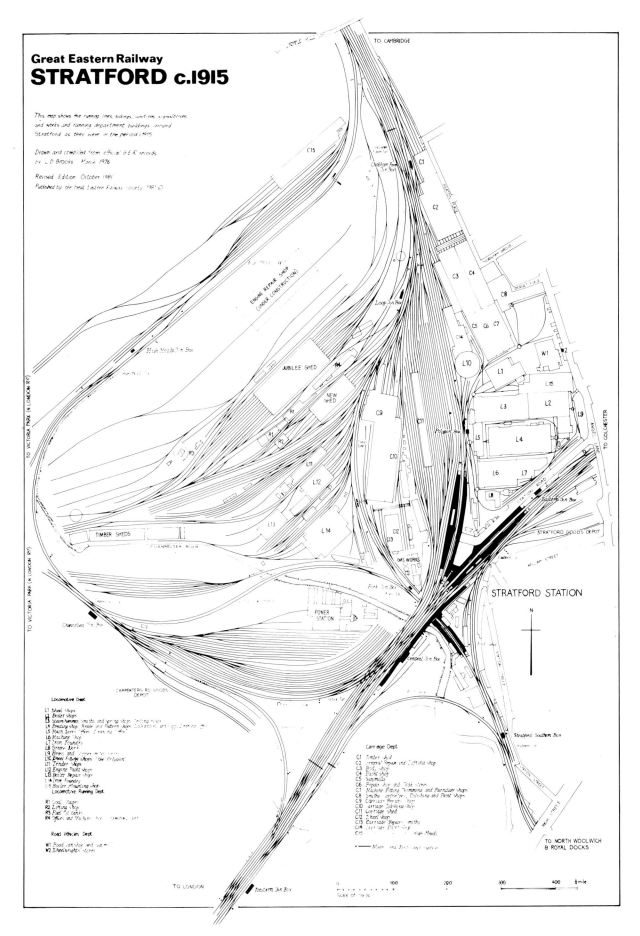

Layout of main lines, yards, depots etc around Stratford station. (Drawing copyright L. D. Brooks, Great Eastern Railway Society)

After Grouping, locomotive building ceased at Stratford in order to provide unemployment relief in the North. The last engines were built, to GER orders, in 1924. The very last locomotive was Class N7 0-6-2T No 999E (BR No 69621) now preserved on the Stour Valley railway at Chappel & Wakes Colne in Essex. The last new carriages to be built were four-wheel passenger brakes in 1929 to LNER designs, while the last new wagons, a batch of forty eight-ton refrigerator vans, were constructed at Temple Mills in 1926.

Stratford Works continued to carry out repair work until 1963, when the 'Old' works was closed in December that year, although latterly repairs had been confined to diesel locomotives and railcars. Repair work was transferred to what was originally the 'engine repair shop', and this still carries out repairs to diesel locomotives as well as some carriage repairs, dmus being dealt with at Doncaster.

Apart from these two workshops which were

Stratford *GER workshop facilities were concentrated at Stratford on both sides of the former Northern & Eastern route to Cambridge and integrally linked with the locomotive running shed. In addition to locomotive and wagon overhaul, the latter at Temple Mills, Stratford maintained the GER carriage fleet. This view of the carriage shop in 1934 includes a Pullman car beneath the gantry. C. R. L. Coles*

retained until BR days, London had several important works in the past. The two smallest were Plaistow, opened in 1881 by the LTSR and closed with the transfer of work to Bow in the summer of 1925 after the Grouping, and New Cross where the LBSCR established a small workshop in the 1840s, developing new carriage and wagon shops between 1881 and 1883. Very much linked with the large adjacent locomotive shed, New Cross became an important depot, together with its associated locomotive repair facilities, by the early twentieth century before electrification of the suburban lines, the construction of new depots at Norwood and Hither Green and the transfer of work to nearby Bricklayers Arms. Locomotive repair ceased in 1949 and the site was taken-over by the carriage and wagon department. Shed facilities, damaged from World War II and severely run down, were abandoned in stages, although locomotives still used the depot into the early 1950s.

The other two main workshops moved from London, Nine Elms of the LSWR and Longhedge of the LCDR, located nearby to each other, both closed within a matter of years in the early twentieth century, the work of Nine Elms transferring to Eastleigh and Longhedge to Ashford.

Nine Elms locomotive, carriage and wagon work-

shops were opened in 1839 and the construction of loco-motives began in 1843. After the closure of the original London & Southampton terminus, the station was partly used as a works extension for carriage work and partly as new running shed accommodation. In 1865 the shed and works were transferred to a new site on the other side of the main line, which had room for expansion, and the original station area was made over completely to a goods depot. As a result of the need to expand the goods facilities further, the main line from Waterloo was shifted, requiring the engine shed to be moved yet again. This time a large semi-circular roundhouse, radiating from two turntables, was built to the south of the works. To meet the ever-expanding needs, the first part of the final shed building was erected in the late 1880s, and as space began to become limited the carriage and wagon works were transferred to Eastleigh in 1890. The need for yet further extension of goods facilities, following the development of Southampton Docks, resulted in the transfer of the locomotive works to Eastleigh by 1909, the last locomotive being built at Nine Elms in the summer of 1908. Closure of the roundhouse also led to the con-struction of a new straight shed alongside the existing one, giving the depot layout as it remained until closure in 1967.

Longhedge, like Nine Elms, was also closely associated with its running shed, renamed Stewarts Lane in 1934. The workshops were established in about

1862, and in 1881 the locomotive shed was recon-structed from a 'half-moon' roundhouse to a straight shed, together with further extensions to the work-shops. By this time, for a railway of its size the LCDR possessed excellent workshop facilities, but after the working merger with the SER in 1899 it was soon decided that the location was too cramped and transfer was made to Ashford. The last locomotive was built in 1904, a Wainwright Class C goods engine, and general repair and rebuilding, with which the works had been heavily involved, ceased in 1912. Part of the site was leased to industry but some was transferred to other railway uses. The former erecting shop was retained for repairs as part of the locomotive depot and the carriage works was rebuilt as a carriage shed when the works moved to Ashford. The shed itself was further improved in 1934 in conjunction with the closure of Battersea Park and the electrification of the Brighton main line, and was equipped to service about 170 locomotives. With further electrification, the shed was run down and closed to steam in 1963 and most of the old works buildings still retained were demolished by 1979.

On London Transport, Acton is the main overhaul workshops for the Underground, but Neasden provided workshops for the Metropolitan from 1888 when a substantial shed was also built to service the Metropolitan's locomotive stock. Extension of electrification and transfer of goods work to the LNER in the 1930s resulted in run-down, but steam had its finale on LT in 1971 from the two small depots retained at Lillie Bridge and Neasden.

Housing

The influence of railways on housing development is well-known and recorded, while railwaymen's cottages are still to be found throughout the London area. There are, however, few remaining easily recognisable large-scale housing areas built by the railway companies to house their employees, examples such as 'Hudson's Town' at Stratford having largely succumbed to the redevelopers. Stephenson Street and Crewe Place at Willesden reflect their past, but it is Neasden which possibly provides the best example of railway housing. Built for employees at the Metropolitan Railway's workshops and locomotive depot Quainton Street and Verney Street are a far cry from their rural counterparts of North Buckinghamshire. Indeed, Claydon House, former home of Sir Harry Verney who, with the Duke of Buckingham, helped develop the railways of Buckinghamshire, would have little in common with those in the street which has inherited the family name.

TABLE 2

LOCOMOTIVE DEPOTS AND SERVICING POINTS IN THE LONDON AREA, TAKEN OVER BY BRITISH RAILWAYS IN 1948

Notes:

Shed codes were introduced on all Regions in 1950, based on the LMSR system. Prior to then, only former GWR locomotives displayed a letter code on the frames.

Some depots were transferred between regions – the previous codes indicate this – while some came into London areas from other districts.

Shed types are: R = wholly or partially 'roundhouse'; 1 = Main line depots; 2 = suburban and local work depots; 3 = more specialist freight operating depots; 4 = depots for branch, miscellaneous, and minor operating. These classifications are broadly-based only.

Dates are included only where positively established. Dashes indicate where facilities are still in use, although not necessarily on same site.

LONDON MIDLAND REGION

BR code (final)	Name	Previous code	Type	Opened	Closed (steam)	Closed (final)
1A	WILLESDEN		3R	1873	1965	—
1B	CAMDEN		1	1837/8	1962	1966
1C	WATFORD		2	c1856	1965	1965
1E	BLETCHLEY	2B; 4A	2	c1851	1965	—
	Leighton Buzzard		4	1859	1962	1962
	Newport Pagnell		4	1866	1955	1955
1J	DEVONS ROAD (BOW)	13B; 1D	3	1882	1958	1964
14A	CRICKLEWOOD		3R	1882	1964	—
	Bedford	15D; 14E; 14C	2	1868	1963	1971
14B	KENTISH TOWN		1R	1867/8	1963	1963
14C	ST ALBANS		2	1868	1960	1960
14D	NEASDEN	34E	1	1899	1962	1962
	Aylesbury Town		4	1863	1962	1962
	Chesham		4		1961	1961
	Rickmansworth		4	1925	1961	1961

EASTERN REGION

BR code (final)	Name	Previous code	Type	Opened	Closed (steam)	Closed (final)
30A	STRATFORD		1	1841	1962	—
	Brentwood		2		1949	1949
	Chelmsford		2		1958	1958
	Epping		2		1957	1957
	Spitalfields		3			

BR code	Name	Previous code	Type	Opened	Closed (steam)	Closed (final)
	Wood St (Walthamstow)		2	1879	1960	1960
	Ongar		4	1865	1949	1949
	Palace Gates		2		1954	1954
	Enfield Town		2		1960	1960
	Ware		4	c1930	1960	1960
	Tilbury	13C; 33B	4		1962	1962
30B	HERTFORD EAST		2	1843	1960	1960
	Buntingford		4	1863	1959	1959
30C	BISHOPS STORTFORD		2	1842	1960	1960
30D	SOUTHEND (VICTORIA)		2		1959	1959
	Southminster		4		1956	1956
	Wickford		4	c1890	1953	1953
33A	PLAISTOW	13A	2		1959	1962
	Upminster	13E	4		1956	1956
33C	SHOEBURYNESS	13D	2		1962	1962
34A	KINGS CROSS		1	1850	1963	1963
34B	HORNSEY		3	1899 (a)	1961	(b)
34C	HATFIELD		2		1961	1961
34D	HITCHIN		2		1961	(c)

(a) Reconstruction of earlier GNR shed
(b) Closed to diesel servicing in early 1970s but still used partly for overhead line maintenance
(c) Original depot replaced by diesel depot north of station now used for track machines and diesel shunters.

SOUTHERN REGION

BR code (final)	Name	Previous code	Type	Opened	Closed (steam)	Closed (final)
70A	NINE ELMS		1	1838	1967	1967
70B	FELTHAM		3	c1923	1967	1970
70C	GUILDFORD		2R	1887	1967	
	Bordon		4	1905	1949	1949
	Reading South	70E	2	c1852	1965	1969
(Sub 70D)	Basingstoke SR	70D	1	1905	1967	1967
73B	BRICKLAYERS ARMS		1	1844	1962	
	Ewer Street		1	c1899	1961	1961
	New Cross Gate		2R	1839	1949	1957
73C	HITHER GREEN		3	1933	1961	—
(Sub 73J)	Gillingham (Kent)	73D	2	c1885	1960	1960
(Sub 73F)	Tonbridge	74D; 73J	2	c1842	1964	1965
75B	REDHILL		2	c1855	1965	1965
	Three Bridges	75E; sub 75A; sub 75B	2	1909	1964	1965
	Tunbridge Wells West	75F; sub 75A; sub 75B	2	1890	1963	1965
75C	NORWOOD JUNCTION		3	1935	1964	1965
75D	STEWARTS LANE	73A	1	1862	1963	—
(Sub 75A)	Horsham	75D; sub 75E	2R	1896	1964	1964

Note: 70D – Eastleigh; 75A Brighton

WESTERN REGION

BR code (final)	Name	Previous code	Type	Opened	Closed (steam)	Closed (final)
81A	OLD OAK COMMON	PDN	1R	1906	1965	—
81B	SLOUGH	SLO	2	1868	1964	1964
	Marlow		4	1872	1962	1962
	Watlington		4	1872	1957	1957
81C	SOUTHALL	SHL	3	1884	1965	—
	Staines		4	1885	1952	1952
81D	READING	RDG	2	c1880	1965	—
	Henley-on-Thames		4	c1857	1958	1958
	Basingstoke GWR		4	c1850	1950	1950

12
HARDLY A TRACE

Services Lost

Railway closures have occurred in the area covered by this book like they have in the rest of the country. The growth of road competition and the legacy of duplication from pre-grouping companies are always the general reasons for closure but in the London area there are certain special factors at work. Looking at closed stations or lines, or what remains of them, an observer wonders what particular factors lead to closure. Of course the general reasons were present but were there particular circumstances to each case? The aim of this chapter is to look at four stations and try to find the reasons why each closed.

However, a general examination is worthwhile to set the background against which each case can be studied. The first step is to divide the area into urban London (ie the built-up area) and its more rural surroundings. Closures in this latter area include such lines as the Great Eastern Buntingford and the Great Northern St Albans branches, the Midland line from Hitchin to Bedford, the LNWR Aylesbury branch, the GWR line from Bourne End to High Wycombe, the LSWR Bisley branch, the LBSCR line from Three Bridges to Groombridge and the SECR Westerham branch. Looking at these, rationalisation of duplicating facilities is apparent in the St Albans and Aylesbury lines; other pre-grouping companies had provided more convenient routes, and closure came relatively early in the 1950s. The Bisley branch performed a specialist function of serving the rifle ranges – operated only when meetings were held, it closed in 1952. Bedford to Hitchin had originally formed part of the Midland route to London, and the opening of the St Pancras Extension in 1868 had left the earlier line an uneasy role as a rural branch, so it joined the rest of the examples as victims of the round of closures from 1960, where road competition had left them with little traffic.

In the urban area of London, while duplication of facilities was one reason for closure, changes in population or travel patterns as well as competition from other forms of public transport were the principal

causes. Examples of branch closures in this area are those by the GER to Palace Gates, the GNR to Alexandra Palace, the LNWR to Stanmore, and the GWR lines to Uxbridge. Further casualties have been the LSWR Kensington to Hammersmith line, the SECR Greenwich Park branch and the North & South Western Junction line to Hammersmith & Chiswick. A particular cause is more difficult to identify in this group, as all suffered competition from more convenient services but the Palace Gates branch was especially affected by changed travel patterns. The Alexandra Palace line would have been incorporated into the Underground system but for the interruption of World War II. In the 1950s buses were thought a better alternative, so the line closed.

Station closures on lines which remain open are again difficult to attribute to one cause. Generally these are in the inner suburban area, where road transport is better placed to serve passenger traffic or where the line does not fit travel patterns. An example of the first is Mildmay Park on the North London Line and Chelsea & Fulham on the West London illustrates the second. A further reason for closure can be that alternative facilities were provided. Coburn Road, between Stratford and Bethnal Green on the GE main line, was closed in 1946 because the Central Line Extension provided a better route to Liverpool Street from its Mile End and Bethnal Green stations, and closure would speed up the train service and increase line capacity.

To develop these themes further sample stations have been selected for more detailed study. Gravesend (West Street) has closed completely as has the line that served it. Dudding Hill has also closed for all services although the line that served it continues to be used by freight trains. Camberwell is again totally closed, but the line remains open for passenger traffic. Stratford Market has closed to passengers but is open for freight; both types of traffic continue to use the line that serves it.

Gravesend (West Street):
To understand the reasons for the closure of the LCDR

Railway Cartage *A memory of a former railway service is given by this view of an LNER parcels van at Marylebone in 1948. The railway cartage fleet passed to National Carriers in 1969 and the collection and delivery of parcels ceased from 1 July 1981, although a restricted service is again offered. Nowadays BR concentrates on its Red Star premium parcels service, limited to a station to station service.*
Rev A. W. V. Mace

Necropolis Funeral Train *A very specialist traffic was that in funerals from the Necropolis station at Waterloo to Brookwood Cemetery with special trains restricted to coffins and mourners. A very Victorian 'improving' mixture of public health and steam railways, it was inaugurated in 1854 and lasted until 1941. In 1902 a train for a double funeral passes Wimbledon on the 50 minute run from Waterloo to Brookwood.* Lens of Sutton/Pamlin Prints

Belmont *After 1952 passenger services on the former LNWR Stanmore branch were truncated at Belmont, a halt which had been opened in 1932 to serve the newly developed suburb. Increased business caused reconstruction into an island platform by 1937 but bus competition and mounting losses brought closure in 1964.* Harrow Observer

Hammersmith & Chiswick *This was the terminus of a 1½ mile branch from the North & South Western Junction at South Acton. Its construction was controversial as the shareholders saw no reason for it, reasonably enough as it was a mile west of Hammersmith. Passenger services, which eventually served three intermediate halts, were withdrawn in 1916 and freight in 1965.*
Locomotive & General Railway Photographs

Gravesend Station and the line from Fawkham Junction, it is first necessary to understand the reason for its construction. Gravesend, and particularly the Rosherville Gardens, had considerable importance for leisure traffic from London. Bank holidays would see considerable traffic to the Gardens from their opening in 1840, which was at first catered for by steamers. This traffic was obviously attractive to railways and was first served by the South Eastern Railway North Kent line, opened in 1849. Five years later an alternative route was established when the LTSR opened its line to Tilbury with a ferry service to Gravesend. Matters remained unchanged until 1881 when an Act for this line to Gravesend was obtained. The LCDR had begun life as the East Kent Railway in 1853, to build a line from

Strood to Dover as an extension of the South Eastern. Subsequent developments changed the name of the company and its objective to a line to London of its own. As a first stage, it opened a line from Strood to Bickley in 1860 and in the open competition it indulged in with the SER, would no doubt wish to obtain its share of the Gravesend traffic. So it comes as no surprise that the junction with its main line faced London, or that the LCDR took-over the local company before the first sod had been cut.

Opening of the line on 10 May 1886 took place on the same day as the opening of the LCDR terminus at St Paul's, the company having previously stated that the line would have to await the increased terminal capacity. The initial train service was 14 trains each way on weekdays and eight on Sundays; all were through trains to and from London. With a small engine shed at Rosherville, two locomotives could be stabled overnight. Rosherville station was of the island type and had two wide stairways to cater for the crowds going to the gardens. Alas, the lush days for Rosherville were short. The gardens closed in 1900, re-opened in 1903 but closed for good in 1910, so the line served the gardens for only 21 years. After this traffic ceased, Rosherville station lost its importance. It was reduced to an unstaffed halt in 1928 and closed on 15 July 1933. A brief role as a Continental boat train route to serve the Dutch Batavier line from the pier that extended beyond Gravesend West Street station did not last; by the 1950s the pier was reduced to serving a pleasure ship during the summer season.

In an attempt to increase local traffic, a service of push-and-pull trains was introduced in July 1913 when Longfield Halt was opened. The service operated from Swanley Junction, a practice which continued until closure, although in latter years some terminated at Farningham Road. Drastic cuts in service during World War II left three morning and two afternoon trains, catering mainly for workmen and school children. Closure to passengers of Gravesend (West), as the station was renamed on 26 September 1949, and its branch to passengers on 3 August 1953 therefore came as no surprise. The branch had lost the major reason for its existence with the closure of Rosherville Gardens, and left it a role to cater for such local traffic as was available. With the SER line from Gravesend Central providing a satisfactory service to London there was little purpose left for the LCDR line. Perhaps the rationalisation should have occurred after the SER and LCDR formed a working union in 1899, or perhaps after the Southern Railway was formed in 1923, both being times where these lines came under common management. In the event it had to wait until BR days. The station at Gravesend (West) had a further 15 years

Edgware Edgware was reached by the London Electric Railway in 1924; subsequent housing development was rapid based upon bus and tube services. Realised and anticipated suburban growth was one reason for the 1935 plan to integrate the LNER Edgware branch of 1867 into the Underground system and use the LPTB Edgware station. Although work commenced in October 1937, it was ultimately abandoned, but traces still remain today. B. R. Hardy

Palace Gates Palace Gates was the terminus of the Great Eastern's 2¾ mile branch to serve Alexandra Palace. Opened in 1878, this 1911 view towards Seven Sisters clearly shows its through station layout. Whilst the Palace did not produce the traffic anticipated, housing development, notably at Noel Park, provided its passengers until alternative transport facilities and changed travel patterns led to closure in 1963. British Rail

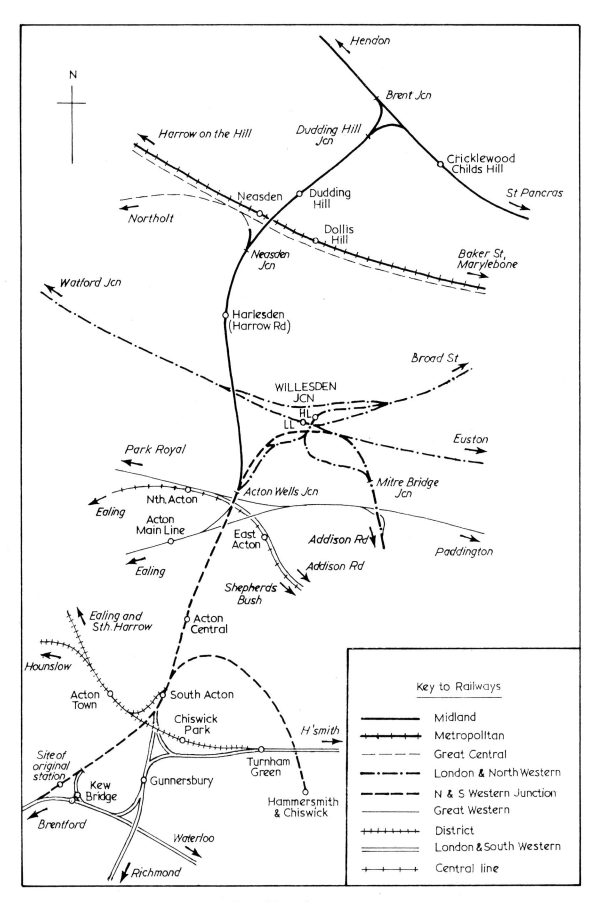

N

Hendon

Brent Jcn

Dudding Hill Jcn

Cricklewood Childs Hill

St Pancras

Harrow on the Hill

Neasden

Dudding Hill

Dollis Hill

Northolt

Neasden Jcn

Baker St, Marylebone

Watford Jcn

Harlesden (Harrow Rd)

Broad St

WILLESDEN JCN

HL

LL

Euston

Mitre Bridge Jcn

Park Royal

Acton Wells Jcn

Nth. Acton

Ealing

Acton Main Line

East Acton

Addison Rd

Ealing

Addison Rd

Paddington

Shepherds Bush

Ealing and Sth. Harrow

Acton Central

Hounslow

Acton Town

South Acton

Chiswick Park

H'smith

Site of original station

Kew Bridge

Gunnersbury

Turnham Green

Brentford

Waterloo

Hammersmith & Chiswick

Richmond

Key to Railways

————————	Midland
—+—+—+—	Metropolitan
– – – – – –	Great Central
—·—·—·—	London & North Western
— — — —	N & S Western Junction
————————	Great Western
+++++++++	District
══════════	London & South Western
+—+—+—+	Central line

The North & South Western Junction Railway, Dudding Hill loop and their connections.

of life as a goods depot since the former SER station at Gravesend was in a very restricted site. On 25 March 1968 all services were withdrawn.

Dudding Hill:

Dudding Hill station was situated on the link from the Midland main line to Acton Wells Junction. 3¾ miles in length, the line was opened in 1868 and at its northern end formed a triangular junction with the main line, one facing Cricklewood and one Hendon. Promoted by an independent company, the Midland did not absorb it until 1874, but its value must have been apparent to the Midland from the opening of its independent route into St Pancras from Bedford in 1868. 150 acres of land had been purchased at Brent Junction by the Midland for locomotive sheds and for a marshalling yard. The link, the Dudding Hill loop, enabled the London & South Western to be reached, and by use of running powers in course of time would enable the Midland to develop its coal traffic to depots in West London, such as High Street Kensington. The principal purpose of the line was therefore freight.

However, the Midland determined to develop passenger traffic on this link, opening two stations in 1875. Dudding Hill station, built in red brick with two side platforms, was situated in a cutting immediately before the line passed under a road overbridge. The initial service ran from Moorgate, Kentish Town and St Pancras to Richmond, which was reached over the LSWR line through Gunnersbury. The service only lasted for seven months and was replaced by a shuttle service from Harrow Road, the other station on the line, to Childs Hill, to-day's Cricklewood. Connections were arranged at Childs Hill with trains in each direction on the Midland main line.

Two years later the Midland experimented with a revised service in an attempt to increase patronage, when the line formed part of a 'Super Outer Circle'. Starting from St Pancras, these trains gained the LSWR at Acton, to reach the District for the run to the other terminus at Earl's Court. This service met with as little success as its predecessor, so the Midland reverted to the former shuttle. By 1887 there were ten trains each way in a day, although two only in each direction ran on Saturdays. Workers would seem to have been the principal traffic as services were concentrated in morning and evening peaks with a gap from approximately 10.00 to 16.00. This gap was only broken by trains bringing passengers home after a morning's work. Patronage must again have been light as the Midland closed the line to passengers from 2 July 1888.

Uxbridge Vine Street *Uxbridge Vine Street, seen here in November 1931, was the first of the town's three stations. It opened in 1856 and until 1904, with the opening of the Metropolitan line, had the monopoly of rail transport. Extension of the Metropolitan to the High Street in 1938 by the LPTB dealt passenger traffic at Vine Street a mortal blow from which it finally expired in 1962. Hillingdon Borough Libraries*

South Acton *In order to run the shuttle between Acton Town and South Acton, London Transport in 1939 modified two G cars to operate as single units for one-man operation. From a special short platform at Acton Town, the 1950s saw a service about every ten minutes to the LT platform at South Acton seen in January 1959, a month before the last train.* T. Wright

Determined to try once more, the shuttle resumed on 1 March 1893, but was attended by no greater success than before. Despite an extension of services to Gunnersbury in 1894, the Midland bowed to the inevitable and withdrew all passenger services on the line in 1902, one of the few closures to passengers in the London area before World War I.

Perhaps a reason for closure can be found in the nature of the service that the Midland provided. It was a circular service around the western side of London, whereas passengers required a radial line into the centre of London. This was to hand in the shape of the Metropolitan which had opened its line to Willesden Green in 1879 and on to Harrow in the next year. With its station at Neasden, the Metropolitan was much better placed to serve the same area as Dudding Hill and this would appear to be the principal reason for the demise of Midland passenger services.

For freight traffic the situation was the reverse, as the Metropolitan stations were for passengers only, and so long as freight reached its destination the routing was less important. Located close to the Midland yard at Brent, a service by local trip freights was comparatively easy to arrange and so Dudding Hill remained open for freight until 1964.

Camberwell:

When the LCDR set its sights on London, it decided to have both a City and a West End terminus. Victoria fulfilled the latter function and as part of its extension to London, the LCDR promoted a line from Herne Hill to the Metropolitan at Farringdon. An impecunious railway, it realised the value of this link to other companies to enable them to work their trains across London. It managed to persuade the LSWR and the GNR to contribute towards the cost of the line, which was opened in sections. Camberwell was built on the first stage to Elephant & Castle, opened in 1862, but the final link to the Metropolitan was not completed until 1866. In addition, spurs were provided to the South London Line at Brixton and Denmark Hill from Loughborough Junction in 1863 and 1872 respectively.

A wide range of services was soon developed using the new cross-London link. The LSWR operated services from Ludgate Hill first to Kingston, then to

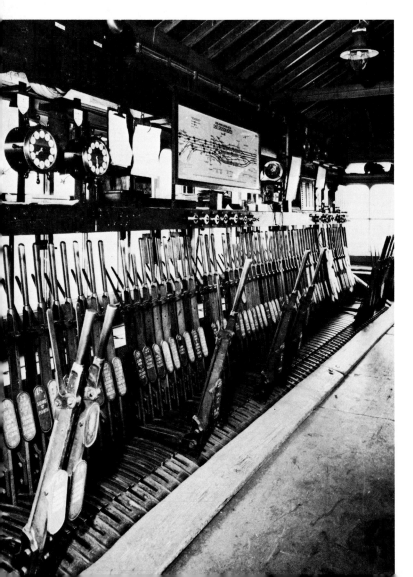

East Croydon *As resignalling progresses, manual signalboxes are replaced by power boxes. An early casualty was the 84-lever East Croydon North displaced in the final stage of the Brighton line colour-light resignalling scheme and demolished in July 1955. Prominent in this interior view of the box are the Walkers' Rotary Train Describers, the track layout diagram and the gas lighting.* London Borough of Croydon

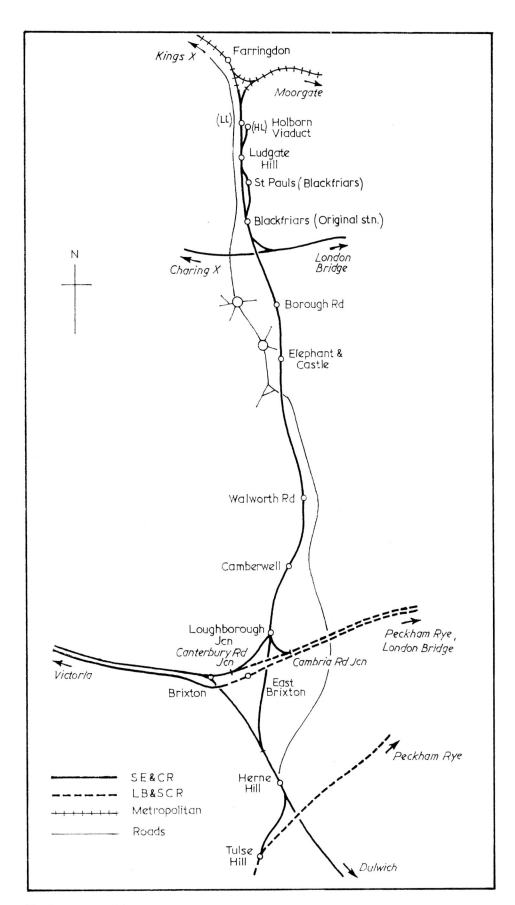

The City extension of the LCDR.

Richmond and Wimbledon. The LCDR ran one from Clapham Junction, as well as a joint service with the GNR to destinations like Barnet, Edgware and Hatfield. Similarly, the LCDR joined with the Midland in working to such places as Hendon. The services between the GNR and SER, although using this link, left it at Blackfriars Junction before Camberwell station was reached. In addition, the importance of the route through Camberwell for freight traffic has been shown elsewhere.

Interesting as these cross-London facilities no doubt were, it was the statutory workmen's service that would have been of most importance to Camberwell. Parliament had realised that the construction of this railway would involve the demolition of a large amount of property, largely occupied by unskilled workmen. To cater for those displaced, who it was presumed would be rehoused further from the centre of London, a train service was instituted in 1865 between Victoria and Ludgate Hill. Leaving each terminus at 04.55, each of the two trains returned at 18.15, except on Saturday when they returned at 14.30. Weekly tickets, good for six return journeys, were sold for 1s 0d [5p], valid between any station on the route and one of the termini.

Camberwell, although provided on the Extension from the outset, was not at the heart of suburban development for a number of years, and while the line was quadrupled between Loughborough Junction and Blackfriars within a year of its opening this was to cater for flows coming on to the line rather than local traffic. While it is difficult to generalise, it would seem that before 1870 train fares were not cheap enough for local families whose budgets hardly permitted a daily journey to work. It was the workman's ticket which really developed Camberwell. The LCDR's arrangements already mentioned were supplemented from 1883 by the Cheap Trains Act, compelling all railway companies to introduce workmen's fares as and when required by the Board of Trade. Camberwell's story in the last thirty years of the century was an increase of traffic as the suburb expanded.

But as rail traffic grew, so it did also on the trams and buses that were finally to cause closure of Camberwell. The Extension was paralleled for all its length by roads which enabled effective tramway competition to develop from 1872, radically strengthened in the first decade of the twentieth century when the LCC took over the horse tramway system and electrified it. Trains continued to call at Camberwell until 1916, when the Victoria to Ludgate Hill service was withdrawn. After World War I, the Southern Railway took the obvious step. Receipts at Camberwell had declined from £3,800 in 1905 to £700 in 1914 and there seemed no prospect of

regaining the passengers that had deserted to tram and bus. Accordingly, the wooden viaduct structure was demolished around the end of 1923.

Stratford Market:

Stratford Market station is an example of the rare situation where a station is only open for goods traffic, although the line that serves it continues to see passenger and freight services. Its location was on the Stratford to North Woolwich branch, a ¼-mile towards Woolwich from Stratford Low Level platforms. The branch, whose history is told elsewhere, was opened in two parts. Stratford Market opened with the second stage on 14 June 1847, when with Canning Town it was one of the two intermediate stations. It was located alongside the High Street, the main road into Essex, later to become the A11, and because the road crossed the railway by a bridge, at first took the obvious name of Stratford Bridge. It might be wondered why this station was necessary when the main Stratford station was so close; the principal reason was the pattern of the initial service. In order to provide a through service from Bishopsgate to North Woolwich, a south-to-west spur had been constructed at Stratford. This meant that Woolwich trains had to leave the main line before reaching Stratford station and join the branch after it had passed under the main line. Stratford was too important to be missed and so Stratford Bridge station was built. If a station had to be provided, it made sense to locate it by the main road to serve the centre of Stratford.

The change of name to Stratford Market came on 1 November 1880 and recognised the establishment of the Great Eastern Railway's market in the previous year. Seeking to develop its agricultural traffic, the company set up a fruit and vegetable market on the London side of the line to the south of the station. Alongside it was the company's goods and coal depot, and the principal road access was from Burford Road.

As traffic on the North Woolwich line grew, it became necessary to increase the two tracks through Stratford Market to four. This necessitated rebuilding the station and the bridge under the High Street. The original station building was in Bridge Road parallel to the line, with a footbridge link between platforms. Under the new arrangements the buildings were on the High Street bridge with a flight of stairs to each platform, although there were only platforms on the two passenger lines.

Intensive passenger services on the Woolwich line continued until the outbreak of World War II. However, the beginnings of competition came in 1938 when London Transport opened a trolleybus service from Stratford to North Woolwich. Previously water

Lordship Lane *The LCDR served the Crystal Palace by a branch which climbed from Peckham Rye. As it crossed Dulwich College lands, special architectural treatment was given to the intermediate station of Lordship Lane. Some idea of the villas it served in 1871 can be obtained from this painting by the French impressionist Camille Pissarro.* Courtauld Institute Galleries

Dunton Green *On the fringe of the London area, the branch from Dunton Green to Westerham remained steam operated by a push-pull unit until closure in 1961. While hopes were entertained that services could be resumed by a preservation society, the construction of the Sevenoaks By-Pass put paid to the idea. Here Class H 0-4-4T No 31177 with the branch train is seen alongside the main line in 1959.* C. G. Maggs

and rail barriers had restricted competition from road transport, but the construction of Silvertown Way changed this. World War II saw the evacuation of labour from Dockland and considerable bomb damage to housing in the area. When these factors are put together, it is not surprising that the reduced level of traffic after the war was better catered for by road transport. The inevitable result of this was the closure of Stratford Market on 6 May 1957; the real need for it had disappeared when the train service was withdrawn from the south-to-west spur at Stratford and instead diverted into the low-level platforms at Stratford. It no longer made sense to operate two stations so close together, and Stratford station could serve the commercial centre as well as Stratford Market. That left the goods service in operation, a situation which remains today, although the vegetable market is largely road-served.

Summary

Summarising the predominant reasons for closure to passengers, it can be seen that Gravesend closed because

187

Bishopsgate *Opened in 1840 as the Eastern Counties Railway terminus, Bishopsgate was replaced by Liverpool Street in 1875. Six years later it took up a new role as a goods depot which continued until it was destroyed by fire in 1964. This August 1912 view shows a miscellany of wagons, a good selection of horse-drawn cartage, and roof repairs in progress.* British Rail

the traffic it was built to serve ceased and an alternative rail route met the town's transport requirements. Dudding Hill's services failed to match the journeys that many of its intending passengers required. Road transport provided a more convenient service than rail services at Camberwell, a situation which was also true at Stratford Market, although in the latter case movement in population reduced demand and the routing of train services was altered.

Preservation

While this chapter has been principally concerned with closed railways or facilities in the London area, some comment on specific preservation activities is helpful. A convenient division is between official preservation and the activities of enthusiasts.

The two prominent examples of official preservation are the Science Museum and the London Transport Museum. The Land Transport Collection in the Science Museum features a number of railway exhibits, some like the City & South London Railway electric locomotive with a specifically London flavour, although others like the prototype *Deltic* were regularly seen at work in the Capital. The Science Museum main collection is held at the National Railway Museum at York, where further facets of London's railways may be studied. The second official preservation project is the London Transport Museum. Originally housed in the Museum of British Transport at Clapham, LT's exhibits moved to Syon Park in 1973 but their present home, the former flower market at Covent Garden, was

King Cross *The station was resignalled with colour lights in 1932, controlled from a 232 lever frame in the signalbox at the platform ends. The complex trackwork between the platforms and the tunnel mouths imposed low speed levels and restrictions on train operation. Replaced by a new power signalbox in 1973, which can be seen behind the old structure, a station landmark disappeared.* E. Wilmshurst

Battersea Park *This view of LBSCR locomotives inside Battersea Park shed in 1921 shows one of its three covered roundhouses whose tracks radiated from a central turntable. Electrification of the Brighton line led to its closure in 1934 and the transfer of its locomotives to the former LCDR shed at Longhedge which was renamed Stewarts Lane.* H. C. Casserley

opened in 1980. Among the railway exhibits are former Metropolitan Railway A Class 4-4-0T No 23, an Aveling & Porter geared locomotive from the Brill branch, a District Line Q23 driving motor car and a Metropolitan Railway compartment coach.

There are many examples of enthusiast preservation projects, although these tend to be at some distance from Central London and to lie outside the area of this book. Projects are at present in the early stages of development at Crystal Palace, alongside the former LBSCR station, and at North Woolwich the station building and one platform will be incorporated into a Great Eastern Railway museum. Looking a little further afield, Great Western practice is well represented at Didcot, Southern operations feature prominently on the Bluebell Railway between Horstead Keynes and Sheffield Park, and a wide variety of rolling stock is to be found at the Quainton Railway Centre, north of Aylesbury. Although these projects touch upon aspects of the London railway scene, there is no centre specifically concentrating on this.

Although it is costly to re-instate and maintain operational facilities with historical links, these do form part of Britain's architectural heritage, and the London termini retain several examples of listed buildings of considerable historical and architectural merit. Their preservation does great credit to British Rail. For the discerning eye there is still much to be seen on and along London's railways. It is to be hoped that examples of this heritage can be saved before the march of progress sweeps everything aside in the effort to create London's railways of tomorrow.

Quainton Road *Now on the BR single-line connection from Aylesbury to Claydon, Quainton Road has adopted a new role of a preservation centre. Steam trips are offered from the former Brill branch platform on the right while stock awaiting restoration can be seen in the yard on the other side of the BR line. DMUs have operated special shuttle services to Aylesbury on certain open days. M. D. Grant*

SOURCES AND BIBLIOGRAPHY

This section provides a comprehensive selection of available material for further reading, although it is not an exhaustive list.

General

Baker, S. K. *Rail Atlas of Britain* (Oxford 1978)
Bennet, A. E. and Borley, H. V. *London Transport Railways* (Dawlish 1963)
—— *British Railways Pre-Grouping Atlas and Gazetteer* (Shepperton 1963)
Clinker, C. R. *Clinker's Register of Closed Passenger Stations and Goods Depots in England, Scotland and Wales 1830–1977* (Bristol 1978)
Cockman, F. G. *The Railways of Hertfordshire* (Hertford 1979)
Course, E. *London Railways* (1962)
Course, E. *The Railways of Southern England: The Main Lines* (1973)
Jackson, Alan A. *London's Local Railways* (Newton Abbot 1978)
Jackson, Alan A. *London's Termini* (Newton Abbot 1969)
Klapper, Charles *London's Lost Railways* (1976)
Klapper, Charles *Roads and Rails of London 1900–1933* (1976)
Morrison, Brian *London Steam in the Fifties* (1975)
—— *Railway Junction Diagrams 1915* (Reprinted Newton Abbot 1969)
White, H. P. *A Regional History of the Railways of Great Britain.*
  Volume III Greater London (1963)
In addition Oakwood Press has published a series of company and line histories.

1 Setting the Scene

Barker, T. C. and Robbins, Michael *A History of London Transport.*
  Volume I The Nineteenth Century (1963)
  Volume II The Twentieth Century to 1970 (1974)
Grinling, Charles H. *The History of the Great Northern Railway* (Supplemented by H. V. Borley and C. Hamilton Ellis) (1966)
Jackson, Alan A. *Semi-Detached London* (1973)
Jackson, Alan A. 'Romford to Grays' *Railway World* (December 1979)
Robbins, Michael *The Railway Age* (1965)

2 In the Beginning

Bennett, Alfred Rosling *The First Railway in London* (1972)
Dendy Marshall, C. F. *A History of the Southern Railway* (Second (Enlarged) Edition in Two Volumes. Revised by R. W. Kidner) (1963)
Dickenson, H. W. and Titley, A. *Richard Trevithick* (Cambridge 1934)
Hadfield, Charles *Atmospheric Railways* (Newton Abbot 1967)
Hopwood, H. L. 'The London and Blackwall Railway' *Railway Magazine* (May 1927)

Lane, Philip 'Croydon, Merstham & Godstone discoveries' *Railway World* (August 1972)

Lee, Charles E. 'Early Railways in Surrey' *Transactions of the Newcomen Society for the History of Engineering & Technology* (Volume XX1-1940)

—— 'The Gauge of the Surrey Iron Railway' *Railway Magazine* (August 1967)

Thomas, R. H. G. *London's First Railway – The London & Greenwich* (1972)

Townsend, Charles E. C. 'Further Notes on Early Railways in Surrey' *Transactions of the Newcomen Society for the History of Engineering & Technology* (Volume XXVIII-1949)

Whishaw, Francis *Whishaw's Railways of Great Britain & Ireland* (1842, reprinted Newton Abbot 1969)

3 Termini

Allen, Cecil J. 'The St. Pancras Centenary' *Railway World* (October 1968)

Betjeman, John *London's Historic Railway Stations* (1971)

Curtis, J. S. 'Old Euston, Parts 1-3' *Railway World* (Sept.-Nov. 1965)

Jackson, Alan A. 'First Hundred Years of Liverpool Street' *Railway Magazine* (February 1974)

Jackson, Alan A. *London's Termini* (Newton Abbot 1969)

Lee, Charles E. 'Cannon Street 1866–1966' *Railway Magazine* (Aug./Sept. 1966)

Lee, Charles E. 'Charing Cross Station 1864–1964' *Railway Magazine* (January 1964)

Lee, Charles E. 'St. Pancras Station 1868–1968' *Railway Magazine* (Sept./Oct. 1968)

Lee, Charles E. 'Useful but Unloved' (Ludgate Hill) *Railway Magazine* (December 1964, February 1965)

'Liverpool Street and the G.E. line' *Railway World* (November 1969)

—— *Liverpool Street Station* (1978)

Marx, Klaus 'Waterloo's Waterloo' *Railway World* (July 1977)

Marsden, Colin J. *This is Waterloo* (1981)

Perren, Brian 'Kings Cross Today' *Railway World* (March 1969)

—— *Discovering London Railway Stations* (1970)

Simmons, Jack *St. Pancras Station* (1968)

Weight, R. A. H. 'Behind the scenes and up front' (St. Pancras) *Railway World* (December 1967, June 1968)

Whitehead, Alan 'Steam behind the Propylaeum' (Euston) *Railway World* (February 1978)

4 Main Lines

Allen, Cecil J. *The Great Eastern Railway* (1955)

Butler, P. 'The Midland before Electrification' *Railway World* (July 1981)

Cooper, B. K. 'Worldwide from Gatwick' *Railway World* (June 1975)

Fellows, Reginald B. *London to Cambridge by Train* (Cambridge Reprinted 1976)

Gadsden, E. J. S. 'Last rites on the GC' *Railway World* (November 1966)

Hamilton, Ellis C. *The London, Brighton & South Coast Railway* (1972)

Harris, Michael 'When "Schools" worked to Hastings' *Railway World* (December 1977)

Kidner, R. W. *The Reading to Tunbridge Line* (1974)

Neve, Eric 'Hatfield – a once busy Junction' *Railway World* (April 1980)

Neve, Eric 'Kings Cross Steam Finale' *Railway World* (March 1978)

Neve, Eric 'The Great Northern route to Cambridge' *Railway World* (Nov./Dec. 1977)

Rounthwaite, T. E. *The Midland Railway London Extension 1868–1968* (1968)

Rugman, W. J. 'The Croydon & Oxted Joint and Woodside & South Croydon Railways' *Railway World* (December 1974)

Stanton, Henry 'South Eastern into Sussex' *Railway World* (October 1974)
Treby, Edward 'The Central Croydon branch' *Railway World* (March 1974)
Webster, V. R. 'Via Reading' *Railway World* (March 1979)
Winkworth, D. W. 'Belle Trains' *Railway Magazine* (May 1972)

5 For Business

Allen, Cecil J. 'Olympia and the West London line' *Railway World* (August 1969)
—— Bedford – Moorgate Electrics' *Railway Magazine* (February 1977)
Bonavia, Michael R. 'The Waterloo & City Railway' *Railway World* (July 1979)
Burnham, T. G. 'Branch to Bromley North' *Railway Magazine* (February 1975)
Farr, K. S. 'Seen in the GN Suburbs' *Railway World* (February 1976)
Faulkner, J. N. 'The Shepperton Branch of the Southern Region' *Railway World* (February 1964)
Fenton, Mike 'The Maidenhead to Marlow Branch' *Railway World* (February 1976)
Hessleton, Kenneth Y. *Sunbury & Thames Valley Railway* (Sunbury 1976)
Hodge, Peter *The Hertford Loop* (Southgate 1977)
Jackson, Alan A. 'Brent Valley Railcars' *Railway World* (May 1979)
Jackson, Alan A. 'Racing to Residential: the Wimbledon & Epsom line' *Railway World* (July 1980)
Jackson, Alan A. 'The Wimbledon & Sutton Railway' *Railway Magazine* (December 1966)
Kerr, G. M. 'Trans-Thames to Richmond' *Railway Magazine* (Aug./Sept. 1980)
Kichenside, G. M. 'End of the Quad-arts' *Railway World* (May 1966)
Kichenside, G. M. 'The North London Line' *Railway World* (April/June 1967)
Klapper, C. F. 'Cannon Street and the Suburban Services of the SER' *Railway World* (Sept./Oct. 1966)
Leigh, Chris 'The End of the Staines branch' *Railway World* (May 1981)
—— *North London Railway* (HMSO 1979)
Pond, C. C. *The Chingford Line* (Walthamstow 1975)
—— 'Revival of London Links' *Railway Magazine* (April 1979)
—— 'Routes of Cross-London trains' *Railway World* (November 1976)
Scott, Peter G. *The Harrow & Stanmore Railway* (1972)
Sillince, D. 'Railways and Eton College' *Railway Magazine* (April 1968)
Siminster, T. A. 'All Stations to Liverpool Street' *Railway World* (May 1981)
Treby, Edward 'By Central line to Ongar' *Railway Magazine* (September 1968)
Treby, Edward 'Kentish Town to Barking' *Railway Magazine* (August 1981)
Whitehead, Alan 'Midland Commuter in the Thirties' *Railway World* (December 1977)
Young, J. N. *GN Suburban* (1977)

6 For Pleasure

Delgado, Alan *The Annual Outing and other Excursions* (1977)
Jackson, Alan A. 'Rails to Tattenham Corner' *Railway Magazine* (June 1975)
Webster, V. R. 'To the Sunny South' *Railway World* (Oct./Dec. 1980)

7 Southern Electric

Dendy Marshall, C. F. *A History of the Southern Railway* (Second (Enlarged) Edition in Two Volumes. Revised by R. W. Kidner) (1963)
Klapper, C. F. *Sir Herbert Walker's Southern Railway* (1973)
Moody, G. T. *Southern Electric* (1968)
Owen, N. *The Brighton Belle* (1972)

Jackson, Alan A. 'Chessington – Southern suburban swansong' *Railway Magazine* (January 1974)

Klapper, Charles & Williams, Alan '30 Years of the Portsmouth Electrics' *Railway World* (July/Sept. 1967)

Klapper, Charles 'South Western Electric' *Railway World* (October 1965)

Lee, Charles E. 'London's "Elevated Electric"' *Railway Magazine* (December 1959)

—— 'New Southern Railway Suburban Line' *Railway Magazine* (July 1938)

—— 'New Wimbledon and Sutton Line, Southern Railway' *Railway Magazine* (February 1930)

8 London Transport's Railways

Lee, Charles E. 'A Hundred Years of the Hammersmith & City Line' *Railway World* (August 1964)

Barman, Christian *The Man who Built London Transport* (1979)

Bruce, J. Graeme *Steam to Silver* (1970)

Bruce, J. Graeme *The Big Tube (GN & City)* (1976)

Bruce, J. Graeme *Tube Trains under London* (1969)

Day, John and Fenton, William *The Last Drop: LT Steam 1863–1971* (1971)

Edwards, Dennis & Pigram, Ron *Metro Memories* (1977)

Edwards, Dennis & Pigram, Ron *The Romance of Metro-land* (1979)

Jackson, Alan A. 'Almost a Tube' *Railway Magazine* (May/June 1973)

Jackson, Alan A. 'Beyond Edgware' *Railway Magazine* (February 1967)

Klapper, Charles 'Centenary of the East London line' *Railway World* (February 1970)

Klapper, Charles 'Diamond Jubilee of the Bakerloo' *Railway World* (April 1966)

Lee, Charles E. 'District Railway Centenary' *Railway Magazine* (December 1968)

Lee, Charles E. 'Mixed Gauge to Hammersmith' *Railway Magazine* (June 1964)

Lee, Charles E. *100 Years of the District* (1969)

Lee, Charles E. *Sixty Years of the Piccadilly* (1967)

Lee, Charles E. *The East London Line and the Thames Tunnel* (1976)

Lee, Charles E. 'Tower Hill and its Stations' *Railway Magazine* (January 1966)

Treby, Edward 'Branch to Stanmore' *Railway Magazine* (May 1979)

Treby, Edward 'Closed London Underground Stations' *Railway World* (May 1974)

Willis, David 'Wood Lane memories' *Railway World* (July 1975)

9 Freight

British Railways Board *The Reshaping of British Railways Part I Report* (1963)

Klapper, Charles F. *Sir Herbert Walker's Southern Railway* (1973)

Course, Edwin 'The Foreign Goods Depots of South London' *Railway Magazine* (November 1960)

Marshall, R. J. 'Smithfield Goods Depot' *Railway World* (July 1962)

—— 'Ripple Lane Starts Work' *Trains Illustrated* (August 1958)

—— 'Temple Mills Marshalling Yard' *Railway Magazine* (July 1959)

10 To the Docks and the River

Bird, J. *The Geography of the Port of London* (1957)

Peacock, T. B. *The Port of London Authority Railways* (1952)

Taylor, D. J. *Great Eastern Railway Society Information Sheet P102 North Woolwich, Gallions & Beckton Lines 6", 25" & 50" OS Plans* (1981)

Welch, H. D. *The London, Tilbury & Southend Railway* (1963)

Holmes, J. G. 'The North Woolwich Branch' *Railway Magazine* (May & June 1946)

Kirkland, R. K. 'The Great Western & Brentford Railway' *Railway Magazine* (February 1960)

Rugman, W. J. 'Deptford Wharf in the Early Twenties' *Railway World* (July 1973)

Treby, Edward 'From Custom House to Gallions' *Railway Magazine* (February 1975)

Young, J. N. 'Angerstein Wharf and Railway' *Railway Magazine* (October 1973)

11 Depots and Works

Casserley, H. C. *The later years of Metropolitan Steam* (1978)

Hardy, R. H. N. 'Memories of Stewarts Lane' *Railway World* (Oct./Nov. 1967)

Hardy, R. H. N. *Steam in the Blood* (1971)

Hawkins, Chris & Reeve, George *An Historical Survey of Southern Sheds* (1979)

Jackman, Michael *Thirty Years at Bricklayers Arms* (1976)

Lyons, E. *An Historical Survey of GW Engine Sheds* 1947 (1974)

Martin, Kirk 'Lillie Bridge Loco memories' *Railway World* (October 1973)

—— 'Recollections of Bow Works and the North London Railway' *Railway World* (November 1978)

Townend, P. N. *Top Shed* (1976)

Winding, Peter F. 'Longhedge' *Railway World* (February 1980)

Winding, Peter F. 'New Cross' *Railway World* (December 1978)

Winding, Peter F. 'Nine Elms' *Railway World* (November 1980)

Youell, R. F. 'A Great Eastern Veteran Returns Home' (Stratford's last loco) *Railway World* (January 1974)

12 Hardly a Trace

Dyos, H. J. *Victorian Suburb* (Leicester 1961)

Taylor, D. J. *Great Eastern Railway Society Information Sheet P102 North Woolwich, Gallions & Beckton Lines 6", 25" & 50" OS Plans* (1981)

—— 'Capital Collection' *Railway Magazine* (June 1980)

Holmes, J. G. 'The North Woolwich Branch' *Railway Magazine* (May & June 1946)

Millar, C. D. 'The Cricklewood-Acton Branch of the Midland (LM & S) Railway' *Railway Magazine* (June 1923)

Morss, Jeffrey 'The Palace Gates to North Woolwich Line' *Railway Magazine* (September 1962)

Riley, R. C. 'The Gravesend Railway' *Railway Magazine* (October 1953)

Winding, P. F. 'Longhedge' *Railway World* (February 1980)

ACKNOWLEDGEMENTS

Anybody who is about to add another to the flood of railway books ought to explain the purpose of the new volume. Primarily it is intended to capture some of the many aspects of the Capital's railways in word and picture, and to bring them alive, rather than provide a complete history of London's railways. Those who wish to obtain more information on particular topics should consult the bibliography where they will find suggestions for further reading. In short this book is selective, acting in part as a complement to the present publisher's *Regional Railway History* volumes and other books such as *London's Local Railways* and *London's Termini*, yet standing on its own.

No work of this scale can be achieved without much assistance from others. We are of course particularly grateful to those who have contributed photographs, an aspect on which we have placed great importance. The written sections, however, have drawn on a wealth of sources and we wish to record our thanks to all who have helped. Our especial thanks go to the staff of the library services throughout London, particularly at the Guildhall Library and the London Borough of Brent Libraries, to Alan A. Jackson, Chris Hawkins and H. V. Borley, who have read sections and provided valuable comments and corrections, members of the Great Eastern Railway Society, in particular Lyn Brooks and D. J. Taylor, who have given invaluable assistance particularly for *Depots and Works*, and Klaus Marx of the Bluebell Railway Preservation Society. Finally *Clinker's Register* and the files of *The Railway Magazine, Railway World* and *Trains Illustrated* have considerably lightened our task of research.

We are greatly indebted to all for their kind assistance, although we must take responsibility for any errors of fact which remain in the book.

INDEX